D0768743

SWINBURNE'S
MEDIEVALISM

SWINBURNE'S MEDIEVALISM

A STUDY IN VICTORIAN LOVE POETRY

Antony H. Harrison

LOUISIANA STATE UNIVERSITY PRESS
Baton Rouge and London

Designer: Sylvia Loftin
Typeface: Meridian
Typesetter: G & S Typesetters, Inc.
Printer: Thomson-Shore, Inc.
Binder: John H. Dekker & Sons, Inc.

10 9 8 7 6 5 4 3 2 1

Library of Congress Cataloging-in-Publication Data
Harrison, Antony H.
   Swinburne's medievalism.

   Bibliography: p.
   Includes index.
   1. Swinburne, Algernon Charles, 1837–1909—
Criticism and interpretation. 2. Medievalism in
literature. 3. Middle Ages in literature. 4. Love
poetry, English—History and criticism. 5. Courtly
love in literature. I. Title.
PR5517.M42H3 1987   821'.8   87-3345
ISBN 0-8071-1327-1

Chapter 1 was first published as "'Love Strong as Death and Valour Strong as Love':
Swinburne and Courtly Love," in *Victorian Poetry*, XVIII (1980), 61–73. Chapter 3 was
first published as "The Medievalism of Swinburne's *Poems and Ballads, First Series*: Historicity and Erotic Aestheticism," in *Papers on Language and Literature*, XXI (Spring,
1985). Copyright © 1985 by the Board of Trustees, Southern Illinois University at Ed-
wardsville. Reprinted by permission. Chapter 5 was first published as "Swinburne's *Tristram of Lyonesse*: Visionary and Courtly Epic," in *Modern Language Quarterly*, XXXVII
(1976), 370–89. Chapter 7 was first published as "'For Love of This My Brother': Medievalism and Tragedy in Swinburne's *The Tale of Balen*," *Texas Studies in Literature and
Language*, XXV (1983), 471–94, published by the University of Texas Press, Austin. I
am grateful to the British Library, owner of Swinburne's manuscript Ashley 5069, and
to William Heinemann Ltd., holder of the Swinburne copyright, for permission to tran-
scribe and publish (as Appendix II) Swinburne's manuscript notebook of undergraduate essays on medieval subjects and his reading notes on Hallam's *Middle Ages*. Copyright © 1987 by The Estate of A. C. Swinburne.

For my parents,
EUGENE and PAMELA HARRISON

Contents

Acknowledgments

Surely my greatest intellectual debt is to Jerome J. McGann, without whose inspiration this book would never have been written. As all his students would agree, he is a teacher who opens up new and exciting directions for criticism and for thinking about criticism. I am indebted, also, to a number of Victorianists who read earlier versions of the text or portions of it and made suggestions for its improvement. For such assistance I would like to thank Cecil Lang, Elizabeth Helsinger, Jerome Bump, John Hodgson, George Landow, Terry Meyers, Clyde de L. Ryals, and Donald Gray. My colleague Tom Hester was also one of my most helpful critics; but more than this, he kept me at work upon this study when I was most deeply frustrated with its inadequacies. For his generous assistance in guiding me through Swinburne manuscripts at the British Library, I am grateful to T. A. J. Burnett. Deborah Wyrick was an invaluable source of intellectual challenges that helped shape many paragraphs in this book. To Margaret Dalrymple, an ideally astute and supportive editor, I am grateful for unstinting advice and encouragement. To the National Humanities Center I am obliged for providing time away from teaching and superb facilities for research. To my department heads, Larry S. Champion and John Bassett, I owe much for their confidence in my work. Linda Lomperis helped with my translations of French originals. And to Charlene Turner I am grateful for meticulous and efficient typing.

My most profound debt is to my wife, Linda. Throughout the writing of this book she has constructively challenged my ideas and assumptions, and she has been patient, understanding, and generous in all ways.

Abbreviations

References to the following frequently cited works will appear parenthetically in the text.

Bonchurch	*The Complete Works of Algernon Charles Swinburne.* Bonchurch Edition, edited by Sir Edmund Gosse and Thomas J. Wise. 20 vols. London, 1925–27.
Poems	*The Poems of Algernon Charles Swinburne.* 6 vols. London, 1904.
Tragedies	*The Tragedies of Algernon Charles Swinburne.* 5 vols. New York, 1906.
Jeunesse	Lafourcade, Georges. *La Jeunesse de Swinburne (1837–1867).* Vol. 2. London, 1928.
Letters	Lang, Cecil Y., ed. *The Swinburne Letters.* 6 vols. New Haven, 1959–62.
McGann	McGann, Jerome J. *Swinburne: An Experiment in Criticism.* Chicago, 1972.
Press	*The Anthology of Troubadour Lyric Poetry.* Edited and translated by Alan R. Press. Austin, 1971.

SWINBURNE'S
MEDIEVALISM

Introduction

In his review "The Poems of Dante Gabriel Rossetti" (1870), Swinburne warns readers against judging any author solely on the grounds of his subject matter or the settings chosen for his works; he thus obliquely attacks the growing emphasis among Victorian writers and readers upon topical and didactic literature. He insists that "all the ineffably foolish jargon and jangle of criticasters about classic subjects and romantic, remote or immediate interests, duties of the poet to face and handle this thing instead of that or his own age instead of another, can only serve to darken counsel by words without knowledge: a poet of the first order raises all subjects to the first rank, puts the life-blood of an equal interest into Hebrew forms or Greek, medieval or modern, yesterday or yesterage" (*Bonchurch*, XV, 38). As one of the most versatile Victorian poets, Swinburne attempted with great success throughout his career to be "a poet of the first order"; thus his invective in this passage is not merely a renewal of his repeated calls in *William Blake* (published two years earlier) for an appreciation of art for art's sake. Rather, it suggests Swinburne's more consistent critical gospel that the greatest poets must assimilate past literary traditions and achievements while remaining torchbearers (to recall Swinburne's own recurrent use of Appollonian metaphors) illuminating fundamental and eternal truths of human experience and the human condition, no matter the extent to which modern issues and modern advances may formally or ideologically supersede tradition.

Thus, like Pope before him, Arnold among his contemporaries, and

1

T. S. Eliot after him, Swinburne was a perplexing and paradoxical literary figure who is simultaneously a traditionalist and a radical innovator. His innovations were not only formal and stylistic but also, and especially, ideological: in his poetry he rebelled against the limited and limiting moral, political, and religious values of his own historical era. Iconoclastic as Swinburne was—writing in the traditions of Blake, Shelley, Baudelaire, and Hugo—his prophetic function, as he conceived it, required that he adopt a poetic stance outside his historical moment in order to transmit to his reader transcendental truths about universal human needs, passions, compulsions, and ambitions; about the inevitable fate of disappointment or betrayal that all human aspirations eventually yield to; but also about the potentially sublime power of nature to inspire and uplift man despite the failure and tragedy that finally shape our lives. In order to perceive and express the unchanging qualities of human experience as well as to attain his ideal of detachment, Swinburne was necessarily a student of history, of past cultures, traditional literary forms, and the varied functions and voices of the poet as prophet from biblical to contemporary times.

Swinburne was appropriately, therefore, a model of the scholar-poet who molds public taste with both his critical and creative efforts. Apart from being the author in 1866 of the scandalous volume *Poems and Ballads, First Series,* which previewed the decadence as well as the subsequent sexual revolution, Swinburne was a dominant force in the Victorian renewal of interest in the Renaissance and in Hellenism. In addition, he almost single-handedly and with great success introduced contemporary French literature (especially Hugo, Baudelaire, and Gautier) to England while announcing to his provincial countrymen the virtues of previously neglected American writers such as Whitman and Poe. As significant as any of these innovative activities, however, was Swinburne's participation in the popular, backward-looking Gothic revival, which powerfully affected not only the arts in Victorian England but also, and more subtly, the social and political directions of the country.

Nineteenth-century medievalism is a subject often mentioned but little studied until the late 1960s among Victorianists,[1] most of whom

1. The most significant discussions appear in Mark Girouard, *The Return to*

have focused attention on the topicality of Victorian literature (whether in its social, political, or psychological aspects) or studied it as a premodern body of documents, following Walter Houghton's assertion that "to look into the Victorian mind is to see some primary sources of the modern mind." And yet Victorian medievalism is an extraordinary phenomenon that cannot safely be ignored by students of the period, for it was not merely a mode of post-Romantic escapism but equally as often a means of glossing, evaluating, and redirecting contemporary developments in history, politics, literature, and art. Involved were thinkers representing the spectrum of English culture: from men like Disraeli to Sir Frederic Madden, who as assistant keeper of manuscripts was prolifically editing medieval texts at the British Museum; from the anti-establishment Pre-Raphaelite painters, who frequently chose medieval subjects and styles, to some of the most prominent architects (including Pugin and Gilbert Scott) and the most successful social thinkers, such as Carlyle, Ruskin, and William Morris. As Alice Chandler has demonstrated, nineteenth-century medievalists from Scott to Morris used medieval settings, forms, and themes in their works to achieve emotional and spiritual effects, as well as to inculcate political and social values. The complexity of Victorian medievalism cannot be overestimated.

Yet one generalization holds firm for most Victorian literary figures who were medievalists: they looked back nostalgically upon what they perceived as a period of uniform social and spiritual values, of social integration, of political and cultural stability. Such is clearly the case in the works of Carlyle, Ruskin, Arnold, and Morris (later in his career). These writers followed the examples of Sir Walter Scott and Coleridge. As a corollary to their idealization of medieval culture, they

---

Camelot: Chivalry and the English Gentleman (New Haven, 1981); *Browning Institute Studies*, VIII, devoted to the topic of Victorian medievalism (New York, 1980); Alice Chandler, *A Dream of Order: The Medieval Ideal in Nineteenth-Century English Literature* (Lincoln, Neb., 1970); and John Dixon Hunt, *The Pre-Raphaelite Imagination, 1848–1900* (Lincoln, Neb., 1968), 33–72. Two treatments of Swinburne in the medievalist context deal exclusively with his Arthurian poems and discuss only his use of sources. They are David Staines, "Swinburne's Arthurian World: Swinburne's Arthurian Poetry and Its Medieval Sources," *Studia Neophilologica*, L (1978), 53–70; and Mary Byrd Davis, "Swinburne's Use of His Sources in *Tristram of Lyonesse*," *Philological Quarterly*, LV (1977), 96–112.

perceived medieval man and his society as existing in idyllic harmony with nature. Victorian depictions of the medieval world usually emphasize (often with startling simplicity) a life of fulfilling industry, of heroic achievement and endurance, of shared values, of filial devotion, and of integration with nature.

Two exceptions to this rule are Tennyson and Swinburne. Tennyson, though a scholar of the Middle Ages as was Swinburne, wrote only one major work that makes significant use of a medieval setting, the *Idylls of the King*. Yet even in his Arthurian epic, Tennyson radically Victorianizes the characters, events, and moral significance of his materials. As every commentator has observed, he rewrites Malory to allegorize for almost evangelical purposes the conflict between "sense and soul." Swinburne, by contrast, wrote numerous major works, both prose and poetry, which embody a notably different treatment of his medieval subjects than is found in Tennyson or in the works of his contemporaries. If Swinburne "idealizes" the period in any way, he does so by consistently depicting it as a golden age—like the Hellenic age—of tragic heroism and tragic love; these appear in a society realistically characterized as disharmonious and corrupt, populated with men and women who are fickle in their emotional attachments, capricious in their loyalties, and misguided in their adherence to Christianity. All such characters are victims of an ostensibly malevolent fate, including even Swinburne's stoical pantheistic heroes, who are often transiently aware of a sublime and transcendent spiritual world that generates and infuses the material world in which they live. Their lives are dominated by frustrated love and inexorable strife which result usually in suffering rather than fulfillment or harmony.

Swinburne produced a considerable body of medievalist works, including his *Chronicle of Queen Fredegond, Rosamond* (set during the reign of Henry II), "Laus Veneris," numerous border ballads and translations of Villon, *Tristram of Lyonesse, Marino Faliero,* and *The Tale of Balen,* as well as many more minor poems, essays, and prose pieces on medieval subjects (see Appendix I). Throughout his career Swinburne conscientiously studied medieval texts, pursuing fidelity to original sources in his own creative efforts and reviving medieval literary forms such as the *aubade* or *alba,* the ballad, and the rondel. He

4

thus holds a significant place among Victorian medievalists who extended the "discoveries" begun in the eighteenth century that much of the greatest English literature has its roots in the medieval period. Moreover, beyond his works set in medieval times or based upon medieval literary traditions or founded upon ostensibly medieval systems of value, Swinburne's frequent use of the Middle Ages and its literature as a frame of reference when evaluating literary developments in his own era makes clear that the impact of medieval literature and values upon the poet was enormous. However, no thorough study of Swinburne's medievalism has yet been published, though extensive discussions of the other major literary traditions in which Swinburne holds a place have been forthcoming since Georges Lafourcade's pioneering studies appeared in 1928.[2] As the general estimate of Swinburne's importance to Victorian and modern literature continues to rise with startling (but not unwarranted) rapidity, analysis of his medievalist works in their proper context helps us to see him steadily and see him whole. Such analysis reinforces our perception of Swinburne not only as an extraordinary scholar and major poet but also as a relentless iconoclast and great innovator who had in common with his contemporaries only the subject matter of his medievalist poetry. Swinburne radically diverged from Tennyson, Arnold, and even Wil-

2. See Edith D. Linsey, "Medievalism in the Poetry of Swinburne" (Ph.D. dissertation, University of Alabama, 1974), for an approach to the topic markedly different from my own. Lafourcade's *La Jeunesse de Swinburne* is still the standard source for all discussions of Swinburne's works before 1868. The finest and most comprehensive subsequent treatment of Swinburne's poetry is Jerome McGann's *Swinburne: An Experiment in Criticism*. Apart from pursuing at length the issue of Swinburne's Romanticism, McGann more fully than any other critic discusses the influence of nineteenth-century French literature on the poet. In wide-ranging remarks on Swinburne's Greek tragedies and poems, McGann also deals with his Hellenism, though the standard sources for such commentaries are William Rutland's *Swinburne: A Nineteenth-Century Hellene* (Oxford, 1931) and Robert A. Greenberg, "Swinburne and the Redefinition of Classical Myth," *Victorian Poetry,* XIV (1976), 175–96. The issue of Swinburne's modernism is broached by Ross C. Murfin in *Swinburne, Hardy, Lawrence, and the Burden of Belief* (Chicago, 1978). Finally, the most thorough discussions of Swinburne's Romanticism appear in David G. Riede's *Swinburne: A Study in Romantic Mythmaking* (Charlottesville, 1978) and Kerry McSweeney's *Tennyson and Swinburne as Romantic Naturalists* (Toronto, 1981).

liam Morris, for instance, in his fidelity to Arthurian sources and in the scope of his tragic sensibility when writing on Arthurian themes. Moreover, he went well beyond any of his contemporaries in the breadth and diversity of medieval materials he treated and assimilated.

Although Swinburne's medievalist poems of epic scope did not appear till the second half of his career, it is clear from the evidence of letters, unpublished manuscripts, and his best biographers that Swinburne read most widely and enthusiastically in medieval authors from 1857 to 1860, as an undergraduate at Oxford, and during his first years in London (1860–1862). In this period of apprenticeship he considered himself to be under the tutelage of William Morris and D. G. Rossetti, whom he always regarded as expert medievalists. Yet Swinburne appears to have read more extensively in medieval literature, to have studied it more thoughtfully, and to have retained more of what he read than did either Morris or Rossetti. Long before he met his two friends, much of his reading, especially in medieval French history, poetry, and romance, as well as in medieval theology, was done in the library of his uncle, the Earl of Ashburnham, who specialized in medieval manuscripts and early Renaissance texts. In a letter to Sydney Cockerell late in Swinburne's life (January 11, 1906), the poet pays tribute to his uncle's library when discussing what Cecil Lang describes as "a magnificent thirteenth-century MS. of *Lancelot du Lac.*" Swinburne effusively confesses "how much both Watts-Dunton and myself would enjoy a sight of your San Graal MS. I wish my uncle Ashburnham, whose collection is now scattered to the winds, were alive to see it—as well as Burne-Jones and Morris" (*Letters,* VI, 198).[3] Swinburne's remarkable knowledge of medieval literature and tradition and his extreme sensitivity as a bibliophile are not at all surprising in light of the many hours of his childhood spent in his uncle's library. Edmund Gosse observes that it was there probably that "Swinburne gained his . . . intimacy with the Frankish Kings of France. He once told me that the medieval and French sections of his uncle's famous collection had been a source of unfailing enjoyment to him" (*Bonchurch,* XIX, 76). But Lord Ashburnham's library provided only the introduction to Swinburne's medieval studies, which were pur-

3. Ironically, as Lang notes, this manuscript happened to come originally from Lord Ashburnham's collection (*Letters,* VI, 198).

sued as an undergratuate at Oxford and, more discursively, later in his career while at work on his major Arthurian poems.[4]

Early in 1886 the *Pall Mall Gazette* asked a number of major English authors to list the one hundred books that each believed to be "most precious to humanity in general." On Swinburne's list (from which he excluded all living authors) appear eight writers or groups of works from the Middle Ages: Dante, Chaucer, Boccaccio, Ballads of North England (from Percy, Scott, Motherwell and others), the story of the Volsungs and Niblungs, the saga of Burnt Njal, Malory's *Morte D'Arthur,* and early English metrical romances from the collections of Weber, Ritson, and Wright. These selections are in no way surprising for such a long list, but the significance of medieval works to Swinburne becomes more striking as one realizes that Greek authors occupy only seven positions on the same list and Romantic writers appear in just nine places.[5] From such references and from allusions to medieval literature in his letters and essays, two facts emerge clearly: that Swinburne's favorite writers of the Middle Ages were Dante, Villon, Chaucer, and Boccaccio; and that throughout his career he read these authors while expanding his appreciation of other medieval texts, including history, poetry, and romance.

As his *Chronicle of Queen Fredegond* (1859–62) indicates, Swinburne was intimate at an early age with Gregory of Tours' *Historia Francorum,* a rare 1561 edition of which was housed in his uncle's library. Gosse notes that "the earlier part of Swinburne's Chapter I is closely paraphrased and reduced from the Book V of Gregory . . . from whom he continues to help himself to incidents until the end" (*Bonchurch,* XX, 305). At Balliol, he continued to read a good deal in medieval history, especially French. On April 15, 1860, he wrote to

4. See Appendix II for his essays on medieval subjects written at Balliol College. Over the years Swinburne gained what seems, especially for an avowed and iconoclastic atheist, to be more than a passing acquaintance with the church fathers and with medieval theology. His knowledge of the saints' lives is indicated not only in works such as "St. Dorothy" (dated 1860 by Lafourcade) but also in his correspondence (see, for instance, *Letters,* V, 101).

5. The Greek authors: Aeschylus, Homer, Sophocles, Aristophanes, Pindar, Epictetus, Theocritus; the Romantics: Shelley, Landor, Lamb, Coleridge, Scott, Blake, Wordsworth, Keats, and Hunt (*Letters,* V, 131–36).

his mother that "I am . . . taking in . . . either Charlemagne or St. Louis—possibly both. That is the sort of history I like—live biographical chronicle not dead constitutional records" (*Letters*, I, 35). Swinburne did indeed study both, along with feudal law, the Crusades, and Hallam's *View of the State of Europe During the Middle Ages.*

His readings of medieval poetry and romance were even more extensive. According to Gosse, well before 1861, Swinburne was familiar with Boccaccio (as well as Malory, Dante, and Chaucer, of course) and with more obscure works, including Marguerite de Navarre's *Nouvelles françoises en prose du xiii^c siècle,* which Morris and he had read in college (*Bonchurch*, XIX, 76). He had also perhaps seen works by Nicholas of Troyes (*Bonchurch*, XIX, 305). As late as 1894, Swinburne wrote to Morris concerning the *Tale of the Emperor Constans and of Over Sea,* "I remember reading the old French romance in the days when we first foregathered at Oxford" (*Letters*, VI, 76). Thirty-five years earlier, Swinburne had written to William Bell Scott, "You must excuse a party who has been prostrate through catching awful colds, etc. with reading French romances on the wet grass about Wallington" (*Letters*, I, 23). By 1859, Swinburne had apparently begun collecting medieval romances for his own library.[6] In addition to French romances and narrative poetry, Swinburne delighted in medieval ballads, especially during his youth. According to Gosse, "At an early age he had been attracted to this class of poetry by the study of Scott's *Border Minstrelsy* of 1802–03, an examination of which will show that it contains, then published for the first time, all the ballads which most powerfully affected Swinburne's imagination."[7]

Swinburne's interest in the medieval world and its literature never waned. After his apprenticeship in medieval studies during the late 1850s and early 1860s, his approach to medieval literature became somewhat more scholarly, especially when he was preparing to write *Tristram of Lyonesse.* On November 4, 1869, he wrote to Burne-Jones:

6. To William Bell Scott on December 16 he wrote, "I have got such a beautiful new old [French romance]—'Floire et Blancheflour'" (*Letters*, I, 28). As Lang notes, it was edited by E. Du Meril and published in Paris in 1856. It was sold in 1916, when Southeby's offered Swinburne's library.
7. Algernon Charles Swinburne, *Posthumous Poems by Algernon Charles Swinburne*, ed. Edmund Gosse and T. J. Wise (London, 1917), vi.

"With 1) Mallory [*sic*], 2) Scott's chaos [his 1804 edition of *Sir Tristrem*] . . . and—if I can get it—3) Michel's collection of every *metrical* fragment on Tristram extant, published by old Pickering, I shall have enough stuff to build my poem on. Besides the French poem, there is one (written at Micklegarth) in medieval Greek of the canine dialect which is at least a good lark" (*Letters*, II, 50). Then on December 28 of the same year to William Michael Rossetti, when discussing his research and objectives for *Tristram*, he explained his need "to look at the romance . . . of father Meladius in the British Museum as well as the Tristan and Lancelot" (*Letters*, II, 78). After this point, one can only speculate on the directions his Arthurian researches took during the almost thirteen years that intervened before the publication of *Tristram*.[8]

Tristram of Lyonesse is not only Swinburne's finest poem with a medieval subject but also perhaps his greatest single poem. Yet Swinburne's irregular studies in medieval literature spanned twenty-five years and resulted in his writing numerous medievalist poems and brief romances. During the four years between 1858 and 1862, Swinburne was most intent upon these endeavors, and they were extremely varied, including such works as "Laus Veneris," "The Leper," "St. Dorothy," and *Rosamond*. But W. H. Hutton writes that Swinburne in 1859 was even composing "Latin medieval hymns . . . with the greatest facility."[9] According to Gosse, Swinburne also "planned an epic poem in the late 1850s on the subject of the Albigenses" (*Bonchurch*, XIX, 54). Soon afterward, in 1860 or 1861,

> Swinburne was . . . occupied with a scheme which had begun to take shape at Oxford and which was not finally abandoned till much later. This was the composition of a cycle of nineteen or twenty prose stories, to be issued as the *Triameron*, in rivalry with Boccaccio and Marguerite de Navarre. . . . The only one of these tales which Swinburne printed was *Dead Love*, which he sent to *Once a Week* in 1862, and published in book form in 1864. But several others were written . . . and three still exist.[10] Moreover, about the year 1861 he wrote a prose *Chronicle of Queen Fredegond*. (*Bonchurch*, XIX, 76)

8. See Davis, "Swinburne's Use of His Sources," 96–112.
9. *The Letters of William Stubbs*, ed. W. H. Hutton (London, 1904), 50.
10. Two of the stories are "The Marriage of the Monna Lisa" and "The Portrait." The title of what Gosse perceives as the third work is uncertain.

The historical studies and notes upon which his *Chronicle* is based are here published for the first time (see Appendix II).

Throughout this period and as early as 1858, Swinburne was at work, too, on his many border ballads. The apparent authenticity of his creations clearly delighted him. On September 15, 1858, he wrote exuberantly to Edwin Hatch: "I must tell you a piece of success on my part: I wrote a ballad lately, which was accepted here [at Capheaton, from the thirteenth century the Swinburne family's Northumbrian home near Newcastle]—in the native land of ballads—as a genuine Border specimen, and of the earliest mediaeval build! The very people I learnt the old ones from when I was a kid of diminutive proportions were wholly taken in—one party was elated at such a discovery, but only wondered where it had been all these years to escape his discovery!!" (*Letters*, I, 22). Despite Swinburne's mastery of pastiche in these and his later medievalist works, most of them clearly reflect his own characteristic philosophical and literary values, as do his commentaries upon medieval writers and upon the medievalism of his contemporaries.

Swinburne's attitude toward the Middle Ages is inherently paradoxical. He is at once vehemently critical of the epoch and nostalgic toward it. Unlike Carlyle, Ruskin, and Arnold, Swinburne does not perceive the millennium generally considered the medieval period as an era of desirable social, political, and spiritual stability founded upon a uniform religious faith. Rather, Swinburne's irrepressible hostility to Christianity skews his vision. A passage from his "Short Notes on the English Poets" reveals his iconoclastic predisposition:

> When Ariosto threw across the windy sea of glittering legend and fluctuant romance the broad summer·lightnings of his large and jocund genius, the dark ages had already returned into the outer darkness where there is weeping and gnashing of teeth—the tears of Dante Alighieri and the laughter of Francois Villon. But the wide warm harvest-field of Chaucer's husbandry was all glorious with gold of ripening sunshine while all the world beside lay in blackness and in bonds, throughout all those ages of death called ages of faith by men who can believe in nothing beyond a building or a book, outside the codified creeds of a Bible or the oecumenical structure of a Church. (*Bonchurch*, XIV, 101)

Swinburne perceives the Middle Ages as centuries of religious oppression, calling them "dark" ages as many of his scientifically oriented contemporaries did, but for different reasons. He sees medieval man as predominantly materialistic rather than spiritual—as pre-Romantic, in fact. At the same time, after the fashion of Morris and Rossetti in their early days, Swinburne is consistently realistic about political events as well as about the tragedies of human interaction that took palce during this period. In his essay on Hugo's *La Légende des siècles* he makes note of "all the blackness of darkness, rank with fumes of blood and loud with cries of torment, which covers in so many quarters the history, not romantic but actual, of the ages called the ages of faith" (*Bonchurch*, XIII, 118). Such critical perceptions seem to be based primarily on Swinburne's knowledge of the period. By contrast, he is nostalgic for the atmosphere as well as the erotic and chivalric ideals of the period, a sentiment that derives from literary rather than historical sources. While discussing another aspect of Hugo's medievalist *Légende,* he remarks that "all the music of morning, all the sunshine of romance, all the sweetness and charm of chivalry, will come back upon all readers at the gracious and radiant name of *Aymerillot*" (*Bonchurch,* XIII, 118). And with even greater exuberance later in his essay Swinburne explains that "the glory of beauty, the loveliness of love, the exultation of noble duty and lofty labour in a stress of arduous joy, these are the influences that pervade the world and permeate the air of the poems which deal with the Christian cycle of heroic legend, whose crowning image is the figure of the Cid" (*Bonchurch,* XIII, 118–19).

Swinburne's remarks on specific medieval writers are less nostalgic and more critically keen than are these mellifluous comments on romantic tradition in general. In an important letter to John Nichol (April 2, 1876), while discussing Nichol's *Tables of European Literature and History,* A.D. *200–1876,* Swinburne crystallizes his essential perceptions on those poets he only half ironically designates as the "Three Persons of the Mediaeval Trinity," each of whom, he asserts,

represented not only his nation, but his class, as it then showed itself for good or evil; Dante the aristocratic class as it ruled in Italy, none the less essentially and typically aristocratic for being commercial or municipal in form; Chaucer the English gentry or prosperous middle class of scholars and professional men, burgesses and small proprietors, or such men as Boccaccio in Italy; Villon, the commons of France, especially the people or populace, if you like, of Paris. Reluctantly in the teeth of patriotism and prepossession, I have long since come to the conclusion that though third in date he is beyond all question second in rank of these three; as indisputably greater than Chaucer as lesser than Dante in natural gift of poetic genius. (*Letters,* III, 164)

Although Swinburne has an appropriate critical respect for the greatness of Dante's work, Villon—whose poems Swinburne often translated—is his favorite among the "Trinity" because of his earthy and rebellious vigor. Despite the similarities between Swinburne's own and Dante's social stations, Swinburne felt a strong spiritual, emotional, and especially ideological kinship with Villon, whom he describes as "a singer of . . . the future; he was the first modern and the last medieval poet. He is of us, in a sense in which it cannot be said that either Chaucer or Dante is of us, or even could have been" (*Bonchurch,* XIV, 100). For Swinburne, Villon is an original in a way that Chaucer, for instance, is not. Among the greatest poets of all nations, "Chaucer borrowed most from abroad, and did most to improve whatever he borrowed. I believe it would be but accurate to admit that in all his poems of serious or tragic narrative we hear a French or Italian tongue speaking with a Teutonic accent through English lips" (*Bonchurch,* XIV, 98). Swinburne reserves quite different criticisms for Dante. The Italian poet's virtue of concreteness suggests to Swinburne dangerous deficiencies in his stature as a metaphysician: "Dante was beyond all other poets a materialist,—and this, I have heard it remarked [probably by Rossetti], is of course what Blake meant to convey by the quaint apparent paradox of his essentially accurate objection to the 'atheism' (as he called it) of Dante; with whom the finest forms of abstract qualities that the scholastic ingenuity of mediaeval metaphysicians could devise and define became hard and sharp and rigid as tempered steel. Give Dante a moral image, he will make of it a living man" (*Bonchurch,* XIV, 102–103). Swinburne is ambivalent about Dante's attempt to establish a poetic cosmos on medieval theological foundations.

If in such commentaries as these and in his poems and fiction Swinburne displays his perspective on the medieval period and its literature, he further clarifies that perspective in his various remarks about the medievalist works of Morris and Rossetti. From the first months of 1857, when Swinburne was prolific in his imitations of Morris, until Morris' death in 1896, Swinburne's admiration for his fellow poet's works was unbounded. Yet his enthusiastic review of *The Life and Death of Jason* (1867) seems now to be detailed and accurate rather than hyperbolic, and it reveals some of the attributes of medieval romance that most appealed to Swinburne. He observes that "in direct narrative power, in clear forthright manner of procedure, not seemingly troubled to select, to pick and sift and winnow, yet never superfluous or verbose, never straggling or jarring; in these high qualities [the poem] resembles the work of Chaucer. Even against the great master his pupil may fairly be matched for simple sense of right, for grace and speed of step, for purity and justice of colour. In all the noble roll of our poets there has been since Chaucer no second teller of tales, no second rhapsode comparable to the first, till the advent of this one" (*Bonchurch*, XV, 55–56). Throughout this passage, Swinburne is suggesting quite correctly that one of the greatest virtues of Morris' art and of Chaucer's as well is an apparent lack of self-consciousness and therefore of strain. In its propriety, its perfect sense of pace and choice of images, the "art" is invisible, the creative sensibility apparently instinctive. Moreover, Swinburne admires the tragic scope, the precision and passionate power of *Jason*. In Swinburne's view, much medieval literature possesses such virtues. He concludes that "rarely but in the ballad and romance periods has such poetry been written, so broad and sad and simple, so full of deep and direct fire, certain of its aim, without finish, without fault" (*Bonchurch*, XV, 60).

Three years later, when reviewing Rossetti's poems, Swinburne reveals his delight in three distinct but complementary qualities he perceives in medieval poetry: its passion, its imagination, and its pervasively tragic view of the human condition. Speaking of "the intimate relations of [Rossetti's] work in verse and his work in painting," Swinburne observes similarities in emotional effect "between the romantic poems and the romantic designs, as for example 'Sister Helen' and the 'Tune of Seven Towers,' which have the same tone and type of tragic romance in their mediaeval touches and notes of passionate fancy" (*Bonchurch*, XV, 40). Earlier in the essay, when discussing Rossetti's translations, Swinburne especially applauds his friend's fidelity to the mood of the original and his reproduction of its emotional effects. He praises Rossetti's "full command of that lyric sentiment and power which give to mediaeval poetry its clear particular charm [and which] is plain alike from the ending given to the 'old song' of Ophelia and

13

from the marvellous visions of Villon's and other French songs. . . .
The very cadence of Villon's matchless ballad of the ladies of old time
is caught and returned. The same exquisite exactitude of translation is
notable in 'John of Tours'—the old provincial song long passed from
mouth to mouth and at last preserved with all its breaks and lapses of
sweet rough metre by Gérard de Nerval" (*Bonchurch*, XV, 32–33). Implicit here once again is Swinburne's perception of the inescapable
continuity of literary tradition from medieval to modern times, a continuity that he demonstrates repeatedly in his own numerous medievalist works.

One of the interlocutors in Jerome J. McGann's *Swinburne: An Experiment in Criticism* makes an incisive general remark about the poet's
philosophical thought, a remark that is essential to any consideration
of Swinburne's literary treatment of medieval subjects, but also—
more broadly and profoundly—to the implied theory of history that
informs all his work. "One of Swinburne's most important intuitions," Murdoch insists, "is that discoveries are not made at the end of
something, or even along the way, but at the beginning. So, . . . his
poetry is constantly turning back upon itself in an attempt to reveal
the significance of something in the past, something that he has already seen but that will bear further scrutiny in the light of the still
more recent past" (4). Swinburne's literary beginnings, especially
under the tutelage of Morris and Rossetti, are very largely medievalist,
and thus it comes as no surprise that the poet should return at intervals throughout his career to the composition of medievalist poems.
Nor is it unexpected that each of these works embodies a developing
but fundamentally identical set of moral, spiritual, amatory, and intellectual values, whose varied treatment from one work to another
merely expands their scope and depth.

What must become clear, however, to any serious student of Swinburne and his position in the history of ideas during the nineteenth
century, is that he saw the human condition as essentially static, tragically but paradoxically so. Thus, Murdoch's statement is true in relation not only to the poet's own biography but also to his sense of human history as a whole. Prophetic truth, that is, complete human
truth, emerges from a poetic "scrutiny" of the past in which ephemeral historical contexts are penetrated and exposed. To the extent that

Swinburne saw human nature and the constraints governing human life as unchanging and universal, he possesses more of the neoclassical temper than do any of his literary contemporaries, including Matthew Arnold, whose cyclical theory of human history is frequently belied in his later years by history's implicit and sometimes explicit depiction as a perfectibilianist spiral. With equal felicity Swinburne could set his poetic representations of human passion, aspiration, and suffering in ancient Greece, in medieval France, Wales, Northumberland, or in Renaissance England because the fundamental conditions surrounding human motivations and endeavors do not vary from era to era, according to Swinburne's philosophy of history. Despite his very visible concern with the political events of his own day, therefore, Swinburne's entire literary enterprise can be seen to be anti-historicist precisely because it is philosophically idealistic. As he explains in "Hertha"—which he believed to contain his philosophical thought in its most concentrated form—man is only the supreme manifestation of an ageless and unchanging generative spirit active in the world.

Why, then, focus attention on Swinburne's medievalist works, rather than on his "Renaissance" closet dramas, or his "Greek" tragedies, or his multifarious "philosophical" and aestheticist lyrics? Apart from the fact that, by comparison with Swinburne's other major works, his medievalist poems have been neglected by critics, one can justify examining the medievalist poems on at least two important grounds.

First, for Swinburne, as for most of his contemporaries, the end of the medieval period signaled the beginning of the modern world. His description of Villon as "the first modern and the last medieval poet," one of us in a way that neither Chaucer nor Dante is, suggests that Swinburne thought Chaucer and Dante were thralls of a socially hierarchical culture constrained by an unyielding system of religious beliefs that denied free play to their imaginations. By contrast, Villon—energetically receptive to life and experience of all kinds, wholly engaged with the lives and loves he sang of—possessed a fully liberated imagination, a democratizing instinct, a feel for the transcendent within the quotidian that was foreign to Chaucer and Dante. In important ways, then, for Swinburne the medieval millennium until the twelfth century represents an era inhospitable in its cultural surfaces and institutions, stubbornly foreign to Swinburne's own predominantly Hellenic and Romantic value system. At the same time Swinburne found lacunae—in literary forms and mythologies generated by particular medieval writers—through which he could emphatically project his own view of the human condition as passionate and aspiring, but finally tragic. Thus by exploiting selected literary forms, traditions, topoi, and mythologies from the medieval period, especially from medieval France, Swinburne could, as it were, poetically rewrite medieval cultural history from a revisionist or modernist— that is, Romantic—perspective. Doing so would serve a corrective prophetic function because Swinburne's poetic re-creations of medieval myths and their characters would not yield to the social or religious constraints that thwarted Dante and Chaucer, for instance, at their least imaginative. Using the traditions of love poetry that originated in late-medieval France, and especially the Arthurian matter that represents the culmination of such traditions, Swinburne perceived that he could unveil the universal truths of human experience for the medieval era that otherwise would remain buried beneath the surfaces of medieval culture. Swinburne perceived the medieval courtly love and Arthurian mythologies as in themselves iconoclastic: attempts to revive light and life in an era otherwise dark, oppressed by a religiously grounded system of social and moral values that denied the most profound elements of human nature and experience.

Unlike Tennyson, his sometime Hegelian contemporary, Swinburne must be described finally as a historical, as well as a philosophical, monist.[11] Throughout his major philosophical works he describes the generations of mankind emerging through history as the composite material revelation of a single, changeless spiritual Being, which he sometimes calls God:

> Not each man of all men is God, but God is
>   the fruit of the whole;
> Indivisible spirit and blood, indiscernable
>   body from Soul. ("Hymn of Man," *Poems*, II, 96)

More complexly in the same poem he describes individual men in history as the "multiform features of man": "whatsoever we be," we

11. Henry Kozicki provides the clearest and most reliable study of Tennyson's theory of history in *Tennyson and Clio: History in the Major Poems* (Baltimore, 1979). His chapter on the *Idylls* (112–49) fully discusses the Hegelian influence.

"Recreate him of whom we are creatures, and we only are he." History therefore becomes a mere superflux of putative change:

> In the sea whereof centuries are waves
>   the live God plunges and swims;
> His bed is in all men's graves, but the
>   worm hath not hold on his limbs.
> Night puts out not his eyes, nor time
>   sheds change on his head. (*Poems,* II, 96)

The material universe at once nourishes and embodies this comprehensive spiritual force, as man—in Swinburne's metaphorical myth—moves through its Being both as essential lifeblood and transient consciousness:

> With such fire as the stars of the sky are the
>   roots of his heart are fed.
> Men are the thoughts passing through it, the
>   veins that fulfill it with blood,
> With spirit of sense to renew it as springs
>   fulfilling a flood. (*Poems,* II, 96)

The generations of man generate God and vice versa. History at its most accurate, therefore, and literature at its greatest, repeatedly record the same phenomena: human passions, aspirations, failures, and suffering—an endless, timeless tragedy.[12]

The second rationale for examining Swinburne's medievalist works derives from the first. Just as Swinburne's anti-historicism compels him always to place his works in clear and specific historical settings only to undercut the significance of those settings, his sense of biography—the history of the individual and that most representative of individuals, the poet—compels him insistently to demonstrate the non-developmental quality, the psychological, moral, and spiritual stasis of every man's adult life. Swinburne's own life and work as a poet largely begins with a focus on medieval poetry and romance. Works such as "Dead Love," *Queen Yseult,* "Joyeuse Garde," *Chronicle of Queen Fredegond,* and *Rosamond* constitute his beginnings—formal and stylistic, as well as philosophical—to which he almost compulsively

12. An incisive discussion of Swinburne's complex tragic vision appears in Murfin, *Swinburne, Hardy, Lawrence and the Burden of Belief,* 22–47. See also my article, "Swinburne's Losses: The Poetics of Passion," *ELH,* XLIX (1982), 689–706.

returns until the very last decade of his life. As a cohesive body of materials, Swinburne's medievalist poems therefore represent systematically and coherently his moral, literary, philosophical, and religious values, as they take on varied shapes and emphases during his career. This body of works, when set against the poetry of his contemporaries, fully demonstrates Swinburne's uniqueness as a major Victorian poet.

To illustrate Swinburne's manipulations of medieval literary forms and topoi, as well as his role in the Victorian medieval revival, I have chosen in the following chapters to discuss at length only those poems I consider to be Swinburne's finest that rely upon medieval settings or that are based upon what the poet considered to be a medievalist system of values. These poems—from *Queen Yseult* through *Rosamond*, some of his *Poems and Ballads, Tristram of Lyonesse,* and *The Tale of Balen*—span a period of forty years, constituting about 80 percent of Swinburne's literary career. My judgment of many of these as important Victorian poems is either explicit or implicit in all I have to say about them. Beyond their intrinsic virtues, however, I hope to demonstrate something of their cultural significance as documents in the extraordinary phenomenon of Victorian medievalism.

Further explanation of Swinburne's reasons for choosing medieval subjects and settings for many of his best poems appears in the chapters that follow. Clearly, his early exposure to medieval literature and the influence of Morris, Rossetti, and Burne-Jones had a good deal to do with such choices, as did his almost constitutional fondness for action-filled depictions of chivalric warfare. But as I have indicated, Swinburne's philosophical and ideological stances also drew him to medieval subjects. Setting his work in the age of faith allowed Swinburne to continue his attacks on the misguided values of Christianity, but in a manner less iconoclastic and in a context more palatable to his Victorian readers than he managed, for example, in the lyrics of *Songs before Sunrise.* His medieval subjects further enabled him to correct his own era's unwarranted and contagious idealization of an age that was more socially chaotic than harmonious and that remained more primitive but therefore closer to nature than was the industrial age. Swinburne could thus exploit the greater dangers and brutality of daily life in the Middle Ages to express his relentlessly fatalistic world view. Finally and most important, for Swinburne, as for his contemporaries, the age of faith was also the age of love literature, and so the poet in his medievalist works could fill out his philosophical vision that held Love—whether erotic, fraternal, or spiritual—to be the presiding albeit fatal impulse in all human lives and the power ultimately governing all activity in the world.

1

Swinburne and
Courtly Love

From *Queen Yseult* to *Chastelard* and *Poems and Ballads, First Series,*
Swinburne's early works begin to formulate his private mythology of
love. Their pattern is most frequently sadomasochistic, involving a
lover wracked by unquenchable desires for an often cruel woman and
concluding with a wish for death as the only adequate release from
and consummation of love's torture. But these poems often also emphasize less carnal, more metaphysical issues, especially the poet's intuition that death will yield a return to elemental nature, to organic
unity with the natural world. As Jerome J. McGann has suggested,
Swinburne's mythology of passion is derived primarily from courtly
love literature.[1] "Swinburne's work is dominated from the start by a
fascination with . . . the theme of a lost love and the sorrows of a memorial poet-lover. . . . Swinburne was not only absorbed by the figures of powerful and/or unattainable women at a very early age; he

1. See especially McGann, *Swinburne,* 210−20 *passim.* The term *courtly
love (amour courtois)* is one that Swinburne himself is very unlikely, even late
in his life, to have known. It is, as Francis X. Newman observes, a "descriptive
and heuristic" term, one "medievalists invented for themselves." It was introduced by Gaston Paris in a famous article that appeared during 1883 in *Ro-
mania.* Still, the existence of a code of behavior and values connected with an
"idolatrous passion" (D. W. Robertson's term) and its frequent expression in
medieval literature is undeniable. The best discussions of the phenomenon
and the controversy that still fairly rages among scholars appear in *The Meaning of Courtly Love,* ed. F. X. Newman (Albany, 1968). Newman's words are
taken from page x.

also seems always to have been fascinated by the idea of ill-starred love. . . . [His] obsession . . . is essentially a slightly modernized, that is, romanticized version of the topos of the Provençal poet-lover" (McGann, 216).

In a complementary observation, Lionel Stevenson, commenting on *Rosamond* and *The Queen Mother*, notes that "the predominant role of women in both plays is to some extent derived from the chivalric exaltation of the sex in the Courts of Love."[2] But no commentator has yet explored in depth Swinburne's revisionist and Romantic uses of the values embodied in courtly love literature, as he formulates his private mythology of passion, even in his early, most visceral works.

Before we proceed with such an exploration, some explanation of Swinburne's special interest in medieval *French* literature is in order. More than in medieval Italian, German, or even English poetry, Swinburne found in the literary traditions descended from the troubadours, at least in potential, a system of amatory, intellectual, philosophical, and political values compatible with his own. Moreover, Swinburne was himself a Francophile, propagating from his early years a myth of his own French lineage and consistently looking to France for new literary figures to champion. Such interests were, however, in large part a response to his early reading and studies. By his early adulthood, Swinburne read and spoke French fluently and knew French history better than that of any other country but England. His affinity for things French and his taste for French literature (and even the French landscape) were self-consciously cultivated throughout his life. Only in the works of Chaucer, and there less often than in medieval French literary traditions and their Romantic progeny, did Swinburne discover congenial literary forms and values that covered the entire range of human experience. One might argue that even his admiration for English Renaissance poetry and drama results from the fact that much of it is grounded in passions and amatory conflicts that derive from troubadour poetry and courtly romance as transmitted through late-medieval Italian literature, especially the works of Dante, Petrarch, and Boccaccio.

Swinburne's fascination with medieval French culture and history appears not only in his statement to Gosse that the medieval and

2. Lionel Stevenson, *The Pre-Raphaelite Poets* (New York, 1974), 198.

21

French sections of his uncle's famous library had provided "a source of unfailing enjoyment to him" in his youth but more particularly in his unpublished historical essays on French medieval subjects (see Appendix II). These include discussions of Roman and feudal law, of Charlemagne and the Crusades, as well as of Saint Louis and his biographer, Joinville. The last two of these papers are relatively long and surprisingly knowledgeable and speculative. Like Swinburne's extensive notes on Hallam's *Middle Ages,* which appear in the same autograph notebook, these essays present the young scholar attempting to interpret an enormous amount of data, to mediate between supposed facts and the truth they reveal. What he says about the Crusades demonstrates the difficulty Swinburne felt in coming to terms with the distinction he intuited between reality and its spiritual underpinnings: "To understand the crusades," he insists, "we now think, we should be able to go back to their time: and when that was done, the loss of all later experience and of all analogy would perhaps have the fact actually occurring before our eyes as hard as ever to explain fully."

It was perhaps such difficulties in attaining any genuine "historical" understanding of a plethora of facts from the past that discouraged Swinburne from pursuing professionally his early "leaning towards history," described in a letter to his mother, Lady Jane Swinburne, in April of 1860. At about that time, he was writing his essays on medieval (as opposed to classical) history with William Stubbs, who became Regius Professor of Modern History at Oxford in 1866. With Stubbs he studied law as well as history, but throughout that winter and early spring, Swinburne appears enthralled only with some of his historical studies. He writes to his mother, "When I have done with routine work I think of taking *periods* to read in contemporary books if I can keep up my present leaning towards history. I got out (the last time I was at Wallington) all sorts of things about Mary Stuart of the most exciting kind, down to an inventory of her gowns, which gave me great satisfaction. . . . I am in the meantime taking in (at Oxford) either Charlemagne or St. Louis—possibly both. That is the sort of history I like—live biographical chronicle not dead constitutional records" (*Letters,* I, 35). Swinburne's fascination with "live biographical chronicle" is, of course, reflected in the titles of most of his longer works of poetry and fiction, which focus on individual protagonists: Fredegond, Rosamond, Atalanta, Mary Stuart, Bothwell,

Chastelard, Lesbia Brandon, Erechtheus, Tristram, Balen. But that fascination also appears unmistakably in the topics of his 1860 essays, where he shows a keen interest in differentiating the true and the false heroes of history. The latter are exemplified by Charlemagne, whose human and religious values conflict with Swinburne's own. Concerned at the frequency with which Charlemagne appears as the "central figure of a wide and various body of legends," a "constantly reappearing Deus e machinâ of mediaeval poetry at least as far as the 13th century," Swinburne protests:

> Witness the legends, to take only two instances out of many, of Amis and Amiloun and Floris and Blancheflor. From these and such as these his name passed over into England and assumed a similar prestige there. Even late and grave historians have not thoroughly disengaged the idea of the historical warrior and reformer from that of the man who had been made by anticipation a model of chivalrous action, a centre of chivalrous tradition. The deep and wide anachronism, afterwards taken up by the Italians, which made of Charlemagne an Amadis or a Lancelot has to this day confused and impaired the appreciation of his real position and influence on his time.

Apart from being a "lawgiver of the most clear intuition and profound skill," he was, as Swinburne sees him, "liable to be guided and misguided by the religion of the time in which he lived and acted," a man, in short, incapable of true spiritual vision, despite his enormous political successes.

By contrast, Swinburne perceives Louis IX (1214–1270) as a truly heroic historical figure. Swinburne admires him for two clear reasons. One is that his failures in the Crusades were of genuinely tragic proportions; the other is that he lived at the end of the medieval millennium, the "dark" age—according to Swinburne—of Christian faith. During Louis's lifetime, however, "everywhere the intellectual revolt was begun or beginning," a revolt that would at last enlighten the world. For Swinburne, Louis is a man redeemed by his courage and devotion to his people, which is greater, significantly, than his religious faith. Swinburne characterizes Louis—after his second, disastrous crusade—as an incipient tragic hero:

> The failure of his expedition had been utter: and such was his despondency. All Christendom, he said, was disgraced in him and by him. (There was never an completer instance of the growth of a man's greatest glory

from a noble failure.⟩ Nevertheless it was from this mistimed and mismanged attempt that the chief reputation of St. Louis was to grow. Admitting all the impolicy and aimless misconduct which have to be deducted from the sum of his glory, yet the true valour and purity of purpose, the heroism and the patience he displayed in battle and in worse than battle—his faithful care of his people—his pity of their lost lives—his tenderness for their dishonoured bodies—all these things, even for those who need not regard him as saint or martyr, make his name and his memory among the most pure, noble, worthy of love and loving honour, in all history.

In such commentaries we see Swinburne's early compulsion to admire historical figures who appear to be touchstones of the inescapably tragic human condition, to perceive their engagement with what is at once a deep human reality and a profound spiritual one, but we also must be struck by his refusal to relinquish historical contexts and details, which he can use to empower his imaginative perceptions. It is not surprising, then, that in his finest long poems we repeatedly find imaginative or spiritual interpretations of material and often historical reality. Although many of his lyrics are predominantly abstract, his longer poems are inevitably balanced between concrete details of historical setting and characterization, and abstract, often metaphysical speculations and perceptions. Swinburne emphasizes the mimetic and realistic requirements of literature in his essay on John Webster (1886): "The crowning gift of imagination [is] to make us realize that thus and not otherwise it was" (*Bonchurch*, XIV, 168–69). At the same time, however, as Thomas Connolly has observed, "the typical Swinburnean terms *sublimity* and *spiritual instinct* are used whenever he speaks of the perfect or 'real' imagination."[3] Hence, the historical poet, like a Carlylean historian, according to Swinburne, distills the permanent, spiritual meaning from representative lives, their events and circumstances. In his 1860 notebook essay on Joinville, Swinburne gropes toward this fundamentally Romantic ideal of literary history: "The debatable ground between history and biography is a ground attractive to all men for all reasons. It seems likely to give us a true and clear notion of all that lies choked in an overgrowth of statistics or wanders before modern eyes in the mist of speculation. It is also dangerous ground. A thoroughly bad historical memoir is about the most thoroughly bad book that can well be writ-

---

3. Thomas E. Connolly, *Swinburne's Theory of Poetry* (Albany, 1964), 62.

ten. It has claims beyond the classics of romance, and duties less strict than the duties of history." Most of Swinburne's long historical poems are imaginative biographies that traverse the ground between romance and history. Many of these, like his early works influenced by Morris and Rossetti, have medieval settings because in the Victorian mind the medieval world itself, so frequently mythicized, poeticized, fictionalized, and in other ways idealized, existed on the borderline between romance and history.[4]

Not only do many of Swinburne's undergraduate poems have medieval French or Arthurian settings and deal explicitly with courtly love themes, but they also attempt to authenticate those themes and settings through careful use of historical details and literary forms while extrapolating from them philosophical propositions that embody his fundamentally Romantic ideology. Two of his first long works of some merit, *Rosamond* (begun in 1858) and *Chastelard* (begun in 1859 or 1860), verify his early fascination with the convergence of historically accurate biography and courtly love tradition. He probably had the idea for *Rosamond* before he met the Pre-Raphaelites.[5] This Elizabethan tragedy in five scenes interprets the courtly love ethos that, in historical fact, dominated the court of Henry II. Eleanor of Aquitaine,

4. This is the thrust of Mark Girouard's argument throughout *The Return to Camelot*. His commentary (p. 8) on the Victorians' chivalric idealization of Sir John Franklin's failed polar expedition is telling in a tangential way, especially since it was, coincidentally, the topic of the "first poem in which Swinburne struck a really original style," according to Georges Lafourcade (*Swinburne: A Literary Biography* [New York, 1932], 76).

5. In his commentary on *Rosamond,* Georges Lafourcade notes that "l'histoire de la belle concubine était . . . un thème presque classique parmi les préraphaélites: en 1861, D. G. Rossetti peint *La Belle Rosamond,* et Burne-Jones, en 1862, *Rosamonde* et *Eleanor et Rosamonde.* Mais la Rose du Monde était connue du poète avant sa rencontre avec les préraphaélites. G. B. Hill écrit en date 3 mai 1857" ("The story of the beautiful mistress was . . . an almost classic theme among the Pre-Raphaelites: in 1861, D. G. Rossetti painted *Fair Rosamund,* and in 1862 Burne-Jones painted *Rosamund* and *Fair Rosamund and Queen Eleanor.* But the Rose of the World was known by the poet before he met the Pre-Raphaelites. On May 3, 1857, G. B. Hill wrote"): "'Tomorrow I believe that Old Mortality intends to take a pic-nic up the river and make merry. We shall go to Godstow and dream of fair Rosamond there, I suppose, and the old days of the nunnery'" (*Jeunesse,* 236). This letter was written seven months before Swinburne met Morris, Burne-Jones, and Rossetti.

Henry's wife, was famous for upholding courtly fashions, and for providing literature connected with them, long before Henry married her, and she brought her trouvère courtiers with her to England. In Swinburne's play, however, Henry's beautiful mistress, rather than Eleanor, becomes the rapturous exponent of courtly love doctrine and is the victim of the queen's jealousy. But Swinburne does include suggestions of the latter's notoriety as a courtly lady. Courtly love themes dominate this play, whose tragedy is precipitated by the kind of adulterous relationship the troubadour poets idealized, and is consummated in murder by Eleanor. At her death Rosamond requests from her lover even the conventional courtly *consolamentum*, "one strong kiss out of your heart" (*Tragedies,* I, 265), and she tries to approach death as a new lover:

> Use me the best way found in thee, fair death,
> And thou shalt have a pleasure of mine end,
> For I will kiss thee with a patient lip. (*Tragedies,* I, 264)

Similarly, in the play named for him, Chastelard's love for Mary Stuart fits the courtly pattern, even to his projecting upon her the image of a *belle dame sans merci.* Swinburne represents Mary's largely fictionalized French lover as the traditional, impassioned warrior-bard.

Although it remains impossible to prove unequivocally that Swinburne had become enchanted by courtly love literature long before going to Oxford, it is clear that he had been steeped in it at a very early age. In addition to the evidence from Gosse's biography, some remarks appear in his letters. He writes to Paul Hamilton Hayne (May 2, 1877) that "the [Tristram] story was my delight (as far as a child could understand it) before I was ten years old" (*Letters,* III, 332). In fact, Swinburne worked at creating his own version of the myth from the time of *Queen Yseult* to the completion of his masterwork, *Tristram of Lyonesse,* in 1882. Swinburne's knowledge of medieval French romance and courtly love poetry is further substantiated by James K. Robinson, who speaks at length of French influences. Robinson specifically notes, for instance, that Swinburne "studied and imitated the Middle French *Violier des Histoires Romaines*" and observes that "A Match" (1862) "consisted of a chain of imperfect triolets adapted from an Old French wooing-song, 'Les Transformations.'" In this context, Ezra Pound acknowledges the mastery of Swinburne's imitation of the

Pastorela (as revived by Guiraut Riquier) in "An Interlude."[6] "In the Orchard," also of *Poems and Ballads, First Series,* is a superb pastiche of a troubadour *alba,* as is a passage in "The Queen's Pleasance" from *Tristram of Lyonesse* (see *Poems,* IV, 51). And the form of "Laus Veneris" constitutes a clever inversion of the *alba's* conventions.

Both formal and thematic similarities are easily discernable in Swinburne's works and troubadour poetry, as well as courtly romance. These similarities demonstrate his deep engagement with the values and ethos of courtly love literature, expressed most fully in the highly rhetorical poetry of the troubadours. For them, as for Swinburne, love provided material for art. More important, however, is the fact that for the original troubadours and their successors, love became an obsession to which everything else in life was, at least in theory, subordinate. It encompassed spiritual passions and physical lusts, both of which depended for their perpetuation upon the art that expressed them. Moreover, the substance of their chansons was essentially that of young Swinburne's poetry: "Many of the troubadours extolled the purer forms of Catharsis, and dwelt on the dolorous joy of unsatisfied longing. . . . They sang of a passion which can never be requited in this world, of death as preferable to any human reward and of the duty of separation from the beloved." In light of Swinburne's own permanently unrequited passion for Mary Gordon, it seems appropriate that he alludes to Jaufré Rudel's courtly devotion to the Countess of Tripoli in "The Triumph of Time," which is almost always read as an autobiographical statement.[7] Rudel's poetry, like

6. James K. Robinson, "A Neglected Phase of the Aesthetic Movement: English Parnassianism," *Publications of the Modern Language Association,* LXVIII (1953), 735–36; Ezra Pound, "Troubadours—Their Sorts and Conditions," in T. S. Eliot (ed.), *Literary Essays of Ezra Pound* (New York, 1954), 103. The essay was first printed in the *Quarterly Review,* 1913.

7. M. C. D'Arcy, S.J., *The Mind and Heart of Love: Lion and Unicorn, A Study in Eros and Agape* (New York, 1947), 33–34; Cecil Y. Lang, "Swinburne's Lost Love," *Publications of the Modern Language Association,* LXXIV (1959), 123–30. That Swinburne, in almost devout courtly fashion, idealized women he admired is made clear repeatedly in his letters. For instance, he writes to Edwin Hatch (February 17, 1858) concerning the intense relationship between William Morris and Jane Burden: "The idea of his marrying her is insane. To kiss her feet is the utmost man should dream of doing" (*Letters,* I, 18). Swinburne is quite serious here in advocating an attitude of aloof submission and reverence before a female idol.

Swinburne's, embodied a highly developed mythology of tragic love, and his life emulated the courtly pattern of his art.

Whatever the settings of his poems, Swinburne's dominant subject from 1857 to 1882 is Love. He dwells either upon passions that are so "strange" (or masochistic) as to be by definition insatiable (those of Chastelard, Tannhäuser, Sappho, Baudelaire), or upon passions that cannot ever be happily fulfilled because of obstacles (Rosamond's, Meleager's, Phaedra's, Tristram's). In fact, for Swinburne, only man's devotion to an ideal of love can immortalize him, love that

> though body and soul were overthrown
> Should live for love's sake of itself alone,
> Though spirit and flesh were one thing doomed and dead,
> Not wholly annihilated. (*Poems*, III, 299)

Swinburne's own devotion to his cousin Mary Gordon has even been understood in this way; McGann sees her as "an avatar of the woman doomed to be loved by and lost to him from eternity" (McGann, 218). Similarly, of course, it is most often the exclusive and total commitment of a lover to his beloved, in spite of (if not because of) insuperable obstacles, that ennobles a man and renders him worthy of reputation in courtly love lore.

Although Swinburne's temperament allowed him to be open to varied and complex influences, the evidence presented here suggests that courtly ideals, as projected in the works of medieval poets and romanceurs, represent one important source of Swinburne's own mythology of love and, as we shall see, of his slightly idiosyncratic brand of mysticism. That evidence is reinforced by the very flexibility of the courtly tradition and of courtly values, which prove remarkably compatible with aspects of Swinburne's life and work that critics have found irreconcilable. They do not conflict with his republicanism, his philosophical monism, his Hellenism, his advocacy of art for art's sake, or his attraction to Sade.[8] If Swinburne was as captivated by courtly love topoi and values as the themes of his poetry and the lost-love myth to which his life conformed suggest, we can understand

8. See, for instance, Ezra Pound's essay "Psychology and Troubadours," which suggests an intriguing reconciliation of Swinburne's Hellenism and his delight in courtly literature. In his *Spirit of Romance* (New York, n.d.), 91.

how political, moral, aesthetic, and fundamental religious considerations must all have merged for him in art, as they did for the troubadours. In *Woman as Image in Medieval Literature,* Joan M. Ferrante explains that in courtly literature beloved women often "personify cosmological forces that govern man's life; in lyric and romance they represent his ideals, his aspirations, the values of his society."[9] For the troubadours and courtly romanceurs, love as a topos became a flexible artistic convention that served to comprehend religious aspirations, to espouse moral values, to cope with carnal lusts, and to etherealize political issues, which resulted in wars fought in the name of love and under the auspices of the beloved.

For instance, in one of his best-known lyrics, "Rassa, domn'al qu'es frescha e fine," Bertran de Born not only indulges in the obligatory praise of his lady but moves on to a general philosophical discussion of the virtues and pastimes of great men. He concludes with some highly topical remarks on local politics.

> Rassa! A lady have I who is fresh and pure, a graceful and gay young girl, golden-haired with tints of ruby, with skin as white as hawthorn flower, supple of arm, firm of breast, and like a young rabbit's is her back. . . . Rassa! This I pray you to agree with: for a great man not to weary of war and not to renounce it for any threat till one has desisted from doing him harm, is worth more than river-sports and hunting, for thereby he wins and thereby upholds high merit. Maurin, against his lord Sir Aigar, is deemed a fine warrior; so let the viscount fight for his lands and title, and let the count seek them from him by force, and let us see him here soon, at Eastertide! (Press, 156–58)

Such a blending of the *canso* and *sirvente* forms is also characteristic of Peire Vidal, who is described by Alan Press as alternating "the role of public spokesman with that of impassioned lover" (Press, 194). Similarly, Swinburne could be composing the highly political lyrics of *Songs before Sunrise,* which are much in the tradition of the troubadour *sirvente* (they are addressed to a political patron), while he was simultaneously at work on the impassioned lyrical verses of *Tristram,* portions of which often seem to be epic transpositions of troubadour *cansos.*

Indeed, for Swinburne, there was a fundamental and articulable

9. Joan M. Ferrante, *Woman as Image in Medieval Literature: From the Twelfth Century to Dante* (New York, 1975), 1.

philosophical connection between passion and politics. Of course, the most conspicuous precedents for this connection appear in Swinburne's Romantic precursors, particularly Blake and Shelley. However, no matter how clearly Swinburne's political poems rely upon the precedents set by these two poets, the way in which he perceives passion, especially in its relationship to political philosophy, is more closely aligned to courtly patterns than to Romantic ones, especially in its tragic qualities. Like the troubadours, Swinburne defines passion as a source of suffering, not of Blakean joy or of Shelleyan spiritual redemption. In this he was more like Keats; but in Keats's work we find no systematic relationship between politics and passion, as we do in Blake and Shelley on the one hand, and Swinburne and the troubadours on the other. Swinburne's republicanism originates with the desire for total freedom, a release from the material sufferings of life, which for him are analogous to the sufferings of unrequitable passion. Achieving freedom from a cruel or unattainable lady (the archetype in troubadour poetry) requires precisely what achieving freedom from cruel tyrants necessitates: self-immolation. Chastelard and Meleager, who are martyrs to love, are true brothers to Chthonia, who exults in being a sacrifice to the gods that will prevent Athens' conquest in *Erechtheus*. In his undergraduate poem "The Death of Sir John Franklin," Swinburne suggests—much in the manner of Bertran de Born—that "love" and "valour" are merely separate manifestations of the same basic human impulse. He eulogizes the British explorer and formulates the supreme value of self-sacrifice, which he never abjured:

> neither land nor life
> Nor all soft things whereof the will is fain
> Nor love of friends nor wedded faith of wife
> Nor all of these nor any among these
> Make a man's best, but rather loss and strife,
> Failure, endurance, and high scorn of ease,
> Love strong as death and valour strong as love.[10]

Indeed, by 1879 when Theodore Watts (later Watts-Dunton) rescued him from a wasting alcoholic suicide, Swinburne had nearly completed his own self-destruction and thereby consummated the

10. *Posthumous Poems*, 83–84.

myth of his lost love in his own life. This myth has been perpetuated by the tireless investigations of commentators in the way that Swinburne himself helped to assure the immortality of Tannhäuser, Chastelard, Meleager, and Tristram, all martyrs to love. Prototypes for the passionate and tragic pattern of these heroes' lives abound in troubadour poetry. Jaufré Rudel, in one of his few surviving poems, describes his love as inexorable and devastating: "I am stricken by joy which slays me, and by a pang of love which ravishes my flesh, whence will my body waste away; and never before did it strike me so hard, nor from any blow did I so languish, for that is not fitting, nor seemly" (Press, 34–35). And Marcabrun echoes the sentiment, as many troubadours do: "He whom noble Love singles out lives gay, courtly and wise; and he whom it rejects, it confounds, and commits to total destruction" (Press, 50–51). But, paradoxically, Rudel is joyfully reconciled to the inevitable tragic culmination of his passion (as Chastelard, among Swinburne's early heroes, conspicuously is): "Love, gaily I leave you because now I go seeking my highest good; yet by this much was I fortunate that my heart still rejoices for it" (Press, 38–39).

For Swinburne, as for courtly writers, the beloved woman is often a destructive force, and love possesses the power "to free the soul from the constraints of the world" as well as "the pains of the world." Indeed, Swinburne's personae who are ennobled in dying for causes they exalt—whether erotic or political—are ultimately freed from the bonds of discontinuous existence and demonstrate the fundamental interconnection of those causes, which they transcend through synthesis after death with organic and metaphysical nature, Swinburne's unitary life-force, Hertha.[11]

Nearly all Swinburne's major poems reveal the courtly influence through their radical emphasis on the interrelatedness not only of passion and politics but also of all actions, all ideals, all life. Ultimately, for him a great poem must not work to exclude any sphere of human perception or activity. The experience it describes must be amenable to extension. As Thomas Connolly explains, for Swinburne the greatest poetry always expresses a "moral passion" which "fills verse 'with divine force of meaning' . . . [and] enable[s] the poet to

---

11. Ferrante, *Woman as Image,* 81, 96. See especially the fates of Sappho in "Anactoria," Meleager in *Atalanta in Calydon,* and Merlin and Tristram in *Tristram of Lyonesse.*

transcend the material world to commune with the spiritual."[12] Formal perfection is, of course, a prerequisite for such an achievement. However, the themes of successful poems must not appear in isolation. As McGann contends, the "deep ambiguities" of Swinburne's poetry "generate a process of suggestiveness . . . which can only be terminated by the reader's sense of exhaustion or incapacity. . . . For the poem does not circumscribe its suggestions, and the reader cannot perceive their limits. At the same time, the verse holds its perception of infinite resonances in forms which, by their extremely 'finished' quality, affirm the presence, though not the comprehension, of unity, law, and meaning" (McGann, 170). He adds that Swinburne is one of those poets "who seek to reveal the mysterious order of the universe" and are "forever pursuing the point where multiple worlds of life are felt to impinge upon each other" (McGann, 172). In many of Swinburne's major poems, modes of thought, experience, and aspiration are all intricately related—stages in an endless metamorphosis. As with the troubadours, poetry represented, in Swinburne's view, the ultimate form of experience, the only form pure enough to comprehend—as all kinds of mysticism must—the simultaneous transformation of every type of experience into every other type, the profound unity of consciousness that can only by artificial analysis be reduced to categories of thought: passion, politics, religion, art. For Swinburne art was a very real sphere of life, the only one in fact where the truly binding relations among types and qualities of experience, the "multiform unity of inclusion," can be purely expressed without reduction.[13] Art to be great must be open-ended and all-inclusive, a source of infinite generation. In Swinburne's Blakean concept of creativity, art must not contain but rather reflect experience as a series of endless transformations and have an expansive rather than reductive final effect.

Most of these tenets are at least implicit in courtly love poetry and romance. There, as in Swinburne's poetry, spheres of experience and levels of expression frequently merge, as they do, for instance, in the

12. Connolly, *Swinburne's Theory of Poetry,* 58.
13. Randolph Hughes uses this phrase of Swinburne's as a basic concept crucial in understanding his verse (see *Algernon Charles Swinburne: A Centenary Survey* [London, 1937], 18).

poetry of Bertran de Born, Peire Vidal, and their troubadour successors. Unrequited carnal passions are often spiritually ennobling; political loyalty is transformed into service to the beloved; devotion to the lady is equivalent to devotion to God; valorous death in her service becomes the highest good. Thus passion and service often lead to a desire for self-immolation, and death represents release from, as well as fulfillment of, both physical and spiritual passions. All types and levels of experience are focused in the love convention, which is by definition expansive, and all that it encompasses can be adequately expressed only in art. In this respect, Swinburne is in the tradition of Jaufré Rudel. Alan Press has aptly remarked that for Rudel "love . . . is known and experienced only as the end of an unending aspiration, and . . . is made perceptible only in the self-engendered, unique, and utterly isolated reality of the love-song itself" (Press, 28).

Swinburne's early exposure to the literature of the courtly tradition may well have reinforced or even shaped the enormous but characteristic breadth of his intellectual receptivity. Swinburne could simultaneously admire writers who deal with strikingly different spheres of experience—Malory, Whitman, Blake, Baudelaire, Shelley, Villon, and Hugo. He was able in good conscience to propound art for art's sake in *William Blake* and at the same time compose many of the political and mystical pieces of *Songs before Sunrise.* And in 1872, reviewing Hugo's *L'Année terrible,* he could enigmatically reveal his truly expansive critical canons:

> No work of art has any worth or life in it that is not done on the absolute terms of art. . . . thus far we are at one with the preachers of "art for art." . . . We admit then that the worth of a poem has properly nothing to do with its moral meaning or design . . . but on the other hand we refuse to admit that art of the highest may not ally itself with moral or religious passion, with the ethics or the politics of a nation or an age. It does not detract from the poetic supremacy of Aeschylus and of Dante, or Milton and of Shelley, that they should have been pleased to put their art to such use: nor does it detract from the sovereign greatness of other poets that they should have no note of song for any such theme. In a word, the doctrine of art for art is true in the positive sense, false in the negative; sound as an affirmation, unsound as a prohibition. (*Bonchurch,* XIII, 242–46)

Thus, during one period of his career, Swinburne could compose political lyrics, *Erechtheus,* the plays of the Mary Stuart trilogy, and

Tristram of Lyonesse without feeling that he was moving among incompatible spheres of experience. Passion and politics, history and myth were all mutually inclusive, and I suggest that Swinburne's early fascination with the values embodied in medieval French poetry, which themselves conflated the sources and ends of passion, religion, politics, and art, conditioned his intellect to a versatility of thought aptly characterized by the monistic inclusiveness of "Hertha."

As both M. C. D'Arcy and Denis de Rougement point out, the courtly love tradition was even flexible enough to sustain carnal superstructures built on its ethereal Platonic foundation. We see a devolution from idealism to carnality in the works of William IX, Raimbaut d'Orange, and even Arnaut Daniel, for example. After beginning one poem with the conventional references to nature, and after introducing his "midonz" as "del mon la bellaire," Raimbaut in one stanza idealizes his beloved while in the next he longs to possess her body: "I shall indeed, lady, have great honour if ever the privilege is adjudged me by you of holding you under the cover, naked in my arms, for you are worth the hundred best together, and in this praise I'm not exaggerating; in that merit alone does my heart rejoice more than if I were emperor" (Press, 112–13). And Arnaut Daniel in several poems describes even more graphically the carnal aspect of his usually devout and idealized passion: "Would I were hers in body, not in soul! and that she let me, secretly, into her bedroom! For it wounds my heart more than any blow of a rod, that her servant, there where she is, does not enter. Always I'll be with her as flesh and fingernail, and I'll not heed the warning of friend or uncle" (Press, 188–89).

Rougement, in a chapter specifically relevant to the apparent contradiction between Swinburne's fondness for the effusions of Sade and his courtly literary heritage, urges a surprising relationship between Sade's doctrine and that of orthodox devotees of courtly love. He insists that the obsessions of Swinburne's "divine Marquis" arose from and sustained themselves on "the intolerable tension of a mind" that is wracked by both carnal and ideal passions, torn between the amorous possibilities embodied in the myths of Don Juan and of Tristram. Providing evidence of the influence of courtly love on Sade, Rougement reminds us that "Sade admired the poetry of Petrarch, as he remarks in his. *Crimes de l'amour.* The admiration had been traditional in his family ever since his direct ancestor, Hughes de Sade, married Petrarch's lady, Laure de Noves." Rougement also plausibly insists that the necessary result of the contradictory yearnings of Sade's characters for both sensual and spiritual or ideal gratifications is an insupportable frustration, which demands that one be freed totally from his insatiable passions. For Sade "only murder can restore freedom, and it must be the murder of the beloved, inasmuch as loving is what fetters us." Sade's whole aim, in Rougement's view, is that of morbid courtly lovers and of Swinburne's impassioned personae: to escape the suffering of love through death.[14] But death for Sade meant murder rather than self-immolation. The fact that Swinburne's figures seem equally willing, in their desperation, to grasp either alternative merely reflects the emphasis in his poetry on the urgent human desire to escape from the bonds of passion to the freedom of death and continuity with organic nature, the unitary "Herthian" matrix of us all.[15] The speaker of "The Triumph of Time," for instance, finally yearns for union with the sea, the source of all life, "mother of mutable winds and hours," and for death as the means to achieve that union:

> This woven raiment of nights and days,
>   Were it once cast off and unwound from me,
> Naked and glad would I walk in thy ways,
>   Alive and aware of thy ways and thee;
> Clear of the whole world, hidden at home,
> Clothed with the green and crowned with the foam,
> A pulse of the life of thy straits and bays,
>   A vein in the heart of the streams of the sea. (*Poems*, I, 43)

Swinburne's personae, though often initially afraid of death, always crave their own deaths. Phaedra, Sappho in "Anactoria," Chastelard, Meleager, even Chthonia and Tristram, all share the same goal beyond death. In this respect, too, Swinburne's mythology reflects

14. Denis de Rougement, *Love in the Western World*, trans. Montgomery Belgion (New York, 1956), 211–12; Lafourcade comments upon the relationship between Swinburne's sadism and his highly "intellectual" theory of love (*Jeunesse*, 431) and observes that for Swinburne the laws of suffering and death that govern human passion also dominate the operations of nature.

15. Figures in "Phaedra," "Anactoria," "Les Noyades," and *Chastelard* are all willing to murder those they love and derive gratification from the prospect of doing so.

courtly love tradition. As one of the most astute commentators on post-medieval uses of courtly love convention, Lenora Leet Brodwin, observes,

> The courtly lover does not have a "love of death" but of the Absolute, the Infinite, all that is beyond the sphere of mortal contingency. Rather, he despises death because it is the final proof of the hated contingency and limitations of human life from which he wished to disassociate himself. But the tragic paradox of his love of the Absolute is that it can only be truly realized in that utter transcendence of mortality which involves his death. If he "triumphs in a transfiguring Death," it is because his fearless embrace of death in the name of an infinite love raises him above its power and unites him to the Absolute.[16]

Brodwin's formulation holds for Swinburnean figures as well as for traditional courtly lovers. In his philosophy—as it is illustrated in *Rosamond, Chastelard, Atalanta in Calydon,* the erotic lyrics of *Poems and Ballads, First Series,* and *Tristram of Lyonesse*—passionate experience is finally subordinate to its mystical resolution after death in the divine natural world, the Garden of Proserpine, where "all trouble seems / Dead winds' and spent waves' riot / In doubtful dreams of dreams."

Ultimately for Swinburne, Proserpine's "languid lips" are sweeter than love's, because the vision of ideal passion that he dwells on is necessarily superior to any real love relationship that can be formed and consummated in this world of physical constraints. In order to reconcile his intuition of the supremacy of man's immortal spiritual essence with the facts of material existence and carnal passion, Swinburne was forced, even from the first, to conceive of love not primarily in terms of momentary gratifications, but, as did the courtly poets and romanceurs, in ideal terms. For him, timeless intellectual and spiritual experience subsumes and is superior to transient physical and emotional experience. With Swinburne, as with the troubadours, passion resolves finally into philosophy.

16. Lenora Leet Brodwin, *Elizabethan Love Tragedy, 1587–1625* (New York, 1971), 8.

2

Rosamond and *Chastelard*
Courtly Love and
Swinburne's Religion of Beauty

One of Swinburne's earliest works about love is *Rosamond,* a drama in the Elizabethan style, but one that employs a medieval setting and real historical figures as characters. Published in 1860, this play is extraordinarily significant for the poet's future themes and artistic development. *Rosamond* possesses many of the virtues of Swinburne's later tragedy *Chastelard,* which has attracted somewhat more critical attention, but the earlier work is usually dismissed as a mere Pre-Raphaelite exercise.[1] Both plays, however, prove inspired throughout by Swinburne's youthful enchantment with courtly love topoi. In these dramas we can discern the depth of his fascination with the topoi of medieval romance and tourbadour poetry, as well as their effect

1. On the Pre-Raphaelite qualities of *Rosamond,* see Philip Henderson, *Swinburne: Portrait of a Poet* (New York, 1974), 49. For the best analysis of the play and the source of most succeeding commentaries, see *Jeunesse,* 235–45. The most useful additions to Lafourcade's discussion, all of them too brief to do the play justice, appear in: Samuel Chew, *Swinburne* (Boston, 1929), 188–90; Mario Praz, *The Romantic Agony* (London, 1933), 218–19; and Stevenson, *The Pre-Raphaelite Poets,* 196–98. Harold Nicolson was the first to insist upon *Rosamond*'s merits and was understandably perplexed that it should have "escaped the attention, or even the hostility, of contemporary criticism" (*Swinburne* [London, 1926], 66). *Chastelard* (discussed by Praz, 219–23) has begun to receive the critical attention it deserves, especially in two studies that build upon Lafourcade's standard analysis (*Jeunesse,* 261–83). These are Curtis Dahl, "Swinburne's Mary Stuart: A Reading of Ronsard," *Papers in English Language and Literature,* I (1965), 39–49; and Gerald Kinneavy, "Character and Action in Swinburne's *Chastelard*," *Victorian Poetry,* V (1967), 31–36.

on his treatment of the carnal and the ideal aspects of his constant theme, love.

Analysis of these two works with emphasis on their courtly elements reveals the extent of his early assimilation of values fundamental to medieval love literature, which he adapted to his "modern," that is, Romantic world view and to his unique artistic needs. In Swinburne's version of *Rosamond,* the passionate entanglement between Henry II and his mistress culminates with Rosamond's murder by his wife, Eleanor of Aquitaine, perhaps the most famous heroine of courtly love lore.[2] Similarly, an ethos derived from courtly convention underlies Chastelard's love for Mary Stuart.

The first of *Rosamond's* five scenes is the most forceful in demonstrating Swinburne's debt to troubadour conventions as well as to Pre-Raphaelite stylistic influences. Courtly love preoccupations and the medieval setting overshadow elements of Jacobean revenge tragedy throughout the play. Swinburne's Rosamond, rather than the historical queen of the Courts of Love, espouses the religion of love and, as a result of her lived creed, is poisoned by Eleanor out of jealousy. The play's predominantly lyrical psychodramatic vignettes stress highlights of the relationships among the four main characters during the last months of Rosamond's life. The action begins in spring and ends in late summer, but the only explicit time lapse occurs between the fourth and fifth scenes, when Henry is abroad, subduing the French provinces. In addition to the historical characters, Swinburne creates the courtier Bouchard, the serviceable object of the jealous Queen's ambivalent affections. But *Rosamond* is significant primarily for the characterization of its tragic heroine, whose passion for Henry suggests the power of the courtly love influence on young Swinburne. In the "Prelude" to *Tristram of Lyonesse* (written nine years later), Swinburne catalogues "the sweet shining signs of women's names / That

2. Swinburne's preoccupation with actual or simulated adulterous relationships in *Rosamond, A Year's Letters, Tristram of Lyonesse,* and elsewhere agrees perfectly with courtly tradition. Brodwin explains that "true courtly adultery, such as that of Lancelot or Tristan, never looks forward to marriage as the fulfillment of its desire. Indeed, the concept of a love relationship seems framed to include the husband or wife [as in *Rosamond*], in order to provide the intensifying obstruction necessary for the perpetuation of desire" (*Elizabethan Love Tragedy,* 24).

mark the months out and the weeks anew," which Love "moves in changeless change of seasons through / To fill the days up of his dateless year" (*Poems,* IV, 208). Alongside Guenevere, Hero, Cleopatra, and the rest is "The rose-white sphere of flower-named Rosamond." This Swinburnean heroine conceives of herself not as an individual but rather as a type, the beautiful woman who inspires insatiable and potentially destructive passions: "Yea, I am found the woman in all tales, / The face caught always in the story's face." She *is* Helen, Cressida, Hero, and Cleopatra. In her particular "tale," as in Swinburne's versions of stories about Cleopatra, Guenevere, and Yseult, the heroine herself is destroyed. Yet we are conditioned from the play's first scene, as the "flower-white" Rosamond wrestles with the fact of her own mutability, to accept the drama of her death as merely one episode in Love's timeless, cyclic tragedy.

Swinburne's choice of the "rose of the world" as one of his first subjects for verse suggests that he associated his conception of Rosamond with courtly love allegory, specifically the *Roman de la Rose,* in which the rose is the eternal symbol of the beloved and of the perfect beauty that is fearfully transient but simultaneously immortal.[3] As in Swinburne's later lyrics "Before the Mirror" and "The Year of the Rose," *Rosamond*'s central symbol is the rose, and, like them, this play recapitulates the major preoccupations of courtly love poetry: the apotheosis of beauty; love as the necessary consequence of beauty; fear of mutability; and a final insistence on the immortality of both love and beauty, which can be attained, paradoxically, only through death.[4]

3. Swinburne's interest in the *Roman* is demonstrated in a letter to Seymour Kirkup dated August 11, 1865, by Lang. He makes a point of observing that "in the sale of Lord Charlemont's library by auction, there was sold a MS. of the *Roman de la Rose* with many beautiful illuminations, given by the poet Baïf to Charles IX, and having also the autograph of Philippe Desportes" (*Letters,* I, 128–29). His referring to Philippe Desportes and Jean-Antoine de Baïf, both troubadour poets, confirms his familiarity with medieval French verse.

4. Swinburne's infatuation, here and elsewhere, with beauty as the sole cause and sine qua non of love is perhaps a result, direct or indirect, of Andreas Capellanus' influence. As C. S. Lewis notes, for Capellanus in *De Arte Honeste Amandi,* the source of love "is visible beauty: so much so, that the blind are declared incapable of love, or, at least of entering upon love after they have become blind" (*The Allegory of Love* [London, 1936], 33).

The first scene of *Rosamond* characterizes its heroine as simultaneously enchanted with her own beauty, exalted by her love affair with Henry, and insecure about the permanence of her beauty and her love. Surrounded by the ephemeral rose blossoms with which she identifies in the maze at Woodstock, she is alone with her maid, Constance. Here Rosamond reveals her concern with the world's slanderous gossip about her, and as the scene progresses she attempts gradually to rebuild her self-confidence—in her beauty, in Henry's continuing devotion, and in the unassailable value of beauty and of love. At first, she is defensive:

> See,
> If six leaves make a rose, I stay red yet
> And the wind nothing ruins me; who says
> I am at waste? (*Tragedies*, I, 231)

She repeatedly challenges Constance to "say I am not fair," in order to elicit the praise she pretends to despise. She equivocates between self-doubt and unabashed vanity: "Leave off my praise . . . quaint news to hear, / That I am fair, have hair strung through with gold" (*Tragedies*, I, 232). Then she renews herself by remembering Henry's courtly verses of adulation, and concludes by defining her own and the world's goodness purely in terms of beauty, the ultimate value that Swinburne everywhere associates with love:

> But I that am
> Part of the perfect witness for the world,
> How good it is; I chosen in God's eyes
> To fill the lean account of under men,
> The lank and hunger-bitten ugliness
> Of half his people . . . I that am, ah yet,
> And shall be till the worm has share in me,
> Fairer than love or the clean truth of God,
> . . . .
> I . . . have roses in my name, and make
> All flowers glad to set their colour by. (*Tragedies*, I, 236–37)

Earlier, Eleanor has revealed that the source of her jealousy is her homeliness. Angrily and plaintively, she compares herself with Rosamond:

> Sweet stature hath she and fair eyes, men say;
> I am but black, with hair that keeps the braid,

40

And my face hurt and bitten of the sun
Past medicine of all waters. (*Tragedies,* I, 245)

Nonetheless, feelings of jealousy are mutual. Throughout the play
Rosamond schizophrenically alternates between vanity and insecu-
rity. Since she values herself exclusively for her beauty, she needs a
man continually to reinforce her self-esteem, as does every courtly
lady. She nourishes her vanity by goading the king to denigrate his
queen:

As you are king, sir, tell me without shame
Doth not your queen share praise with you, show best
In all crowned ways even as you do? I have heard
Men praise the state in her and the great shape. (*Tragedies,* I, 260)

That Henry can describe Eleanor coldly as "A Frenchwoman, black-
haired and with grey lips / And fingers like a hawk's cut claw" (*Tragedies,* I, 261) explains Eleanor's rabid antagonism toward Rosamond.
In the play's aesthetic theology, ugliness is equivalent to damnation,
and Henry's adulterous relations with so beautiful a mistress as Rosamond entirely undermine the queen's pride and reputation.

Rosamond and Eleanor both need courtly praise and devotion, because the love that beauty inspires is their supreme value. Beauty not
only assures love, it assures immortality: "Love's signet-brand stamps
through the gold o' the years" (*Tragedies,* I, 238). In Scene I, Rosamond articulates the courtly apotheosis of love upon which the whole
action of the play depends. Here, as always, a life of love assures salvation. It is the one crucial sacrament:

God has no plague so perilous as love,
And no such honey for the lips of Christ
To purge them clean of gall and sweet for heaven.
It was to fit the naked limbs of love
He wrought and clothed the world with ordinance.
Yea, let no wiser woman hear me say
I think that whoso shall unclothe his soul
Of all soft raiment coloured custom weaves,
And choose before the cushion-work of looms
Stones rough at edge to stab the tender side,
Put honour off and patience and respect
And veils and relics of remote esteem
To turn quite bare into large arms of love,

41

> God loves him better than those bitter fools
> Whom ignorance makes clean, and bloodless use
> Keeps colder than their dreams. (*Tragedies*, I, 238)

Rosamond's emphasis here on the transcendent value of passion that defies convention and her earlier emphasis on the power of beauty that defies mortality are reminiscent of two arguments implicitly proferred in Morris' "The Defence of Guenevere," composed at about the same time as Swinburne began the first draft of *Rosamond* (see *Jeunesse*, I, 235–36). But Guenevere's values are more strained and tentative than Rosamond's. Of even greater importance in differentiating Morris' attempt at a sternly realistic adaptation of medievalist amatory and religious values and Swinburne's iconoclastic recasting of them, however, is that Guenevere pathetically capitulates in "King Arthur's Tomb," her monologue's companion piece, to conventional religious orthodoxies, as Swinburne's medievalist heroines and heroes often refuse to do.

In the passage from *Rosamond* quoted earlier, we discover the first lengthy formulation of Swinburne's consistently fatalistic "religion" of love and beauty, which "makes the daily flesh an altar-cup / To carry tears and rarest blood within / And touch pained lips with feast of sacramant" (*Tragedies*, I, 239). Indeed, in this play as elsewhere in Swinburne's poetry, the experience of passion temporarily becomes a kind of religious ecstasy. The oblivion it engenders, however, simulates death. In a sad and loving mood, after singing a Swinburnean imitation of a sorrowful troubadour lyric, Rosamond ends Scene III with this plea to Henry:

> Yea, kiss me one strong kiss out of your heart,
> Do not kiss more; I love you with my lips,
> My eyes and heart, your love is in my blood,
> I shall die merely if you hold to me. (*Tragedies*, I, 265)

The hyperbole of this last line is typical of courtly rhetoric. Further, Rosamond's postponement of carnal satisfaction, and her demand for a single kiss, reflects an "orthodox" courtly love convention in which the degree of restraint a lover feels compelled to employ is merely a measure of promised bliss and present woe, the mixed pain and pleasure of passion.

With Rosamond it is not so much the intensity of insatiable love as the fear of forfeiting her beauty and, consequently, her lover's praise that makes her desire death. Although she is terrified and cowardly when actually confronted by Eleanor, Rosamond opens the play's last scene with a weary and sorrowful soliloquy in which she ponders the ugliness age is sure to bring, and because of that inevitability, she prays, "God . . . / get me broken quickly." Finally she meets death as a succedaneum and is consoled to die with her beauty and Henry's love undiminished: "To die grown old were sad, but I die worth / Being kissed of you" (*Tragedies,* I, 287). It is appropriate that the heroine should end this play receiving the traditional kiss or *consolamentum* of courtly love, for Swinburne has produced in *Rosamond* an only slightly modified—that is, sensualized—recapitulation of what he perceived to be the essential values and basic conventions of medieval love literature.

Chastelard reflects the same adherence to the courtly love ethos as does *Rosamond.* However, Swinburne's religion of love by 1865 contained Sadean elements with which the poet was unacquainted five years before. In *Chastelard* we find the ideals of *Rosamond* sensationalized with a graphic carnal awareness. Moreover, the desire for death as love's supreme consummation had become more than a convention. By 1865, Swinburne's own mythology of passion had subsumed the ideology of medieval love literature that had earlier inspired his work. The reciprocal influences of London life and Swinburne's own artistic experiments of the early 1860s are reflected in a play that crystallizes Pre-Raphaelite, Sadean, *and* courtly love influences. But in it, historically empty conventions of courtly love are presented dramatically as earnest and moving solutions to the problem of human passion.

Chastelard constitutes an even more convincing transposition of courtly love values than does *Rosamond,* partly because of Swinburne's improved dramatic technique and partly because of his ability to write more vigorous verse, but primarily because of an ostensibly deeper personal involvement in the emotional issues that the play dramatizes. Although *Chastelard* was not published until 1865, it was—as Georges Lafourcade plausibly asserts—the focus of Swinburne's attention immediately after, if not simultaneously with, "The Triumph of Time," his own elegy on the loss through marriage of Mary Gordon.[5] We know, however, by Swinburne's own assertion, that *Chastelard* was first conceived and begun in 1859 or 1860 and that it went through numerous revisions (*Letters,* II, 235). Following *Rosamond* so closely, early drafts of *Chastelard* perhaps laid more stress on Swinburne's unsophisticated acceptance of courtly love ideals than the final version does. The play's hero, who describes Ronsard as "The sweet chief poet, my dear friend long since" and as "my old lord" (*Tragedies,* II, 139), not only espouses courtly love values but acts them out in his life. Whether additions to the original version of *Chastelard* resulted from Swinburne's disappointment with Mary Gordon, as "The Triumph of Time" is assumed to have done, or simply from a more epic conception of his evolving mythology of insatiable passion, *Chastelard* in its final form is a palpable and artistically successful reflection of Swinburne's ethos of love. Dramatic tension in the play is generated almost exclusively by the dynamic and suicidal passion of the hero for the dark and capricious heroine.

Chastelard is depicted from the start as a warrior-poet who is also Mary Stuart's courtier and lover. Lafourcade has pointed out the play's biographical significance: Swinburne's identification with the ideals that Chastelard embodies is transparent. The poet's most important early critic remarks that Swinburne "crée, comme Dieu, à son image. . . . Chastelard est poète comme Swinburne; et ce dernier ne manque pas de lui donner l'auréole qu'il avait, adolescent, ambitionnée: celle des armes et de la gloire militaire; il mêle ses rêves de Mary à des visions de bataille" (*Jeunesse,* 280).[6]

Lafourcade does not perceive, however, that all the attributes with which Swinburne invests Chastelard belong also traditionally to the

5. "The year 1863 comes as an anti-climax after the many events and intense literary activity of the months that preceded. Apart from *The Triumph of Time,* it seems that Swinburne set himself as his chief task during the first half of the year to complete and give some sort of definite shape to the much-modified and rewritten *Chastelard*" (Lafourcade, *Swinburne,* 107).

6. Swinburne "created, like God, after his own image. . . . Chastelard is a poet, like Swinburne; and he did not neglect to give Chastelard the aura which he himself had, as an ambitious adolescent; the aura of arms and military glory; he mixes his dreams of Mary with his vision of battle."

troubadours and their successors. Chastelard is represented in the play as a sixteenth-century trouvère whose devotion to the ideal of his love is fanatically orthodox. When the object of his passion proves inaccessible and viciously changeable, his commitment to the ideal supersedes his passion for the beloved. It becomes a passion for death.

Curtis Dahl has already verified the significance of Swinburne's use of Ronsard in the play. Chastelard's "old lord" is the author of the book that Mary in the last act brings to Chastelard's prison cell and that Chastelard reads as he approaches the block. Indeed, Dahl claims that Swinburne's conception of Mary Stuart was inspired by a misreading of Ronsard, who was writing about Mary Stuart "in a highly artificial convention of courtly compliment developed in the Middle Ages and raised to a paean to physical love in the early Renaissance." Dahl accurately observes:

> By consciously or unconsciously ignoring the conventional quality of Ronsard's diction and attitudes toward his beloved mistress, Swinburne transforms what is really graceful and beautiful but not unusual flattery by a court poet to a lovely and unfortunate Queen into characterization of a fabulously seductive, partly historical but largely mythological goddess of aesthetic beauty and cruel passion. Whereas in Ronsard the emphasis on Mary's many physical charms is conventional cataloguing compliment, Swinburne (whether unknowingly or with conscious literary intention) reads into it an almost morbid eroticism.[7]

Swinburne was aware of the convention Ronsard was working in and deliberately undertook to literalize the courtier-poet's typical love song—to employ courtly rhetoric and hyperbole in earnest. Mary Stuart is thus transformed by Swinburne into a truly threatening *femme fatale,* and Chastelard becomes a powerfully realized extension of the representative courtly poet-lover, a literary ideologist with troubadour conditioning.

As a result, the play is punctuated with Swinburnean imitations of sorrowful love lyrics. Mary Beaton appropriately sings one as the play begins, for her futile love of Chastelard represents the sad, steadfast, and ethereal counterpart of Chastelard's carnal and aesthetic passion for Mary Stuart. Mary Beaton and Mary Stuart both sing his songs in

7. Dahl, "Swinburne's Mary Stuart," 44.

the second act, and in the last play of the trilogy that *Chastelard* begins, Mary Stuart's fate rests on her being able to recognize the author
of a lyric composed years before by Chastelard. As with all Swinburne's pastiches, the verses attributed to Chastelard in the play are
authentic reproductions of conventional courtly love lyrics. But they
have special significance here, foreshadowing the play's action and
echoing the imagery used to depict it. For instance, the last two stanzas of Mary Beaton's opening song characterize the religious quality
as well as the consuming intensity of Chastelard's love for Mary Stuart, which he sustains to his death and which, in fact, transforms his
violent end into the final, sacramental act of his passion:

> Et l'amour
> C'est ma flamme,
> Mon grand jour,
> Ma chandelle
> Blanche et belle,
> Ma chapelle
> De séjour.
> .   .   .   .
> Toi, mon âme
> Et ma foi,
> Sois ma dame
> Et ma loi;
> Sois ma mie,
> Sois Marie,
> Sois ma vie,
> Toute à moi! (*Tragedies*, II, 14)[8]

The paradox of Chastelard's passion is that it is at once what he lives
for and what kills him. Life without his love is not only futile but
equivalent to damnation, and after Mary jealously and spitefully
chooses Darnley as her husband, fulfillment is impossible. Yet Chastelard's devotion is complete and inevitable, wrongheaded as he knows
it is. His conditioning apparently does not allow for the caprice of traditional courtly lovers, expected as well as displayed by Mary Stuart.

8. "Love is my passion, it is my light, my great day, my beautiful white
candle, my shrine. You, my soul and my faith, be my lady and my law; be my
love, be Marie, be my life, everything to me."

As in Swinburne's lived mythology, Chastelard is both made and broken by an irretrievable commitment to one love. However, Mary, in spite of her desire to be loved with devotion like Chastelard's, can honestly yet remorsefully describe her own fickle nature this way:

> I would to God
> You loved me less; I give you all I can
> For all this love of yours, and yet I am sure
> I shall live out the sorrow of your death
> And be glad afterwards. You know I am sorry.
> . . . .
> God made me hard, I think. Alas, you see
> I had been fain other than I am. (*Tragedies*, II, 75)

Thus, with severe irony, Mary can remark upon expected infidelities after singing one of Chastelard's mutablity lyrics, which, in Swinburne's usual manner, associates love with roses:

> As-tu vu jamais au monde
> Vénus chasser et courir?
> Fille de l'onde, avec l'onde
>   Doit-elle mourir?
>
> Aux jours de neige et de givre
> L'amour s'effeuille et s'endort;
> Avec mai doit-il revivre,
>   Ou bien est-il mort?
>
> Qui sait où s'en vont les roses?
> Qui sait où s'en va le vent?
> En songeant à telles choses,
>   J'ai pleuré souvent. (*Tragedies,* II, 56)[9]

The Venus of the first stanza has already been identified in Act I as Mary herself. "A Venus crowned, that eats the hearts of men" (*Tragedies*, II, 25) is represented on a breastclasp given her by an admiring artist. As a later incarnation of the archetypal *femme fatale* with whom Rosamond has identified, this beautiful Queen, fearful of death but

9. "Have you ever seen Venus chasing and running? Daughter of the sea, should she die with the sea?

"In days of frost and snow love sheds its petals and goes to sleep, with May should it awaken or is it really dead?

"Who knows where the roses have gone? Who knows where the wind goes? One dreams of such things. I have often cried."

doomed to be beheaded, is, in fact, immortal. "Doit-elle mourir?" in connection with Mary Stuart is a doubly ironic rhetorical question.

The power of Mary Stuart's beauty makes her, like Rosamond, the eternal object of men's desires. For Chastelard, as for Swinburne's earlier courtly lovers, beauty is the supreme and literally captivating attribute of woman. Because of it, he becomes Mary's suicidal "sweet fool." To love in irrevocable earnest is Chastelard's fatal "flaw." Yet it is a fault that is most easily understood in terms of the erotic aestheticism of Chastelard's courtly heritage. Even Mary at first cannot fathom the obstinate depths of his devotion to her beauty. Gradually, however, she begins to perceive the passionate spirit of his unique supplication, along with the power it confers upon her:

> Though he be mad indeed,
> It is the goodliest madness ever smote
> Upon man's heart. A kingly knight—in faith,
> Meseems my face can yet make faith in men
> And break their brains with beauty: for a word,
> An eyelid's twitch, an eye's turn, tie them fast
> And make their souls cleave to me. (*Tragedies*, II, 115)

Like any religious fanatic, Chastelard appears mad. For him, as for Rosamond, beauty is the chief measure of goodness in the world. In his last moments with Mary, he explains,

> You have all the beauty; let mean women's lips
> Be pitiful, and speak truth: they will not be
> Such perfect things as yours. Be not ashamed
> That hands not made like these that snare men's souls
> Should do men good, give alms, relieve men's pain;
> You have the better, being more fair than they,
> They are half foul, being rather good than fair;
> You are quite fair: to be quite fair is best. (*Tragedies*, II, 138)

Chastelard is finally vindicated in his worship of a pitiless and capricious beauty not only by the traditional courtly apotheosis of "fairness" but also by the representation of Mary's beauty as a characteristic ethereally detached from her other attributes. All the play's major figures at some point remark upon Mary's superb beauty and intuit its tragic counterpart, cruelty. Mary knows that her beauty is the exclusive cause of men's attraction to her and of Chastelard's passion.

Chastelard confirms the fact when Mary Beaton tries to understand why he loves Mary Stuart so fervently. In response, he catalogs her physical splendors:

> She hath fair eyes: may be
> I love her for sweet eyes or brows or hair,
> For the smooth temples, where God touching her
> Made blue with sweeter veins the flower-sweet white;
> Or for the tender turning of her wrist,
> Or marriage of the eyelid with the cheek;
> I cannot tell; or . . . her mouth,
> A flower's lip with a snake's lip, stinging sweet,
> And sweet to sting with: face that one would see
> And then fall blind and die with sight of it
> Held fast between the eyelids. (*Tragedies*, II, 20)

Chastelard in fact dies because of his inalterable devotion to an ideal of beauty, of which Mary Stuart is a typical incarnation. In the mythology of this play, as in *Rosamond*, coalescence with the ideal can be striven for in this world but achieved only in death. His early intuition of some "kindling beyond death / Of some new joys" inspires Chastelard's last hour. In fact, by the time he dies, he has articulated several visions of possible consummations to his passion that death may supply. When in Act III he hides himself in Mary's chamber and confronts her with the fact that his love is undiminished though obstructed by her marriage to Darnley, he articulates his yearning for a union with Mary of the type craved by Sappho in "Anactoria." Between frenzied kisses, he threateningly chides,

> Now I am thinking, if you know it not,
> How I might kill you, kiss your breath clean out,
> And take your soul to bring mine through to God
> That our two souls might close and be one twain
> Or a twain one, and God himself want skill
> To set us either severally apart. (*Tragedies*, II, 72)

Chastelard's ideal is total integration with Mary, his ideal of beauty. Although he can conceive of attaining such a consummation to his passion only in death, in life he assiduously pursues whatever can best approach or simulate it. Thus, he insists on accompanying Mary to Scotland and, later, on exulting in his love of her even after she is married.

Our impression of Chastelard's masochism results from his aggressive pursuit and apparent enjoyment of passions he knows are inherently insatiable. At the play's beginning Chastelard admits to having suffered the unquelled passion of "two years' patience." In Act I, awaiting the Queen in Mary Beaton's chamber, Chastelard joyously anticipates an end to his fever of expectation. When the figure he assumes to be the Queen appears, he at once associates her embrace (and the promise of a final gratification of his desires) with man's final consolation, death. "O sweet," he sighs,

> If you will slay me be not over quick,
> Kill me with some slow heavy kiss that plucks
> The heart out at the lips. (*Tragedies*, II, 35)

His accumulated passion for the Queen is so intense that, discovering Mary Beaton's deception, he impulsively threatens to kill her. When Chastelard does finally gain access to the Queen in her chamber with a promise of impassioned confrontation, he for the first time realizes the inevitably fatal nature of his love. He affirms that "to die thereof, / ... is sweeter than all sorts of life" (*Tragedies*, II, 63). As in Swinburne's other works of passion, death in this play's mythology becomes the desired end of love, the ultimate consummation:

> let me eat sweet fruit and die
> With my lips sweet from it. For one shall have
> This fare for common day's-bread, which to me
> Should be a touch kept always on my sense
> To make hell soft, yea, the keen pain of hell
> Soft as the loosening of wound arms in sleep.
> Ah, love is good, and the worst part of it
> More than all things but death. (*Tragedies*, II, 64–65)

Death is, in fact, superior to love because it guarantees release from the necessary constrictions and the mutability of life, both of which prevent the perfect fulfillment of love. In obviating the further possibility of unrequited or disappointed passion, death paradoxically assures love's permanence, "Held fast between the eyelids." Chastelard's death, then, represents a means to immortal fulfillment. Courtly rhetoric is taken with a fatal seriousness that prevents the play from being melodrama, and Chastelard's example vividly underscores his proposition that death is "sweeter than all sorts of life."

In spite of all the sanguinary images that surround and prepare for Chastelard's death, the event itself comes to represent the ultimate act of love for both the queen and her courtier-poet. Murder and suicide do converge at Chastelard's beheading, but the love talk in the play has prepared us to accept his execution as a specific metaphor for a form of mutual sexual satisfaction. Throughout the play, Chastelard has explicitly identified acts of violence with acts of love. He has explained that in battle "when the time came, there caught hold of me / Such pleasure in the head and hands and blood / As may be kindled under loving lips" (*Tragedies*, II, 52–53). Shortly afterward, he has revealed a further connection between his sensations in battle and his impassioned conception of Mary. He has rapturously explained how "when I rode in war / Your face went floated in among men's helms, / Your voice went through the shriek of slipping swords" (*Tragedies*, II, 71). Mary, for her part, has dwelt at length on her yearnings for participation in the violent physical excitement of battle. Watching "the fight at Corrichie," she claims, "twice my heart swelled out with thirst / To be into the battle."

Death at Mary's violent hands (albeit at one remove) comes to simulate a sexual encounter in the same way that battle does for both Mary and Chastelard. In idle discourse with her devoted courtier in Act II, she says: "I would you might die, when you come to die, / Like a knight slain" (*Tragedies*, II, 55). Chastelard views his execution as precisely such an honorable end. It will prevent his dying "meanlier sometime." In addition, this kind of death preserves passion intact. This way Chastelard is "sure of her face" (as neither Rosamond nor Eleanor is of hers), thus avoiding the profound bitterness of love's decay. In Act II, believing Chastelard had rejected her and conceived a new passion for Mary Beaton, the Queen has dolefully declaimed: "There's nothing broken sleep could hit upon / So bitter as the breaking down of love" (*Tragedies*, II, 46). Later she suggests death as a solution to the problem of love's transience. She asks Chastelard if he agrees that "it were convenient one of us should die," for "there could come no change then; one of us / Would never need to fear our love might turn / To the sad thing that it may grow to be" (*Tragedies*, II, 47). With Chastelard's execution they succeed in raising their love to a condition of permanence through tacit cooperation in an ostensibly brutal, but actually loving series of intuitively grasped moves and countermoves. Mary Stuart and Chastelard act out their own immortal myths of the kind that, Swinburne repeatedly insisted, art strives always to imitate, and that Swinburne himself successfully imitated in his lived, lost-love myth as well as in his art. But it is a myth that was initially legitimized in courtly love lore and formally propagated in troubadour poetry. There, death, as sought after in military service on behalf of the beloved or simply as a release from an ultimately insatiable passion, is represented as the metaphorical solution to problems of transience and consuming love. It served, as it does in *Chastelard*, as self-fulfilling proof of constancy and as a guarantee of love's permanence.

From this point of view, Chastelard and Mary Stuart appear something more than suicidal and merciless. By means of Chastelard's death they are able to gratify their individual inclinations and to consummate an otherwise doomed love in an event that has acquired the significance of a supreme act of passion. It simultaneously fulfills and immortalizes their relationship. Therefore, *Chastelard* is a "tragedy" only from a perspective unsympathetic to the courtly dynamics of the protagonists' love relationship. Mary Beaton represents such a perspective within the play, and it prevents her, as it has prevented a century of commentators, from understanding exactly how a *belle dame sans merci* and ostensibly helpless victim can *both* be full and sympathetic figures. Perhaps better than any of Swinburne's other major works, *Chastelard*, along with its earlier, thematic companion piece *Rosamond*, demonstrates how his unique and complex modern additions to the tradition of courtly love literature depend in part upon an ability to depict hauntingly beautiful women who fit into the archetypal category of *femme fatale* but preserve their integrity as convincing, sympathetic characters.

The sinister reputation that Swinburne's heroines have acquired originated with the work of Georges Lafourcade and Mario Praz. Both critics emphasize the *femmes fatales* who appear in Swinburne's poems of the 1860s, the period of his career in which he was strongly influenced by Sade. They focus on Swinburne's female figures who dominate *Poems and Ballads, First Series*. Close analysis of the major medievalist poems in that volume demonstrates, however, that nearly all the beloved women appear as mute objects of their lovers' affections. They are seen entirely through anguished eyes, and these frequently belong to medieval knights, courtiers, or clerks. Swinburne uses such lovers, who are located in a precise historical situation, not primarily to exalt or excoriate beautiful seductive women, but rather to make unconventional statements about the unchanging relations among passion, orthodox religion, and art over the course of human history.[10]

10. Only by the very end of the 1860s, I believe, did Swinburne's mythology of female "types" fully crystallize. At its base is his concept of Hertha, a transcendent and ubiquitous generative principle eternally active in the world, one that compels the "illimitable" passions that define human relationships as well as interactions among objects and phenomena in nature. For an extended discussion of this topic, see my article, "The Swinburnean Woman," *Philological Quarterly,* LVIII (1979), 90–102.

3

Poems and Ballads, First Series
Historicity and
Erotic Aestheticism

Among the works denounced by the earliest English reviewers of *Poems and Ballads, First Series* (1866) are the medievalist poems "Laus Veneris," "The Leper," and "St. Dorothy."[1] But the volume contains many other pieces—very nearly half the volume, in fact—that are also medievalist in their forms, styles, settings, sources, or subjects. Such are "A Ballad of Life," "A Ballad of Death," "A Litany," "In the Orchard," "A Cameo," "A Ballad of Burdens," "April," "August," "A Christmas Carol," "The Masque of Queen Bersabe," "The Two Dreams," "Madonna Mia," "After Death," and, of course, the ballads "The King's Daughter," "May Janet," "The Sea-Swallows," and "The Bloody Son." That Swinburne conceived this book as one that would appeal especially to contemporary currents of interest in medievalism is clear from the title of the American edition, *Laus Veneris and Other Poems*,[2] which emphasizes as the volume's centerpiece a work that complexly and gracefully brings together Swinburne's historicist,

1. For full discussions of the critical reception of *Poems and Ballads, First Series*, see Clyde K. Hyder, *Swinburne's Literary Career and Fame* (Durham, 1933). A briefer summary of critical attacks and Swinburne's responses to them appears in the same author's "Introduction" to his edition of major essays by the poet, *Swinburne Replies* (Syracuse, 1966), 1–13.

2. Although T. J. Wise insists that the American edition of *Poems and Ballads, First Series* "was fully authorised," he confesses that its new title presents some difficulties. He reaches a conclusion different from my own, suggesting that "possibly the discussion raised by *Laus Veneris . . .* in London had awak-

erotic, formal, and spiritual preoccupations. Examples of his Romantic antiquarianism, as well as his understanding of the complex relations between poetry and history, appear throughout the collection. Like some late-twentieth-century historical thinkers, Swinburne perceived the extent to which the writing of history is a creative act: ultimately the historian is an artist and mythmaker.[3] But Swinburne's medievalist poems in the 1866 volume demonstrate further that poets must be seen, finally, as authentic historians. He makes this point primarily by manipulating various levels of historical framing in the depiction of disparate love relationships.

More fully than any of the other medievalist pieces in *Poems and Ballads, First Series,* "Laus Veneris," "The Leper," and "St. Dorothy" exemplify the ways in which the volume's radical ideology evolves from interactions among Swinburne's historicist, erotic, and formal concerns. In these works, the young poet plays variations upon historically contrary attitudes toward the relations between Christianity and erotic passion, between the orthodox and "satanic" faiths. Each poem is iconoclastic: either passion triumphs over orthodox Christianity as a form of devotion; or, more complexly, erotic passion becomes identified, as the poem develops, with the art that describes it. The poem thus becomes an aestheticist document. In this latter case, the beauty of a beloved woman is gradually overshadowed by the beauty of the sensations she generates in her lover or biographer, and

---

ened curiosity in the United States, and the publisher looked to excite a larger sale for his book by distinctly showing that the most notorious poem was not excluded from its pages" (*A Bibliography of the Writings in Prose and Verse of Algernon Charles Swinburne* [London, 1919], 134). Even were this the case, Swinburne would very probably have concurred in such an advertisement, which would also have drawn attention to the medievalist cast of the volume. The American edition was reprinted three times in three months.

3. See especially Hayden White, *Metahistory: The Historical Imagination in Nineteenth-Century Europe* (Baltimore, 1973), *passim*; and, in White's *Tropics of Discourse: Essays in Cultural Criticism* (Baltimore, 1978), the two essays "The Historical Text as Literary Artifact" (5–80) and "Historicism, History, and the Figurative Imagination" (101–20). Also important in this context are E. D. Hirsch's *Validity in Interpretation* (New Haven, 1967) and Karl Lowith's *Meaning in History* (Chicago, 1949). Valuable in demonstrating where Tennyson overlaps and diverges from Swinburne's philosophy of history is Kozicki, *Tennyson and Clio*.

these sensations are, in turn, superseded by the ideal beauty of the artistic vehicle that embodies them. The beauty of the poem recapitulates, transmutes, and makes permanent the beauty of otherwise ephemeral erotic sensations. Such is one important achievement of "Laus Veneris," "The Leper," and "St. Dorothy," and it reinforces their radically subversive, prophetic functions as well as their effects as romantic tragedies in monologue and lyric forms. This representative group of medievalist poems punctuates the 1866 volume near its beginning, middle, and end, and analysis of them significantly advances our understanding of Swinburne's later treatment of tragic love in medieval settings.

In 1862, the year that "Laus Veneris" was largely composed, Swinburne began to propound his doctrine of art for art's sake in a *Spectator* review of Baudelaire's *Les Fleurs du mal*. "A poet's business," he asserts there, "is presumably to write good verses, and by no means to redeem the age and remould society."[4] Baudelaire, he insists, properly "ventures to profess and act on the conviction that the art of poetry has absolutely nothing to do with didactic matter at all." Thus, Baudelaire's most representative poems treat "failure and sorrow . . . physical beauty and perfection of sound or scent" (*Bonchurch*, XIII, 419). In this respect, the French poet resembles Keats, as well as Poe and "even the sincerer side of Byron." Swinburne is nonetheless careful in this essay, just as he is in his later aestheticist criticism, to make clear that a poem shaped predominantly by aesthetic concerns may still have important implications for moral values and ethical behavior. He explains that "there is not one poem of the *Fleurs du Mal* which has not a distinct and vivid background of morality to it. Only, this moral side of the book is not thrust forward in the foolish and repulsive manner of a half-taught artist; the background is not out of drawing" (*Bonchurch*, XIII, 423). Here, as in his later essays on Blake

4. See *Jeunesse*, 421. Further, in *Notes on Poems and Reviews* (Hyder [ed.], *Swinburne Replies*, 26), Swinburne acknowledges that "Laus Veneris" owes a great deal to Baudelaire's pamphlet on Richard Wagner's opera, published on April 1, 1861. Barbara Charlesworth also briefly examines the influence of Swinburne's aestheticism (as it is expressed in the essay on Baudelaire) upon the contents of *Poems and Ballads, First Series* (*Dark Passages: The Decadent Consciousness in Victorian Literature* [Madison, 1965], 10−21).

and Hugo, which uphold the same aestheticist values, Swinburne identifies form and beauty as the artist's primary concerns, though moral considerations are very likely to support and reinforce the poet's purely aesthetic aims. But, as always, his notions of morality are iconoclastic and revolutionary rather than conventional. Concerned ultimately with "high" forms of morality, rather than with the sexual mores that were, in his era, popularly thought to constitute a basis for all morality, he concludes that any reader "who will look for them may find moralities in plenty behind every poem of M. Baudelaire's" (*Bonchurch*, XIII, 423). To illustrate his point, Swinburne focuses upon Baudelaire's medievalist mode in the poem "Une Martyre." The poet, "like a medieval preacher, when he has drawn the heathen love, . . . puts sin on its right hand, and death on its left. It is not his or any artist's business to warn against evil; but certainly he does not exhort to it, knowing well enough that the one fault is as great as the other" (*Bonchurch*, XIII, 423). Perhaps the most important virtue of art for Swinburne is its absolute integrity—in both senses of the word. The purity and independence of art can in all ages serve as a corrective to narrow and repressive systems of morality, as well as to oppressive political systems.

Even while writing his review of Baudelaire, Swinburne was immersed in his readings of William Blake,[5] and in the book that finally emerged from those readings, Swinburne presents arguments strikingly similar to those in his 1862 essay. In both of these aestheticist treatises, as well as in his later commentary in Hugo's *La Légende des siècles*, Swinburne frequently turns to medieval literary prototypes or medieval topoi to fill out and illustrate his unyielding doctrine of art for art's sake.

In a pronouncement crucial to any full understanding of the interactions among erotic, psychological, literary, and even political elements in his own poetry, Swinburne asserts of his kindred spirit Blake that "to him, as to others of his kind, all faith, all virtue, all moral

5. On October 6, 1862, Swinburne rejected an offer to compose a commentary on Blake's poems for the biography by Alexander Gilchrist, whose premature death had thrust the job of supervising publication into William Michael Rossetti's hands. Swinburne in this letter outlines his plan to write "this . . . year a distinct small commentary of a running kind as full and satisfactory as it could well be made, on Blake's work" (*Letters*, I, 60).

duty or religious necessity, was not so much abrogated or superseded as summed up, included and involved by the one matter of art" (*Bonchurch*, VI, 132–33). Swinburne elaborates upon this conviction by acknowledging the existence and effective power in the world of a "kind" of person, one whose attitude toward the function of art is exactly contrary to that of Blake and Swinburne. This is "the party of those who . . . regard what certain of their leaders call an earnest life or a great acted poem (this is, material virtue or the mere doing and saying of good or instructive deeds and words), as infinitely preferable to any feat of art" (*Bonchurch*, VI, 135). Feats of art, for Swinburne, are primarily concerned with "the shape or style of workmanship." These contrary parties always exist and are always at odds, according to Swinburne, and "all ages which were great enough to have space for both . . . hold room for a fair fighting-field between them" (*Bonchurch*, VI, 135). To illustrate his point, he chooses to focus on "the medieval period in its broadest sense, not to speak of the notably heretical and immoral Albigeois with their exquisite school of heathenish verse" and on such poems as the "Court of Love" (then attributed to Chaucer), which is "absolutely one in tone and handling . . . with the old Albigensian *Aucassin* and all its paganism" (*Bonchurch*, VI, 135). The essential point here is, simply, that "priest and poet, all those times through, were proverbially on terms of reciprocal biting and striking" (*Bonchurch*, VI, 136); the poets, quite properly, maintained the integrity of their art, at whatever price. In Swinburne's view, then, much medieval poetry—like the work of Baudelaire and Blake—reflects the ultimately aestheticist proclivities of its authors and is therefore overtly iconoclastic, attacking the doctrines of the priesthood and therefore the accepted religious values of most readers (or auditors).[6]

6. Significant as an indication of how important Swinburne's *William Blake* was to aestheticist thought in England is Donald Hill's acknowledgment that Walter Pater "probably got his incentive" for the first essay of *The Renaissance* from these "two or three pages of Swinburne's" book. In Hill's superb edition of *The Renaissance* (Berkeley, 1980), 303, he also notes the same perception in Germain d'Hangest's *Walter Pater: L'Homme et l'ouevre* (2 vols.; Paris, 1961), I, 356n57. For further discussion of the subject, see Charlesworth, *Dark Passages*, 33–35.

In an important footnote that glosses these passages from *William Blake* and suggests the historical and aesthetic dimensions of all the medievalist poems of *Poems and Ballads, First Series*, Swinburne alludes to "the Horsel legend," upon which the most important medievalist poem in that volume is based. He does so in the course of discussing *Aucassin and Nicolette*, in which, as Swinburne sees the matter, the poet turns "the favorite edgetool of religious menace," the threat of damnation for sinfulness, "back with point inverted upon those who forged it." In this medieval work, "men and women of religious habit or life punished in the next world" are represented, and they are "beholding afar off with jealous regret the salvation and happiness of Venus and all her servants." For Swinburne the Tannhäuser legend, unlike *Aucassin*, "shows the religious or anti-Satanic view of the matter" (*Bonchurch*, VI, 136). "Laus Veneris," however, like Blake's *Marriage of Heaven and Hell*, undertakes to present for Swinburne's historical era the "Satanic" perspective on the Tannhäuser myth and on the historical conflict between pagan erotic values and Christian notions of sin and renunciation. "Laus Veneris" therefore becomes a psychodrama emblematic for Swinburne of the permanent historical conflict between contrary systems of cultural values that—as in Blake's "Argument" to the *Marriage*—alternately dominate the world. In this respect, "Laus Veneris" is a medievalist poem parallel to Swinburne's Hellenic "Hymn to Proserpine."

In Tannhäuser's meandering monologue the reader can view Swinburne's medieval poet-lover and knight on a number of different levels simultaneously. A tension between opposed forces in his life—between opposed loyalties, for instance, or contradictory psychological impulses—informs each level of perception. The poem may thus be seen as a dramatization of the battle between Blakean contraries within the wracked mind of Tannhäuser. In the course of the poem Swinburne fully exposes the conflicts not only between Tannhäuser's passion and religion but also between his vocation as poet and his career as a knight: the one depends upon service and devotion to an ideal of love, the other upon service and devotion to Christ. Also at odds yet inextricably entangled in Tannhäuser's mind are body and soul; concepts of life and death, virtue and sin (as well as the reward of each), fruitfulness and barrenness, love and happiness, beauty and goodness. In the poem's concluding stanzas, however, out of Tann-häuser's convoluted self-analysis, his analysis of love, his retrospection, and his resignation to the eventual torments of hell he is bound to suffer, evolves Blakean "progress": a powerful affirmation of *eros* that for Tannhäuser constitutes a psychological apocalypse.[7] Addressing the slumbering Venus, who is at once, in the poem, a real woman, an ideal, and a myth, he asserts that there is, ultimately, "no better life than . . . / To have known love." How, he asks, shall those "that know not . . . have such bliss / High up in barren heaven?" (*Poems*, I, 26). He determines to cling passionately to Venus, his ideal of erotic love, to "seal upon [her] with my might" until the Last Judgment, "until God loosen over sea and land / The thunder of the trumpets of the night."

This denouement has been carefully prepared for in the body of the poem, throughout which Venus' role as a mythical and historical ideal predominates. Upon this ideal Tannhäuser guiltily projects his deepest spiritual compulsions—his proclivities to rebel against orthodoxy—as well as his physical compulsions—his erotic and aesthetic appetites. His monologue exposes precisely enough of Tannhäuser's own true value system to inspire his concluding affirmation of *eros* over Christian notions of *agapē*. The conclusion is not merely a belated rationalization, but rather a genuine statement of Satanic or Gnostic faith in the spiritual and aesthetic values that dominate trou-

7. Some important commentators have refused to see the poem's conclusion as a coherent rejection of orthodoxy or a sincere realization and affirmation of the ultimate value Tannhäuser places upon his attraction to Venus' beauty and the life of sensation she has come to symbolize. Among those critics are McGann (*Swinburne*, 255–58) and even Julian Baird, who focuses on important connections between Swinburne's *Blake* and "Laus Veneris" ("Swinburne, Sade, and Blake: The Pleasure-Pain Paradox," *Victorian Poetry,* IX [1971], 49–75). Other important commentaries on "Laus Veneris" include Robert Peters, "The Tannhäuser Theme: Swinburne's 'Laus Veneris,'" *Pre-Raphaelite Review,* III (1979), 12–28; Chris Snodgrass, "Swinburne's Circle of Desire: A Decadent Theme," in Ian Fletcher (ed.), *Decadence and the 1890's* (London, 1979), 61–88; Praz, *The Romantic Agony,* 228–29; Charlesworth, *Dark Passages,* 26–28; Thais E. Morgan, "Swinburne's Dramatic Monologues: Sex and Ideology," *Victorian Poetry,* XXII (1984), 175–95; and Barbara Fass, *La Belle Dame Sans Merci and the Aesthetics of Romanticism* (Detroit, 1974), 181–88.

badour, or minnesänger, tradition.[8] Thus, Tannhäuser's "entrapment" by Venus is ultimately a mode of self-willed liberation, one that is, during the monologue, merely delayed by temporary lapses of his Venerean faith, which proves in the end to be far more compatible than is Christianity with his vocations as soldier and love poet. Thus, on its most fundamental level, "Laus Veneris" is psychogenetic, depicting for Tannhäuser the evolution of true self-knowledge. The poem is an exercise in ideological epistemology. At the same time, on other overlapping levels of interpretation, it is an affirmation of historical dialectics and of the inevitably aestheticist doctrines of "the poet" generically defined by Swinburne: in the case of this poem including both Tannhäuser and the kindred poet who chooses to "record"—that is, project—his monologue.

The poem insists in a number of clear ways upon its own literary-historical dimensions. Even at the very beginning of the poem, as a preface to his own fictitious nineteenth-century work, Swinburne creates an illusion he maintains throughout the poem, of three historical stages in the literary development of the Tannhäuser legend: that of Tannhäuser himself, spoken in his monologue; of "Maistre Antoine Gaget," who is quoted in the epigraph; and of the present poet. These are, of course, only three among dozens of well-known and complementary versions of or stages in the myth's "historicization": innumerable writers have appropriated the Tannhäuser legend. The epigraph from the fictional Maistre Antoine Gaget's imaginary "Livre des grandes merveilles d'amour"—as soon as we realize the deception—betrays the shaping hand of an inventive poet who makes use of both his own and the reader's sense of history in order to regenerate a great myth of love. Swinburne's procedure here suggests that the myth itself, and the history of that myth, are both permanently available to the poetic mind for reconstitution. That is, a myth articulated at any particular historical moment implicitly contains its own previous and possible articulations, and these the poet is privi-

---

8. Peters observes that Tannhäuser, "rejected by Pope Urban (and hence by Christianity)," has, by the time of his monologue, fully evolved as a "knight-artist whose sense of beautiful design and aesthetic effect [has been] enhanced rather than diminished by personal traumas" ("The Tannhäuser Theme," 26).

leged to extrapolate because of his special concern with preserving the beauty—the essential artistic reality—of the myth. Great myths perpetually regenerate themselves by means of such men, and the human truths they embody can never be suppressed as long as there are poets whose ultimate concern in the world is with the beautiful. In short, poets are—uniquely—historians of beauty. Thus, the epigraph here, like the "Prelude" to *Tristram of Lyonesse* or like Swinburne's "Thalassius," reminds us of the dialectical relationship between history and poetry. That the epigraph feigns a Renaissance recapitulation of a medieval myth now appropriated by a nineteenth-century poet reinforces our awareness that matters of literary genealogy are crucial to human "progress." This awareness is ultimately central to our perception that Tannhäuser is an unwitting iconoclast and an elect poetlover who is nonetheless blind to his own election.

Despite his inability to understand the special role he will play in the evolution of the Venerean mythos, Tannhäuser is by no means insensitive to the history of the myth itself. Repeatedly during his monologue he reflects on the changing status of Venus worship over history, especially as it either exalts or victimizes its devotees, according to the dominion, at a given historical moment, of puritans or poets. Gazing intently upon the slumbering form of Venus very early in the poem, Tannhäuser synecdochically contrasts the defunct reign of Venus with the presently triumphant reign of Christ, and in doing so expresses his conflicting allegiances. At the same time he exposes his own dominant and irrepressible, though obsolete, affinities: "Lo, she was thus," he maintains, "when her clear limbs enticed / All lips that now grow sad with kissing Christ" (*Poems,* I, 11). Later, adopting the Christian view of Venus, as he does through most of the poem, Tannhäuser depicts her as an immortal *belle dame sans merci* whose perennial victims' "blood runs round the roots of time like rain" (*Poems,* I, 15), and he cites "the knight Adonis" as among the earliest of her victims.[9] Later still, he envisions those historical devotees of beauty and love

9. Praz, the first critic to insist upon this view of Venus, also reinforces the connections between this poem and Swinburne's interest in Baudelaire. In "Laus Veneris," Praz argues, "the subject of Keats's *Belle Dame Sans Merci* is treated more profoundly and elaborated with all the resources of a grim and satanic Pre-Raphaelite medievalism. Venus who was 'the world's delight' [is] now fallen, in Christian times, to the level of a sinister vampire, . . . she

who have surely, according to Christian doctrine, been condemned to
an eternity in hell. He cites the Provençal courtly lovers, the Albigeois, "the knights that were so great of hand, / The ladies that were
queens of fair green land, / Grown grey and black now" (*Poems*, I, 17).
Also among those in hell, "Trampled and trodden by the fiery feet"
because of their amorous adventures, are Helen of Troy, "the marvellous mouth whereby there fell / Cities and people whom the gods
loved well," and Cleopatra, who "softer than the Egyptian lote-leaf
is, / The queen whose face was worth the world to kiss; / Wearing at
breast a suckling snake of gold" (*Poems*, I, 18). Both these queens have
become exalted as mythical figures, perceptions of their power over
the direction of history also increasing as their stature in myth has
been enhanced by poetic treatments of them. Venus is, of course, their
permanent mythical prototype, and in "praising" her, Tannhäuser the
poet not only tells his own story but also becomes an important
mytho-historiographer, advancing her power over the world and over
perceptions of world history. Similarly, of course, Swinburne has
taken on the dual role of extending and enhancing the power of
Venus—that is, the values of beauty and love that she symbolizes—
while similarly mythicizing and enhancing the power and historical
stature of the poet-lover Tannhäuser.

After establishing the larger context for any historical perspective
on the worship of Venus, Tannhäuser presents his own particular history, which has culminated in devotion to her. He relates the ecstasies
of his military exploits as a knight "of Christ's choosing"; he describes
his career as a famous minnesänger who "Sang of love" and *its*
ecstasies but "knew them not" until he "one dawn . . . rode forth
sorrowing . . . / Up to the Horsel." There he discovered the ideals
of perfect love and perfect beauty in the voluptuous form of Venus.
Entranced, upon the Hörselberge, he viewed "heaps of flowers" and

---

whom the poet evoked again later in the ode on the death of Baudelaire, *Ave
Atque Vale*" (*The Romantic Agony*, 228–29). Both McGann (*Swinburne*, 256)
and Barbara Fass extend Praz's perspective on the Venus of "Laus Veneris" by
using *Ave Atque Vale* as a gloss on the earlier poem. Referring to Swinburne's
concern, in his elegy on Baudelaire, with the "historical process" involved in
treatments of Venus as a symbol and mythological figure, Fass also suggests,
but does not pursue, the implication that Swinburne's interest in historical
matters was crucial in shaping "Laus Veneris" as well (*La Belle Dame*, 181–82).

> The ripe tall grass, and one that walked therein,
> Naked, with her hair shed over to the knee.
>
> She walked between the blossom and the grass;
> I knew the beauty of her, what she was,
> The beauty of her body and her sin,
> And in my flesh the sin of hers, alas! (*Poems*, I, 22)

Tannhäuser's sense of sin here represents only a temporary and puritanically limited perspective on his capitulation to the power of beauty and the fundamental human craving for it: Venus' effect upon him is to inspire an exultant and insatiable erotic passion. He is thus seduced by both aesthetic and erotic appetites, but in his description of his "fall," his aesthetic response is primary and causal. Like his historical predecessors in the grip of Love, he has become an aesthete and, unlike many of them, a *guilty* hedonist.[10] (He speaks, appropriately, in iambic pentameter quatrains; the rhyme follows the pattern of Edward FitzGerald's *Rubáiyát*.) From such a perspective, Tannhäuser is for Swinburne a type of all those who are true poets by nature and thus lovers of beauty. As a memorializing poet, he alludes in his monologue to his predecessors' now mythicized fates, revealing that his value system is ultimately and paradigmatically aestheticist in its preoccupation with the inescapable effects of beauty and sensation upon mankind. Of course, the shaping historical consciousness of the poet "external" to the monologue is aestheticist in complementary ways. By means of this modern poet's evident concern with the genealogy of literature about Venus and Tannhäuser, but also by means of literary allusions sometimes outside Tannhäuser's possible frames of reference, Swinburne extends the aestheticist implications of the poem, which are founded upon Tannhäuser's experiences with love and beauty.

In "Laus Veneris," Swinburne generates from a preexisting myth an entirely new and original poetic artifact that is molded largely by his adaptation of complementary literary strains—medieval, Blakean,

---

10. Fass also describes Tannhäuser as a hedonist and asserts, finally, that in "Laus Veneris," Swinburne "celebrates the delights of sensuality" (*La Belle Dame*, 188). And Peters insists that even Tannhäuser's "Christianity . . . is sensual, suiting his characer" ("The Tannhäuser Theme," 20).

and Keatsian. The influence of Morris' Arthurian and Froissartian poems, along with a number of Rossetti's works with medieval settings, is also visible in superficial ways, though "Laus Veneris" is more overtly erotic, iconoclastic, and ideological than is any medievalist poem by Morris or Rossetti. Like so many of Swinburne's early poems, this poem is to an extent imitative of their work in its atmosphere, while its form parodies medieval originals and its content is at once Blakean and Keatsian. Both despite and because of the poem's diverse sources and influences, however, "Laus Veneris" is finally unique. Formally, the work is a type of inverted and extended medieval *alba*. This poetic form is superimposed upon medieval materials reshaped by Swinburne's understanding of Blake's philosophy of history and Blake's theory of contraries; in the poem Swinburne also appropriates Keatsian erotic aestheticism. Shaping the poem in addition to these influences, however, are Swinburne's own attraction to a kind of erotic militarism and, more important, his obsession with the suffocating, sadomasochistic sensations of passion.

Blake's influence upon the dialectical patterns of historical thought and upon the dialectical psychological patterns of the monologue are already clear, as are Swinburne's perceptions of Blake as a kindred aesthete. Moreover, the major medieval elements of "Laus Veneris" are obvious. They include Tannhäuser's careers as knight and minnesänger, his apparent participation in the Crusades, his unpropitious pilgrimage to the pope, his Catholic view of sexual morality, and his frequently chivalric language. But Swinburne enhances these elements in subtle ways, both formal and substantive, that make the poem organically medievalist. The poem's form as an inverted and extended *alba* requires a lyric lament over the imminent parting of lovers at dawn. Yet, just as Tannhäuser eventually turns against orthodox Christianity and just as the poem becomes thematically an attack upon the religious tyrannies that victimize Tannhäuser, so Swinburne extends the contrariousness of his general procedures and turns the form of the poem against its originary conventions. This poem is, until the last four stanzas, a lament that Tannhäuser *cannot* finally part from his beloved; and in its concluding lines it becomes a complexly tragic affirmation of eternal union with the beloved. Further, with the lovers underground throughout the poem, cycles of night and day here are parodically replaced by Tannhäuser's references to the linear progress of mankind's history that culminates in the apocalypse, the ultimate dawn. But in that "dawn" as envisaged by Tannhäuser, the light of the sun—usually dreaded by the *alba's* speaker—is replaced by the more dreadful glow of hell's flames. Such variations on the *alba* form draw the reader's attention to matters of aesthetics that are corollary to Tannhäuser's personal obsession with beauty and to his artistic vocation.

Like the poem's form, the psychology of its central character appears to be deeply medieval, especially in the conflict between Tannhäuser's professed orthodox values and his subversive, anti-orthodox affinities.[11] Tannhäuser, in fact, represents microcosmically the opposition between Gnostic Albigensian and orthodox faiths in the thirteenth century, when the historical Tannhäuser lived. Swinburne's clear perception of this conflict is, of course, skewed in the same directions that are apparent in Denis de Rougement's reconstruction of twelfth- and thirteenth-century Catharist history. Both writers associate the heretics with the religion of love that dominates troubadour and related strains of European poetry. Thus, Tannhäuser's psychological bifurcation appears as a mirror of the opposition between poet-lovers and priests, which Swinburne believed prevailed during Tannhäuser's age. Such a reinterpretation of medieval history is precisely parallel, as a matter of the poem's thematic substance, to Swinburne's revisionist use of the *alba* form. Again, the effect is to draw attention to matters of artistry and artistic license in the present poet's attempt to reshape historical materials in order to produce a fully integrated poem, one concerned not only with psychology and ideology but, more fundamentally, with the creation of beauty at all levels of representation. These levels include the external poet's shaping of his materials, Tannhäuser's depictions of Venus as an exquisitely beautiful woman, of love and battle as predominantly visceral experiences, and even of Love as Cupid, a poetic emblem standing "hard by [Venus'] head / Crowned with gilt thorns and clothed with flesh like fire, / . . . wan as foam blown up the salt burnt sands" (*Poems*, I, 12).

Such emblems remind us, of course, of similar medievalist tendencies in the poetry of Keats, especially his odes. In "Laus Veneris,"

11. Peters observes that "no matter how symbolic Tannhäuser becomes as a vehicle for Swinburne's religious ideas, he remains a creature of the Middle Ages" ("The Tannhäuser Theme," 23).

Swinburne echoes such tendencies and adapts several of Keats's other aestheticist practices as well.[12] While Swinburne relies upon the medieval backgrounds of his poem primarily for its form and subjects, and upon Blake primarily for its ideology, Swinburne repeatedly alludes to Keats (though perhaps unconsciously) in ways that reinforce his own voluptuous style and display the complex psychology of the poet-lover and aesthete, Tannhäuser, who is inextricably ensnared in a pain-pleasure complex that leaves him always on the verge of wholly languishing in sensation.

The poem begins, appropriately, with a paraphrase of the conclusion to Keats's "Ode to a Nightingale": "Asleep or waking is it?" In "Laus Veneris" this question refers, however, not to the speaker, but rather to the object of his aesthetic and erotic passions. Throughout the first half of the poem Tannhäuser strives repeatedly to project upon Venus the image of a relentless Keatsian *belle dame sans merci.* Psychologically, the attempt is an effort of puritanistic rationalization, in order to escape responsibility for his hedonism and his fate; but it is also a perversely pleasurable act of self-flagellation that reinforces Tannhäuser's deep desire to accept and enjoy a life inescapably devoted to beauty and love. Halfway through the poem he generalizes about love on the basis of his bittersweet experiences with his mythic and celebrated *femme fatale.* Once again personifying Love, Tannhäuser compares pursuing her to tracking a panther, "hidden in deep sedge and reeds," with her "rare scent." Suddenly the hunter

> Is snapped upon by the sweet mouth and bleeds,
>
> His head far down the hot sweet throat of her—
> So one tracks love, whose breath is deadlier,
>   And lo, one springe and you are fast in hell. (*Poems,* I, 20)

12. In his now classic study, *Keats and the Victorians* (New Haven, 1944), George Ford concludes that "in spite of ecstatic outbursts of praise on some occasions, and in spite of early imitations, Swinburne's respect for Keats's art is not very deep. His own poetry is on the periphery of the Keats tradition" (169). Most current critics of Swinburne would, however, agree more fully with Lafourcade's estimate of Keats's profound influence on Swinburne's early concerns and style (see *Jeunesse,* 155–56, 537–38, but also and especially his *Swinburne's Hyperion and Other Poems: With an Essay on Swinburne and Keats* [London, 1927]). See also Fass, *La Belle Dame,* 170–75, 188–90; and Riede, *Swinburne,* 106–107, 114.

But it is an erotically and aesthetically gratifying hell, rich with sensation; it is the cave in the Hörselberge, the domain of Venus the archetypal *belle dame*. The repeated use of vivid sensory images and sonorous language, here and throughout the poem, contagiously communicates Tannhäuser's erotic and aesthetic appetites and instills in the susceptible reader a desire also to pursue "underground" pleasures. Tannhäuser's monologue thus serves what is, for Swinburne, a moral function: it initiates the reader into the ideal realm of erotic aestheticism and thus liberates him from repressive moral and religious values, as many of the other works in *Poems and Ballads, First Series* do.

As "Laus Veneris" proceeds, and it becomes clear that Venus, the putative *belle dame sans merci*, is static and unresponsive—indeed, a virtual symbol, like Love at her side—Tannhäuser's own state of mind becomes increasingly the focus of his attention. He goes considerably further than the admission by the speaker in the "Ode to a Nightingale" that he is "half in love with easeful Death." To resolve the anguish created by the conflict within him between love and religion, Tannhäuser craves the anodyne of death. He does so, however, in voluptuous images that undercut his death wish and betray it as an appetite for beautiful sensation purified of guilt and anguish. Stunned by the beauty of Venus when he looks upon her, he laments that for her "mouth's sweet sake" his "soul is bitter": his "limbs quake / . . . as their heart's vein whose heart goes nigh to break" (*Poems*, I, 16). Using Keatsian language and image patterns, he pleads,

> Ah God, that sleep with flower-sweet finger-tips
> Would crush the fruit of death upon my lips;
>   Ah God, that death would tread the grapes of sleep
> And wring their juice upon me as it drips. (*Poems*, I, 16)

Lush sensual passages like this one punctuate "Laus Veneris," but they are descriptive of Venus or her victims or Tannhäuser's own passions rather than his quest for oblivion. In fact, Tannhäuser's craving for death largely gives way after the first third of the poem to his savoring of sensations associated with passion and thus with Venus' beauty. These culminate in reminiscences upon his return to her after vainly seeking Pope Urban's absolution for his "sin." Shocked once again by the ineffable beauty of Venus—"more beautiful than God"—

he remembers how "she laid hold upon me," and "her mouth / Clove unto mine as soul to body doth." He details Venus' gorgeous "smells," including the "perfume . . . swart kings tread underfoot / For pleasure when their minds wax amorous" (*Poems*, I, 25). Such imagery in its general character and its specific prosodic techniques recalls passages from "The Eve of St. Agnes" and *Lamia*. But more than this, its dominance in the last half of the poem indicates within "Laus Veneris" as a whole a Keatsian movement from a quest for oblivion in death to a luxuriant affirmation of beauty for its own sake, an affirmation parallel to the one that structures the "Ode on Melancholy."

This movement reveals once again that Swinburne in "Laus Veneris" is working at a number of complex levels simultaneously—psychological, moral, mythic, historical, and aesthetic. Yet it is finally the aestheticist concerns that unify all the others. Swinburne appears to write this poem and his other medievalist poems because of their subjects' historically distant tragic beauty. This concern of a nineteenth-century poet with aestheticizing events in the lives of medieval characters who were real or mythical or even wholly invented by Swinburne results usually from the relentless attraction figures from the great age of romance are traditionally depicted as feeling toward sensational experiences of the beautiful in love. Love of all descriptions for Swinburne presented the possibility of enjoying such experiences with the greatest possible intensity. Telling the usually tragic stories of medieval lovers—as Dante, Petrarch, Chaucer, and the troubadours had done—allowed Swinburne, at his poems' most important level of meaning, to propagate in beautiful and passionate poetry his unyielding belief in the preeminent value of beauty and sensation. In his view, the poet's "moral" function in the world, finally, is to uphold that value central to human experience and, through the beauty of his own creations, to liberate readers from systems of belief that interfere with the pursuit and desire of beauty—what Walter Pater was to describe as "passion" that yields the "fruit of a quickened, multiplied consciousness."[13]

Medieval backgrounds and a medieval setting in "The Leper" function in ways significantly different from those apparent in "Laus Veneris"

13. Pater, *The Renaissance*, 190.

but for the same ultimate purpose.[14] Like that poem placed near the beginning of *Poems and Ballads*, "The Leper," which is almost in the middle of the volume, draws attention to the aestheticist implications of its own medievalism, which are rendered by a focus upon the speaker's anguished recognition that any genuine fulfillment of his passion is irretrievably lost to him. The psychology of guilty hedonism that occupies "Laus Veneris" is supplanted in "The Leper" by an exploration of pathetic, failed love. In telling of his love for a beautiful woman who has become a leper and died, the poem's speaker attempts to understand his own encroaching despair that is unassuaged by any pleasures of sensual indulgence. He is only sporadically content with possessing his once beautiful beloved, at least in death, and, before that, during an affliction that had caused all other people to spurn her. Finally, the ideological shock value of the poem exposes Swinburne's iconoclasm and his aestheticism just as forcefully as "Laus Veneris" does. In many other respects, however, "The Leper" serves as an antithesis of "Laus Veneris."

Unlike Tannhäuser, the speaker in "The Leper" from the outset accepts God's repudiation of him—"God always hated me" (*Poems*, I, 119)—and he feels no guilt for his behavior. Rather, he revels in his continuing attentions to his beloved. "Sometimes," he explains,

> when service made me glad
> The sharp tears leapt beween my lids,
> Falling on her, such joy I had
> To do the service God forbids. (*Poems*, I, 122)

Indeed, the "poor scribe" who speaks this monologue is not primarily concerned, as Tannhäuser is, with himself, his present pleasure and his fate, but with his ministry to the woman he loves, and beyond that—both before and after her death—with nurturing an ideal of love that transcends whatever erotic gratification he might de-

14. For commentaries on the backgrounds and possible sources of the poem, see *Jeunesse*, 456–57, 572–73; and Clyde K. Hyder's "The Medieval Backgrounds of Swinburne's *The Leper*," *Publications of the Modern Language Association*, XLVI (1931), 1280–88. Both agree that this is one of Swinburne's earliest poems, a variation upon *A Vigil* (composed in 1857). Lafourcade acknowledges his inability to discover the true source of the poem; Hyder argues for *Amis and Amiloun*, "which Swinburne undoubtedly read in Weber's *Metrical Romances*" (1283–84). Tale xciv of the *Gesta Romanorum* seems to me just as likely a source, though Hyder discounts it (1286).

rive from it. Rather than feeling victimized, as Tannhäuser does, he feels blessed despite his sacrilege. The psychological crisis central to the poem derives only from his fear that he has failed fully to supplant the leper's previous lover in her heart. At the beginning of the first and sixth stanzas, the scribe enunciates the premise upon which he has always based his actions: "Nothing is better, I well think, / Than love" (*Poems*, I, 119). The ideal of love itself is for him "more sweet and comelier / Than a dove's throat strained out to sing" (*Poems*, I, 121). Yet, he finally admits that "all this while I tended her, / I know the old love held fast his part," and he acknowledges that "the old scorn" she had felt for him as a man of lower social station "waxed heavier, / Mixed with sad wonder, in her heart" (*Poems*, I, 123). His anguish at this realization is all the more intense because of his devotion to what must finally be seen as a spiritual ideal of love and because of his unyielding belief in its transcendent value.

The scribe's experience of love thus counterbalances Tannhäuser's in its selflessness and its spirituality. His love does have aesthetic and erotic components, but they are matters of memory and fantasy rather than distraction and obsession, as they are for Tannhäuser. In fact, only once, in stanzas fifteen through seventeen, does the scribe dwell at length on erotic pleasures, and these are largely vicarious. Here he simultaneously envies and disparages the knight who had

> Felt her bright bosom, strained and bare,
> Sigh under him, with short mad cries
> Out of her throat and sobbing mouth
> And body broken up with love. (*Poems*, I, 121)

Yet "he inside whose grasp all night / Her fervent body leapt or lay" eventually "Found her a plague to spurn away" (*Poems*, I, 121). The erotic pleasures this knight presumably enjoyed with the leper well before her illness approach the ecstasies Tannhäuser insists he has learned from Venus, but they have always been unavailable to the humble scribe of this poem, who is no voluptuary, or poet, or—until now—figure of literature and myth.

Also different from "Laus Veneris" is Swinburne's approach in "The Leper" to the issue of historicity. He does not introduce this poem, as he does "Laus Veneris," by quoting as an epigraph a fictive source, which from the start suggests that we become aware of the full artistic significance of the poem's historical genealogy. But Swinburne does cite an alleged historical source for "The Leper" at the end of the poem: the *Grandes Chroniques de France* (1505). The title is an ironic invention, for this hardly "great" love story is raised to significance only by its present author, who pretends to rescue it from oblivion.[15] This source serves three distinct purposes. Most important, it asserts that the perpetual battle between the mentalities of priest and poet (the "scribe" himself) occurred at every level of society during the age of most important rivalry between orthodox religion and the religion of love. The citation also verifies the poem's underlying premise that love of every type and manifestation is the perennially richest aspect of life and therefore the greatest subject of poetry (and *Grandes Chroniques*). Finally, the deception of the invented source demonstrates that poetry as a mode of discourse is uniquely self-authenticating. By citing a source at the end of this particular poem, rather than at its beginning, Swinburne takes advantages of the skepticism about the poem's events that would likely develop among his contemporary readers. The iconoclastic repercussions are twofold: the reader is shocked not only at the outrageously macabre nature and anti-orthodox morality of the events described but also (and again ironically) at their apparent historical veracity. Thus Swinburne exploits his own and all readers' assumed interest in history to advance the cause of art, especially its absolute autonomy and its ability to generate myths that supersede history because of the intense emotional responses they elicit. Although "The Leper" balances sympathy and judgment, as do most dramatic monologues, our memory of the scribe who speaks here is all the more indelible because of Swinburne's note.[16] If the strategy is successful, this poem, like "Laus Veneris," confirms that the reifications of art not only become a part of our larger reality but also subtly alter its constitution. Swinburne's historical consciousness and the fictions he creates insistently to support it in his medievalist poems force the reader to confront this truth in ways that monologues

15. See Hyder, "Medieval Backgrounds," 1282–83.

16. For the standard discussion of the special emotional and intellectual effects of the dramatic monologue, see Robert Langbaum, *The Poetry of Experience* (New York, 1963), 75–108. See also Ralph W. Rader, "Notes on Some Structural Varieties and Variations in Dramatic 'I' Poems and Their Theoretical Implications," *Victorian Poetry,* XXII (1984), 103–20; and Morgan, "Swinburne's Dramatic Monologues," 175–95.

by his contemporaries often do not.[17] The ultimate result of this confrontation is our awareness—Romantic and philosophically idealist—that art can, in fact, shape reality. Beauty is truth of the highest order.

The aestheticism of "The Leper," then, unlike that of "Laus Veneris," is not to be found primarily in the poem's imagery or the sonorities of its music or the richness of its language. These are proper to depictions of the exclusively erotic passion that draws Tannhäuser to Venus, his ideal of beauty. But "The Leper" is a much simpler poem than is "Laus Veneris," even prosodically, with its more schematic rhymes and its briefer, tetrameter lines. The poem is built predominantly upon one-syllable words, rather than the rich, often Latinate and multisyllabic diction of "Laus Veneris." Also, through a careful avoidance of the sibilants, assonance, and consonance that account for the lush musical effects of "Laus Veneris," Swinburne in "The Leper" has produced a poetry that aptly reflects the purity of the speaker's simple devotion to his beloved. Appropriate to the selflessness and spiritual love the narrator feels are the less palpable but equally powerful pathos and compassion that his monologue elicits in response to his own experience as well as that of his beloved, who has been cruelly deceived by the world's vanities. Ultimately, such intense visceral responses are only reinforced by the grotesque circumstances surrounding the bizarre love relationship depicted in "The Leper" and by Swinburne's strategy of alleging the historicity of the story behind it.

Like "The Leper" and "Laus Veneris," "St. Dorothy" serves iconoclastic purposes. It subverts the precepts upon which Swinburne believed the Christian orthodoxy of his contemporaries was founded; it demonstrates the ultimate value (and the inevitable triumph) of aestheticist approaches to erotic and spiritual experience; and it validates the inescapable historiographic functions of the poet. Unlike "Laus Veneris" and "The Leper," however, "St. Dorothy" takes the form of a sequential narrative. In this poem near the end of *Poems and Ballads,*

17. Browning, for instance, insists in "The Book and The Ring" that his art is designed to "tell a truth obliquely," but the moral, intellectual, or spiritual truths his monologues communicate do not usually involve the issue of poetry's relationship to history and our understanding of the ways in which that relationship operates, as Swinburne's do. The same point might be made about Tennyson's monologues.

First Series, Swinburne retells by means of a devout medieval narrator the story of a beautiful woman who lived in the fourth century and was martyred during the persecutions of Diocletian. According to the version of her legend that Swinburne appropriates, she was tortured and beheaded for refusing to repudiate Christianity and return to the worship of Roman gods, especially Venus. Diocletian attempted to enforce such conversions near the end of his reign. The mythology that has come to surround St. Dorothy does have its roots in historical fact, but the *Passio* narrating her life is full of legendary material.[18] She was especially revered during the Middle Ages and a frequent subject in German and Italian paintings during the Renaissance.

Swinburne's adaptation of the legend predictably emphasizes the erotic aspects of Dorothy's persecution and the purely sensory qualities of all the characters' experiences. The poem begins with Theophilus catching sight of and falling in love with Dorothy. Traditionally described as a lawyer, Theophilus is depicted in Swinburne's poem as a wealthy man who leads "a soft life of pleasurable days" and worships Venus. When he first comes upon Dorothy, according to the obtrusive narrator of the poem, he observes that she is "Clothed softly, with sweet herbs about her hair / And bosom flowerful." Her face appears to him "more fair / Than sudden-singing April in soft lands" (*Poems,* I, 238). Wishing to marry Dorothy, Theophilus approaches her, asking that she join him in hedonistic rituals at "the church of Venus painted royally."

When Dorothy refuses Theophilus' proposition, he feels humilated and tries to be avenged by reporting the incident to "The emperor . . . one Gabulus," a lewd and blustering, sadistic voluptuary, who taunts Dorothy, skeptical of her alleged purity: "I pray thee show us something of thy love, / Since thou was maid thy gown is waxen wide" (*Poems,* I, 246). When she protests, the tyrant instructs his men to "draw her with steel gins," Gabulus grinning and "wagging" with delight at the prospect. Indeed, Dorothy is brutally tortured: "her soft blood . . . shed upon her feet, / And all her body's colour bruised and faint" (*Poems,* I, 247).

Gabulus next orders Dorothy's public execution. Just before her beheading, Dorothy is, however, once again approached by Theophilus,

18. *New Catholic Encyclopedia,* IV, 1018.

who now taunts her with the prospect of death, a condition in which all men, he insists, "lie . . . aching to the blood with bitter cold" (*Poems*, I, 247). Dorothy retorts that only "on one side" is death "full poor of bliss." Surprisingly exposing her own sublimated but ultimately aesthetic and erotic motives for a life of renunciation in this world, she relates to Theophilus her vision of death and the afterlife. Its setting is a beautiful garden that gratifies both amorous and aesthetic desires. "On the other side," she explains, death is "good and green." Death is also a lover, and she describes the "soft flower of tender-coloured hair / Grown on his head" and his "red mouth as fair / As may be kissed with lips" (*Poems*, I, 248). Actually, his is "as God's face," and he exists "in a perfect place." The experience of death that Dorothy anticipates is exclusively sensual. Highly sensual, too, if not erotic, is the narrator's delicate description of Dorothy's beheading: "Out of her throat the tender blood full red / Fell suddenly through all her long soft hair" (*Poems*, I, 249).

In Swinburne's poem, as in nearly all versions of the legend, Theophilus is converted to Christianity in the end, after an angel brings him a flower-laden basket Dorothy had promised she would send from the afterworld. He is subsequently hanged for proclaiming his new faith and for witnessing "Before the king of God and love and death" (*Poems*, I, 251). The narrator concludes with a telling description of Theophilus' experience after death: "in his face his lady's face is sweet, / And through his lips her kissing lips are gone" (*Poems*, I, 251). Events thus culminate with a paradoxically noumenal erotic vision.

Not only in this concluding passage but also throughout the poem, the appeal of Dorothy's story and of her religion for the poem's medieval narrator is predominantly erotic and aesthetic, despite her ostensibly ascetic life. Like Tannhäuser and the speaker in "The Leper," this narrator is a hedonist, albeit one who is able at once to veil and intensify his sensual proclivities by embedding them in the myth of a devout and chaste woman. The narrator conceives of his rendering of the myth as a matter of religious devotion, while it is in fact a fantasy that provides aesthetic gratifications for fundamentally erotic impulses. Ultimately for the narrator and for St. Dorothy as he portrays her, *ascesis* and renunciation allow for the suspension and savoring of sensation. In this respect the narrator resembles Morris' narrator in

"Concerning Geffray Teste Noire" or Theophilus himself, who, after first seeing Dorothy, "fell to fancies of her life / And soft half-thoughts that ended suddenly" (*Poems*, I, 238). Because the narrator permanently embodies his fantasies in richly sensory poetry, however, they do not end suddenly.

Rather, Dorothy's spiritual ardor, Gabulus' sadism, and Theophilus' passion all become transmuted through the erotic aestheticism of the narrator's sensibility. In his poetic memorial to Dorothy, voluptuous sensory images and piquant sexual desire are held in balance for expansive moments that anticipate implied forms of gratification but satisfy aroused desires only by the beauty and sensations offered by the poem itself. Such is the case not only in the narrator's ineluctably erotic depiction of Theophilus' union with Dorothy in the afterlife, in his description of Dorothy's beheading, and in Dorothy's vision of the afterworld but also in various lush, synesthetic, Keatsian passages of description that punctuate the narrative. For instance, when Theophilus first sees Dorothy, some of her companions, we are told, "ground perfume out of roots / Gathered by marvellous moons in Asia." These include "Saffron and aloes and wild cassia, / Coloured all through and smelling of the sun" (*Poems*, I, 238). The erotic contexts of this intensely sensory passage appear unmistakably in the young girls' activity with mortar and pestle, but also and more blatantly in the pun that introduces the entire scene: through "a little lattice open down," Theophilus sees "a press of maidens' heads / That sat upon their cold small quiet beds" (*Poems*, I, 238). The last long descriptive passage of the poem is also charged with eroticism. In the penultimate stanza the effect of sexual symbolism and of the dense, lush evocations of sensory experience—visual, olfactory, and tactile—is powerful. The irrepressibly hedonistic narrator of this poem, who thus aesthetically transforms the originary materials he works from, is apparently blind to the identity his narrative eventually insists upon between Theophilus' Venerean religion and that of the God he believes he serves. His narrative becomes, ironically, an unwitting subversion of Christianity, endorsing through the example of its own poetic texture a devotion to beauty, to sensual experience, and to erotic love.

Swinburne's strategy is made even clearer in the poem's introductory stanza, where the narrator asserts the incontrovertible historicity of his own account of the saint's life. Here the narrator implicitly describes himself as a poet-prophet, "wood and simple string" upon which a hedonistic God has "played music sweet as shawm-playing / To please himself with softness of all sound" (*Poems*, I, 237). Despite his "lowliness," the narrator claims that he has finally "waxed imperious" in the world because of his unique ability to construe the truth of past events. He is one of the "tender mouths" through whom "God's praise hath been / made perfect." A latter-day historian-poet, the narrator maintains that through him, "God hath bruised withal the sentences / And evidence of wise men" who actually witnessed the events surrounding the persecution and death of St. Dorothy. By the end of the poem it becomes clear, however, that the narrator's unique perception of the meaning of these events depends not upon the power of his religious devotion—that is, of traditional manifestations of Christian orthodoxy within him—but more fundamentally upon his controlling aesthetic sensibilities. By contrast with the dramatic monologues "Laus Veneris" and "The Leper," the authenticating historical dimensions of "St. Dorothy" are thus provided by the self-depiction of the narrator, rather than by citations to historical sources external to the text of the poem. This narrator who perceives himself as a poet, prophet, historian, and man of God is exposed, by the end of his work, as preeminently an aesthete. In this way Swinburne demonstrates his perception that extraordinarily deep moral perplexities afflicted men of the Middle Ages (and these cannot help but recall the very similar complexities victimizing men of Swinburne's own era). Swinburne also suggests that medieval poets resolved through their art the eternal feud between poet and priest, as the speaker in "St. Dorothy" does; and they do so often without recognizing the nature of their achievement, as is the case with some troubadours, romanceurs, and hagiographers. Swinburne's procedure in "St. Dorothy" further implies his belief that the religion of beauty—as it appeared in the works of Romantics like Blake and Keats, as well as poems by his contemporaries, Morris, Baudelaire, and Rossetti—is simply a modern transmutation, or, rather, an admission without hypocrisy, of the system of values that dominated many medieval ascetics. Renunciation and indulgence, asceticism and aestheticism are to be seen as contrary expressions of the same fundamental human impulse.

Ultimately, "St. Dorothy," like "Laus Veneris" and "The Leper," complexly integrates the erotic, formal, and spiritual preoccupations central to Swinburne's radical ideology early in his career. But these poems also reflect another, less well understood but nonetheless overriding obsession throughout the poems of his 1866 volume. He discusses his own role as a historicist poet who is necessarily a participant in the unceasing feud between artist and priest. In this role he is compelled not only to interpret but also to generate the history of the struggle in which he is involved. As a Dionysian torchbearer for what in Victorian England was stridently disparaged as the devil's party, he attains legitimacy through his own insistent historical self-consciousness, as well as through the various virtues of his seductive artistry. Swinburne's strategy for thus demonstrating his prophetic vocation—his calling as a poet who is also an idealist, an iconoclast, and a social critic—is implemented with greater subtlety in his medievalist poems than in any other cohesive group of his works. Although introduced in his early poetry, the consummate purpose of this strategy is realized only in his two medievalist works of epic scope, *Tristram of Lyonesse* and *The Tale of Balen*. These poems chronicle in verse of dazzling technical virtuousity, beauty, and power diverse tragedies of love and loss fraught with hope. Such tragedies serve both to define and exalt what Swinburne perceived as the inescapable human condition.

4

Queen Yseult
Prelude to Epic

Although composed before the final versions of *Rosamond, Chastelard,* and the medievalist poems of Swinburne's 1866 volume, *Queen Yseult* displays, without technical sophistication, many of the same concerns that characterize these erotic and sadomasochistic poems, as well as a stronger, though also unsophisticated interest in the philosophical possibilities of medieval history and myth, especially Arthurian legend. Throughout, *Queen Yseult* is thematically understated and its eroticism is subdued. It nonetheless demonstrates in subtle ways the same fascination with the relations between history (as biographical legend) and art that appears in the later works. Further, there is the same preoccupation with elegiac treatments of tragic love relationships that in *Poems and Ballads, First Series* operate on both erotic and spiritual planes. *Queen Yseult* also foreshadows Swinburne's often pantheistic and libertarian philosophical concerns, as they come increasingly to dominate his lyric, elegiac, and narrative poems after 1866. As we shall see, his prophetic impulse to unveil the

> Unbeheld, unadored, undivined,
> The cause, the centre, the mind
> The secret and sense of the earth (*Poems,* II, 122)

is at the heart of his poetic endeavor in the redemptive narrative tragedies of *Tristram of Lyonesse* and *The Tale of Balen.*

Swinburne's early interest in medieval French poetry and romance predictably led him to study and interpret the myth of Tristram and

Iseult. His uncle's library may well have contained manuscripts of one or more of the three major twelfth-century versions of the Tristram myth: that by Béroul, or *La Folie Tristan,* or *Le Roman en Prose.* More certainly it included Sir Walter Scott's edition of *Sir Tristrem* by Thomas of Ercildoune, written in the mid-twelfth century, first published in 1804, and frequently reprinted. Because of early encounters with the Tristram legend, as Gosse explains, Swinburne "from school-time onwards . . . never ceased to propose to himself the writing of an epic on the story of Tristram" (*Bonchurch,* XIX, 239). Early in his relationship with William Morris—who was painting the story of Tristram on the Oxford Union walls—Swinburne began writing his medieval pastiche *Queen Yseult,* of which he finished only six cantos. In 1859 he was at work on the theme again, composing "Joyeuse Garde," of which only a fragment remains (*Jeunesse,* 49). In December of 1869 he wrote the "Prelude" to the final version of *Tristram of Lyonesse* (*Letters,* II, 72–73). Over a decade later he resumed work on the epic and labored mightily to complete it by the middle of 1882. Lafourcade quite properly asserts that the composition of *Queen Yseult* itself was largely the result of Morris' early influence on Swinburne: "Le ler novembre 1857, Swinburne est présenté à Morris et l'entend déclamer . . . *Guenevere, Blanche,* et *The Willow and the Red Cliff.* Le 10 novembre, il est en train de composer *Queen Yseult;* le 16 décembre, il a terminé les six premiers chants. L'influence est, on le voit, directe et l'imitation immédiate" (*Jeunesse,* 40).[1] At about that time Morris was also considering a poetic work on the Tristram legend, and the formal similarities between Swinburne's poem and Morris' medieval pastiches, as Lafourcade notes, are indisputable (*Jeunesse,* 40–41). Morris' enthusiasm thus seems to have rekindled a partly dormant interest and demonstrated to Swinburne that a faithful yet modern and successful recasting of the medieval legend was possible.[2] Yet Swin-

1. "On the first of November, 1857, Swinburne is introduced to Morris and listens to him recite . . . *Guenevere, Blanche,* and *The Willow and the Red Cliff.* On the tenth of November, Swinburne is in the process of composing *Queen Yseult;* on the sixteenth of December, he has finished the first six cantos. As one sees, the influence is direct and the imitation immediate."

2. We should recognize the clear connections between *Queen Yseult* and *Rosamond.* After November, 1857, Swinburne was simultaneously writing both works based entirely on medieval love themes and on personages his-

burne was also deeply familiar with Arnold's *Tristram and Iseult* (1852). Although the focus and apparent intent of Arnold's poem are vastly different from those of Swinburne's 1857 fragment, at least Arnold's success in transposing medieval materials for contemporary readers would have provided assurance that, despite the numerous less successful attempts in the nineteenth century to rewrite the Tristram legend, such an endeavor could be worthwhile.[3] In his 1867 essay "Matthew Arnold's New Poems," Swinburne describes Arnold as "an old friend and teacher," whose rare *Empedocles on Etna* volume (1852) he had managed to acquire as a schoolboy. Swinburne especially describes Arnold's *Tristram and Iseult* as a "close and common friend" when he was at Eton, and he proceeds to pay this tribute to Arnold: "I cannot reckon the help and guidance in thought and work, which I owe to him as to all other real and noble artists whose influence it was my fortune to feel when most susceptible of influence, and least conscious of it, and most in want" (*Bonchurch,* V, 63–65).

Like Arnold, as well as Tennyson, Hardy, and Wagner, Swinburne came to perceive in the Tristram myth a profound vision of the power of passion in the world. Tennyson, whose version of the myth had been most influential among his contemporaries by 1882, had, however, employed the Tristram legend as merely one episode in a series of Arthurian legends useful to demonstrate the possibilities for moral decay in a potentially perfectible kingdom. Using Malory as a source where Swinburne used Thomas and the French romances, Tennyson perceived and interpreted the myth allegorically. Arnold also employed the myth in only limited ways, taking advantage of it to at-

---

torically or mythically central to courtly tradition. As far as we know, Swinburne did no additional work on *Queen Yseult* after December, 1857, but a draft of *Rosamond* was finished in 1858. Swinburne may have been writing his tragedy alongside *Queen Yseult,* or the subject of the latter poem may have served as a direct inspiration for the play. In either case, Swinburne could not have ignored the historical connections between twelfth-century versions of the Tristram myth and the atmosphere of the court in which *Rosamond* is set. See Roger Sherman Loomis (ed.), *The Romance of Tristram and Ysolt by Thomas of Britain* (New York, 1918), xix.

3. In *King Arthur's Laureate* (New York, 1971), J. Phillip Eggers provides a useful chronology of Arthurian publications in the nineteenth century (215–252). The great bulk of these are now forgotten works.

tempt an extended character study of Brittanic Iseult.[4] Swinburne, however, saw the Tristram legend as a prophetic and mystical archetypal illustration of the need and modes for expressing heroic men's and women's essential and perpetual condition of passion. That condition was inevitably fated to end in tragedy, but tragedy redeemed by sublime participation in a cosmic and self-fulfilling generative force organically governing history, the interactions of men and women, and the relations between men and nature. By 1869, the myth had come to illustrate for Swinburne life's most crucial informing value. It expressed in narrative form the metaphysic of Love.

Swinburne perceived in the Tristram story the workings of the highest laws that rule men's lives, the topmost of which is Fate. Like Carlyle, the poet believed that the highest "spiritual" truths inevitably realize themselves in history and thus in individual lives. Although Swinburne may not have believed in a strict form of predestination, he did see that patterns of experience perpetually repeat themselves in history. Fate is no intelligent, supernatural force but rather a sort of natural necessity whose active essence is love. All vital men and women succumb to its power and are tormented by the obstacles to its full consummation until death bestows peace and fulfillment. Such men and women are given to the world as signs of the laws that mold all lives, albeit less dramatically and intensely than their own. Swinburne was able therefore to construe the whole cycle of Arthurian romances unambiguously in terms of Greek tragedy. To him, one fundamental intuition of the dynamic forces ruling our lives operated in Greek and Celtic myth alike. Indeed, the philosophical substance of *Atalanta in Calydon* is in complete accord with that of *Tristram* and *The Tale of Balen*. In *Under the Microscope* (1872), while explaining the nature of Tennyson's mistreatment of the composite Arthurian legend, he observes,

> The story as it stood of old had in it something almost of Hellenic dignity and significance; in it as in the great Greek legends we could trace from a seemingly small root of evil the birth and growth of a calamitous fate, not sent by mere malevolence of heaven, yet in its awful weight and mystery of darkness apparently out of all due retributive proportion to the careless sin

4. For the best recent discussion of Arnold's poem, see Barbara Fass Leavy's "Iseult of Brittainy: A New Interpretation of Matthew Arnold's *Tristram and Iseult*," *Victorian Poetry*, XVIII (1980), 1–22.

or folly of presumptuous weakness which first incurred its infliction; so that by mere hasty resistance and return of violence for violence a noble man may unwittingly bring on himself and all his house the curse denounced on parricide, by mere casual indulgence of light love and passing wantonness a hero king may unknowingly bring on himself and all his kingdom the doom imposed on incest. This presence and imminence of Ate inevitable as invisible throughout the tragic course of action [*i.e.*, to the actors] can alone confer on such a story the proper significance and the necessary dignity: without it the action would want meaning and the passion would want nobility.[5]

Tristram and Iseult's accidental drinking of the love potion thus corresponds to Arthur's incestuous intercourse with Morgause. By 1869, Swinburne had realized that the former event was, superficially, the discernible cause of the tragic relationship between Tristram and Iseult and therefore the proper starting point for his epic.

Twelve years earlier, however, Swinburne had only begun to intuit the grounds of his mature understanding that artistic creation must both imitate and explicate fatal Necessity, if myth is to be presented as Truth. Nonetheless, *Queen Yseult* does provide an illuminating introduction to Swinburne's themes, his techniques, and his purpose in *Tristram of Lyonesse.* The monistic philosophy of this Romantic epic derives directly from the medievalist concerns of his early poetry, especially, of course, as they are formulated in *Queen Yseult.*

The poem is an incomplete rendition of the myth of Tristram and Iseult composed in irregular iambic tetrameter rhyming triplets. The same rhyme is often used for stanzas separated at irregular intervals. The diction, most frequently mono- or dissyllabic, along with the versification, contributes to the poem's atmosphere of childlike simplicity and purity, which simultaneously underscores those traits in the three central characters of the poem and counterpoints the complexity of the social, psychological, and emotional entanglements that give substance to the myth.

The six cantos of the poem rehearse the legend from the union of Roland and Blancheflour—Tristram's father and mother—to Tristram's unconsummated marriage to Yseult of Brittany. Canto one stresses the purity of each of Tristram's parents and of their love; it tersely narrates the history of their relationship, Moronde's "false"

5. The authoritative text of this essay appears in Hyder (ed.), *Swinburne Replies,* 58–59.

and "base" murder of Roland in battle, Blancheflour's death in child-birth, Tristram's rearing as an orphan, and his vengeance on Moronde "when twenty years were done." It dwells at length, however, upon descriptions of the tomb Tristram raises to his parents, a "wonder" that is an aesthetic monument to the natural beauty of their love. The first canto, the longest in the sequence, concludes with Tristram's ar-rival in Cornwall at the court of Mark, "the king so lean and cold," who commissions Tristram to seek Yseult of Ireland as Mark's bride.

Canto two begins with a focus on Yseult's unique and devastating beauty and Tristram's resulting captivation. Like the traditional courtly lover, he wishes to die for her, suffers from a burning and breaking heart, and feels deeply unworthy of her. The canto describes the effect of Yseult's song to the crew en route to Cornwall, and Tristram and Yseult's accidentally drinking the love potion intended for her and Mark by her mother. This "little thing" generates "their great love," and the canto concludes:

> Tristram had her body fair,
> And her golden cornripe hair,
> And her golden ring to wear. (*Bonchurch*, I, 31)

In canto three, with the lovers' arrival at the court of King Mark, the narrator recounts the elaborate nuptial festivities for Yseult and the king, focusing upon Tristram's song of praise for Yseult "in the sweet French tongue," upon their most difficult assignation, and upon the pain—"the fierce and bitter kisses"—of their passion before it is be-trayed to Mark after a period of three years.

Canto four depicts Tristram's enforced exile from Cornwall, his so-journ at Camelot, his arrival in Brittany, and the pleasure he takes in Brittanic Yseult's company. This Yseult conceives a painful love for Tristram, whose overheard song of praise for Irish Yseult affirms her hope that her passion is reciprocated. After Tristram undertakes a brief military expedition enhancing his fame, in canto five the wed-ding night takes place, and the poem dwells upon it as Tristram's *Wal-purgisnacht*: he is tortured by his commitment to Irish Yseult, his affection for Brittanic Yseult, and his refusal to dishonor either of them or himself or his marriage vows. Canto six presents a parallel depiction of a tormented Yseult of Ireland, captive to a jealous hus-band while yearning for a lover she fears is dead.

Such a summary of the poem's events and their treatment helps us to perceive the ways in which *Queen Yseult* serves as a very particular kind of prelude to Swinburne's visionary epic on the Tristram legend, significantly different—in its focus and its approach to confronting the problems of writing a long narrative poem—from the exemplary Romantic "preludes to vision" Thomas Vogler discusses in his book of that title.[6] In *Queen Yseult*, Swinburne, unlike his Romantic predecessors, had no pretensions to writing a poem with the scope, philosophical depth, or conventional attributes of "epic." Lafourcade observes that *Queen Yseult* is "la clef du chef-d'oeuvre publié par Swinburne en 1882," and he justifiably admires it for "une richesse d'imagination, une force et une souplesse de technique remarquables" (*Jeunesse*, 42, 45). But he also quite correctly insists that formally and even thematically "*Queen Yseult* n'est pas un fragment épique, mais, comme le disait Swinburne lui-même, une sorte de 'ballade'. Les six chants du fragment, par la clarté et la netteté de leur action, leur accent passionné et leur indépendance relative, constituent plutôt une série de poèmes lyriques utilisant les matériaux d'un ancien roman" (*Jeunesse*, 48).[7]

Swinburne's treatment of his subject in 1857 nonetheless demonstrates his interest in producing a poem more complex than a simple, unembellished balladic narrative. The thematics of *Queen Yseult*, along with its structural and prosodic techniques, suggest a poet exploring a subject rich with potential for an "epic" commentary on fundamental aspects of the human condition: on tragic love; on the operations of a transcendent spiritual power in the world, which is associated with nature; and on the corollary powers of art to memorialize the heroic men and women—the great lovers—who are the victims but paradoxically also the beneficiaries of such a spiritual force.

In *Preludes to Vision*, Vogler discusses a central problem confronting authors of would-be epics, "the absence of an accepted spiritual orientation of the collective consciousness and of a shared sense of

---

6. Thomas Vogler, *Preludes to Vision* (Berkeley, 1971).

7. "*Queen Yseult* is not an epic fragment, but, as Swinburne himself said, a sort of ballad. The six cantos of the fragment, for the lightness and clarity of their action, their passionate qualities and their relative independence, constitute rather a series of lyric poems using the material of an ancient story."

value." As a result, "the nature of the epic challenge to man becomes that of finding rather than preserving, an acceptable collective ideology of some kind. The poet must, in Joyce's words, forge in the smithy of his soul the uncreated consciousness of his race. Before a poet can do this, he must have a firm faith in the power of poetic vision as a mode of finding ultimate truths about the nature of man; he must have the highest possible estimate of the powers of the poetic imagination and complete faith in that estimate."[8] Like his Romantic precursors, Swinburne clearly feels compelled to write poetry that is also prophecy, poetry that will correct the false or fragmented values and beliefs of his contemporaries and project—if not an immediately "acceptable collective ideology"—at least an ideology that requires his own allegiance and one that can be distilled only by means of "the highest possible estimate of the powers of the poetic imagination and complete faith in that estimate." One significant characteristic, however, that distinguishes Swinburne—and indeed all the Pre-Raphaelite poets—from their Romantic forebears as well as the other most distinguished Victorian poets is their unquestioning faith in the power and value of art and the imagination that can successfully shape it. As a result, there is in Swinburne's "prelude" to his epic version of the Tristram myth no problem of finding a subject matter, no self-searching for "firm" poetic faith and mission, and no exploration of consciousness itself and its power as a substitute for the "objective element of the earlier epics."[9]

In *Queen Yseult*, Swinburne from the beginning appears certain of his subject and its validity as an embodiment of supreme emotional, moral, spiritual, and aesthetic values. The Tristram legend for Swinburne conveys a powerfully prophetic vision of life's tragic beauty. Rather than questing, as the Romantics did, for poetic vision and an affirmation of its truth here, Swinburne, both by the example of his poem and the commentaries on art it contains, presents clear statements about the tragic inevitabilities of human passion and the invaluable role art plays in memorializing and perpetuating it.

8. Vogler, *Preludes to Vision*, 9. For a discussion of *Tristram* in these terms, see the best published essay on the poem, John R. Reed's "Swinburne's *Tristram of Lyonesse*: The Poet-Lover's Song of Love," *Victorian Poetry*, IV (1966), 99–120.
9. Vogler, *Preludes to Vision*, 9.

The first such statement appears metaphorically in canto one's lengthy descriptions of the elaborate tomb Tristram builds as a tribute to his parents, but especially in Blancheflour's "great sorrow's praise." The tomb, like Swinburne's poem, is intended to serve as a beacon to all potential lovers, acknowledging the love of Blancheflour and Roland but also glorifying their suffering:

> All was graven deep and fine,
> In and out, and line with line,
> That all men might see it shine.

> So far off it spring and shone,
> Ere ten paces one had gone,
> Showing all the sorrow done. (*Bonchurch,* I, 19)

Insisting upon the harmony between the lovers' experiences and the laws of nature, the roof of the tomb "In wrought flowers" Blanche-flour's "sweet name wore,"

> And in many a tender nook,
> Traced soft as running brook,
> Shone her face's quiet look.

With

> Parted lips and closing eyes,
> All the quiet of the skies
> Fills her beauty where she lies. (*Bonchurch,* I, 19)

And finally, "On her hair the forest crown / Lets the sliding tresses down" (*Bonchurch,* I, 19). Tristram's artistic memorial depicts his parents as extensions of nature, their love a reflection of its governing principles. Like the poet's elegiac tribute to Tristram's tragic love, the tomb serves as a testimonial to the fulfillment earned through suffering in love's service.

As a less formal and ritualized mode of artistic expression that exalts, generates, and perpetuates the value of passion, songs of love are sung repeatedly by the two central characters within the larger "song" of *Queen Yseult*. Song so naturally accompanies the impulse to love or the power to inspire love that, as in *Tristram of Lyonesse* itself, it becomes a virtual metaphor for love, which is here presented as the only worthwhile mode of existence. Further, as the lovers become impassioned singers, love itself becomes a form of art, and a life of tragic love becomes its own memorial, its own aesthetic as well as erotic fulfillment. Appropriately then, Yseult of Ireland's very voice is "as a song," and en route to Cornwall, "her voice the men among / Warmed their spirits like a song." The effect of her singing is to inspire a passion that culminates in beatification: "all faces grew aflame, / And on all great glory came" (*Bonchurch*, I, 27). Similarly, it is Tristram's song that draws both Yseults to him. When he is singing of Irish Yseult's "great grace," she "leant to hear his song." The effect of the same song upon Brittanic Yseult is to make her love Tristram (*Bonchurch*, I, 44). And the only adequate metaphor to describe the cause of his attraction to *her* is song. Although "In his heart he would no wrong, / . . she drew it like a song":

> Some dim song at waking heard
> When the tender gloom is stirr'd
> With the joy of some sweet bird. (*Bonchurch*, I, 42)

Despite *Queen Yseult's* implied apotheosis of tragic love, the pure beauty that inspires it, and the art that commemorates it, this poem, in contrast to *Tristram of Lyonesse*, attempts primarily to recast the legend with as little artistic embellishment as possible. *Queen Yseult* lacks the ecstatic lyric flights as well as the ideological self-consciousness of *Tristram of Lyonesse*. Nor, of course, is it a complete "vision," a tightly organized, unified whole as its sequel is. The poem's six cantos nonetheless exhibit a number of virtues. Up to its abrupt ending, the fragment presents a coherent narrative, balladic in its density and its refusal to succumb to modern demands for narrative causality, transitions, and plausibility.

Unlike *Tristram* but like most successful ballads, *Queen Yseult* is a masterpiece of understatement. In canto three, for example, after being threatened with the "white steel hot" as an ordeal to test her fidelity to Mark, Yseult simply and voluntarily "bade . . . Tristram go." His banishment in most versions is enforced by Mark and in *Tristram* itself is transformed into an unsuccessful attempt by Mark's nobles to murder Iseult's lover. In *Queen Yseult*, however, we are provided with no compelling reason for Yseult's decision, and the canto ends abruptly:

> So he went from her apace;
> And she dwelt by Mark in place
> With a trouble in her face. (*Bonchurch*, I, 39)

Other instances where simple balladic devices are used for the sake of authenticity occur frequently. Matters of probability are once again ignored when, thirsting to see Irish Yseult after winning fame at the court of Arthur, Tristram inexplicably sets off for Brittany. Moreover, as in traditional ballads, characterization in this poem is often accomplished simply by the use of epithets. Mark is described repeatedly as "the king so lean and cold," and even Irish Yseult's existence nearly becomes a function of her "hair of gold," "her golden hair corn-ripe," and her "arrow-straight" hands and body.

Despite the simplicity of its balladic qualities, we do find in *Queen Yseult* at least three of the major narrative devices that organize *Tristram*: the use of repetition, retrospective narration, and parallelism. The most conspicuous use of repetition for thematic purposes occurs in *Queen Yseult* twice, where the Arthurian context is invoked with both its joyous and fatal implications. When first banished from Cornwall, after performing heroically "in wars," Tristram beholds Guinevere at Camelot:

> All her face like light was clear,
> That men shook for loving fear.
>
> And more smooth than steel or glass
> All her happy forehead was,
> Thro' her eyes some dream did pass. (*Bonchurch*, I, 40)

At the end of canto four, once again amid "the noises of his fame,"

> He beheld Queen Guinevere,
> All her face like light was clear.
>
> Thro' her eyes a dream did pass,
> And more smooth than steel or glass
> All her happy forehead was. (*Bonchurch*, I, 47)

Guinevere's radiance each time reminds Tristram of his beloved and absent Yseult and is a source therefore of both joy and sorrow.[10]

10. In *Tristram* the same image, with all its fateful and visionary suggestions, is applied uniquely to Iseult. The first lengthy description of the Queen culminates with it:

> Dream by dream shot through her eyes, and each
> Outshone the last that lightened, and not one
> Showed her such things as should be borne and done. (*Poems*, IV, 15)

Retrospective narration and parallelism, which Swinburne uses to striking effect in *Tristram of Lyonesse,* are employed sparingly, almost hesitantly in *Queen Yseult.* Whereas we discover the former technique only once in the 1857 poem, Swinburne finds it a convenient device in *Tristram* (as Milton does in *Paradise Lost*) to introduce important historical information, which is merely explanatory but does not move the story forward or reinforce thematic emphases.[11] *Queen Yseult* begins with a brief account of Tristram's birth and his later fame as a "good knight" who had "many happy wars" (*Bonchurch,* I, 9). Almost immediately, however, the narrative enters into a lengthy explanation of the circumstances surrounding Tristram's birth, "For long since Queen Blancheflour / Took a knight to paramour." Several pages of the first canto are taken up with descriptions of Blancheflour's devotion to Roland; these include soliloquies that, like Irish Yseult's at the end of canto six, justify her love or explain her delirious flight after Roland's death into a "forest fair" to give birth to Tristram in "great anguish." This formal introduction of the poem's hero followed by so detailed a retrospective narration constitutes one of the very few intrusions of modern technique into *Queen Yseult*'s usually straightforward "ballade" form.

A major instance of parallelism, as distinct from repetition, occurs only once in this poem, though, as Kerry McSweeney points out, it is a basic organizing principle in *Tristram.* He cites the most important instances there as "the matching invocations to Love and Fate which open and close the poem; the contrast . . . between Iseult of Ireland's vigil in Book V, where she prays for Tristram's safety, and the vigil of the other Iseult in Book VII, during which she demands of God that Tristram be damned eternally; and the two carefully contrasted episodes (in Books II and VI) during which Tristram and his Iseult are united, which nicely balance the rising and falling halves of the poem. Finally, twice during the poem Tristram dives . . . into the sea."[12] By comparison, the 1857 poem's parallel between Tristram's and Irish Yseult's seaside vigils in cantos five and six seems obtrusive. On his bridal night with Brittanic Yseult, Tristram, avoiding the temptation

11. In *Tristram,* see especially the beginnings of cantos one and three.
12. Kerry McSweeney, "The Structure of Swinburne's 'Tristram of Lyonesse,'" *Queen's Quarterly,* LXXV (1968), 691.

to consummate his marriage, moves away from his new wife, "Purer than the naked snow,"

> And he bowed his body fair
> Down athwart the window there,
> Weeping for the golden hair. (*Bonchurch*, I, 53)

In a parallel scene immediately after this one, Irish Yseult lies in bed beside Mark, convincing herself that Tristram is dead, because she has heard nothing from him since his banishment. As Tristam had prayed to be faithful for the sake of Yseult's fame, Yseult articulates a more general "praise and prayer for Tristram dead" (*Bonchurch*, I, 56). Like Tristram, she moves away from her spouse. Then in preparation for a languidly erotic scene of bitter prayer, Swinburne inserts one of the poem's few really sensual passages:

> No one saw her girdle slip,
> Saw her loosen it to weep,
> Thinking how he touched her lip.
>
> Heavily her robe sank white,
> Heavily her hair sank bright,
> Rustling down in the dead night.
>
> And her breast was loosened so
> From the hunger of its woe,
> When the samite rustled low. (*Bonchurch*, I, 56)

Then, facing the "white lines of the sea" as Tristram had,

> Down athwart the window bright
> Leant she into the dead light,
> Wept for Tristram the good knight. (*Bonchurch*, I, 57)

The exact verbal parallel in the scenes is reinforced by the repetition of the archaism *athwart*.

It is worth dwelling on this simple instance of parallelism because it is one of the several techniques in *Queen Yseult* upon which Swinburne by 1882 is able to improve enormously. He develops it into a fundamental organizing device for his epic poem. Swinburne thus by no means forgot his early works in the composition of his later ones. But neither do his poems reflect the "arrested development" that has repeatedly been insisted upon by critics. Although every important talent and interest of Swinburne's may be present in the poems before 1869, the poet never complacently assumed he had perfected his art.

91

His formal innovations make the contrast between his later and earlier styles fascinating, especially in light of his ability to adapt old materials to profoundly more sophisticated purposes. He does so when he ends "The Maiden Marriage" in *Tristram* with precisely the same image used to conclude canto five of *Queen Yseult*, but in a context that expands its thematic importance and its pictorial echoes to an extent undreamed of in the ingenuous verse of *Queen Yseult*. Canto five ends:

> So from evening till the day
> At her side in love he lay
> Slept no child as pure as they.
> So her love had all it would
> All night sleeping as she could,
> Sleeping in her maidenhood. (*Bonchurch*, I, 53–54)

The realism and the complexities of prosody and characterization in the parallel passage from *Tristram* are much greater. Despite the nearly exact borrowing of the concluding rhymes, the 1882 version fully reveals the distance between apprentice work and the product of mature genius:

> He kissed her maiden mouth and blameless brow,
> Once, and again his heart within him sighed;
> But all his young blood's yearning toward his bride,
> How hard soe'er it held his life awake
> For passion, and sweet nature's unforbidden sake,
> And will that strove unwillingly with will it might not break,
> Fell silent as a wind abashed, whose breath
> Dies out of heaven, suddenly done to death,
> When in between them on the dumb dusk air
> Floated the bright shade of a face more fair
> Then hers that hard beside him shrank and smiled
> And wist of all no more than might a child.
> So had she all her heart's will, all she would,
> For love's sake that sufficed her, glad and good,
> All night safe sleeping in her maidenhood. (*Poems*, IV, 74–75)

This passage, like many from *Tristram*, employs a number of thematically loaded images that are used throughout the poem and that gain resonance with each use. In fact, John Reed convincingly argues that *Tristram*'s success is largely a function of Swinburne's deft use of recurrent words and of such images as "motifs" that "establish [its]

structural and atmospheric unity."[13] The quoted passage invokes the
themes of will, passion, and transience, as well as complex natural
and philosophical associations already established in the poem for
such images as "wind abashed," "dumb dusk," and "bright shade."

Such sophisticated use of imagery, which continued in Swinburne's
late poetry, extends the typically Pre-Raphaelite use of ostensibly
nonessential detail. Such detail dominates *Queen Yseult* and many of
Swinburne's other early poems. Rossetti has become notorious for his
use of ornamental imagery, and Swinburne's early work imitates
Rossetti's practice.[14] Yseult's seductive disrobing while praying and
weeping for Tristram is one example. There are others in *Queen Yseult*.
Sometimes gratuitous details are clearly added to fill out the meter of
the tercets, as at Tristram's birth when Blancheflour "fain had suckled
him, / There beneath the lindens dim / Round a fountain's weedy
brim" (*Bonchurch*, I, 11). *Weedy* in the context might have all sorts of
useful implications, but none of them is developed in the rest of the
poem. In a similar manner, imagery with potentially significant but
undeveloped religious overtones is occasionally used to describe
Blancheflour and Irish Yseult. After Tristram's birth, his mother is discovered, "Very beautiful and dead / In the lilies white and red"; and
Yseult in various phases of anguish repeatedly appears more pallid
"than a lily dead with dew." Even Tristram's behavior has explicit, but
again unexplored, religious suggestions. For instance, when Tristram
returns to reclaim his father's country, Swinburne invokes the trinity
for no conspicuous reason:

> When he came to Ermonie,
> Bare upon the earth bowed he,
> Kissed the earth with kisses three. (*Bonchurch*, I, 15)

Other passages similarly rich with detail seem purely decorative.

Yet *Queen Yseult* does contain intimations of Swinburne's later, more
consistently significant use of imagery. Irish Yseult's golden hair and
her brightness twice associated with that of Guinevere are suggestive
of the life-giving properties of the sun. The obtrusiveness of that

13. Reed, "Swinburne's *Tristram*," 100.
14. See Jerome McGann's discussion of the matter in "Rossetti's Significant
Details," *Victorian Poetry*, VII (1969), 41–54.

image is retained in *Tristram*, where her hair is first described as a "golden sunrise." Here the condition of Yseult's brightness serves consistently as a sign either of her own or of Tristram's spiritual condition. That she looms on Tristram's wedding night above his bride-bed as a "bright shade" suggests the perfect balance in the myth between the joy and sorrow Yseult brings to Tristram's life. In the poem's final lines, thinking of Tristram dead, Yseult becomes pale as a "lily dead." She merely endures in a state of phlegmatic mournfulness, "gazing through the gloom." Antithetical image patterns are also used to define Brittanic Yseult's harmful potential, especially the repeated contrast of her celebrated whiteness and the dark objects that surround her. She lives in a "great grey castle" located by "ranges of black stone." And on her wedding night she significantly uses a "comb of jet and pearl."

The consistent and successful use of such imagery is, of course, characteristic of any good poet, but it is present in *Queen Yseult* alongside a plethora of inconsequential detail that reflects the Pre-Raphaelite influence. In combination with Swinburne's persistent use of repetitions and epithets, however, this use of imagery also reflects a potential for the kind of stylistic development we see realized in *Tristram*. There, as Reed has observed, repetitions of both theme and imagery serve to reveal developing character; to foreshadow events and imbue them with specific value; and to indicate the ubiquitous presence of governing metaphysical realities. Reed sees the complex use of repeated metaphors as important to define the philosophical touchstones of Swinburne's epic.[15] The metaphysics of *Tristram* are, of course, explicit, whereas Swinburne does not attempt to make *Queen Yseult* an overtly philosophical poem. In fact, he does nothing even to undermine the poem's authenticating background of religious orthodoxy. If we can detect a system of belief to which the narrative subscribes, beyond its insistence upon the supreme value of art and "song" to exalt human passion, it appears in the literary heritage of medieval romance and the courtly lore that dominate the poem and that subtend the action of *Tristram* itself, not obtrusively as in *Rosamond* and *Chastelard*, but as a donnée of the myth.

Blancheflour both represents and articulates the governing courtly

15. Reed, "Swinburne's *Tristram*," 104.

ethos of *Queen Yseult* at its very beginning, when she describes her
union with Roland:

> "Lo!" she said, "I lady free
> Took this man for lord of me
> Where the crowned saints might see.
>
> "And I will not bid him go,
> Not for joyance nor for woe,
> Till my very love he know." (*Bonchurch,* I, 10)

The story of Roland and Blancheflour is a courtly tragedy in its own
right, whose active principles are beauty, fidelity, stoical endurance,
and heroism in the service of love. Roland, in protecting his kingdom
of Ermonie, is, in fact, "Slain for Blancheflour the sweet." The tragedy
of her son Tristram, as Swinburne saw it in 1857, was an extension of
this tragedy, but with more numerous and attractive complications
and therefore of larger proportions. What fascinates Swinburne about
the Tristram myth, finally, is that in it courtly convention is transformed into tragic reality in highly lyrical fashion. It prophetically
embodies essential truths about love and its beneficent as well as disastrous causes and consequences, and it demonstrates the potential
of song to reveal such high truths. In the myth, fame is one consequence of love, and it is achieved by means of the sort of battle and
adventure Swinburne delighted in, becoming for the knight what
beauty is for his lady, demonstrating his worthiness to be loved, reinforcing a passion in progress, and consoling the knight in times of
distress or physical deprivation. In order to prove himself worthy of
Brittanic Yseult, for instance, Tristram must leave her and find an opportunity to display valor. As a result, "great praise he won," and "all
men spake him fair for the wondrous name he bare" (*Bonchurch,* I,
47). Ultimately, it is fame of this sort, the fame that accrues from what
each lover endures for the sake of passion, that establishes the immortality of the Tristram myth and of any courtly lover. Irish Yseult in the
poem's last pages is described as having borne "for very love . . .
Things no woman knew before, / And would bear for evermore"
(*Bonchurch,* I, 59).[16] Queen Yseult is the focus of this poem (as Tris-

16. Indeed, in order to avoid footprints in the snow that would betray the
lovers, Yseult in this early version has quite literally borne Tristram on her
back to her chamber so that they might indulge their passion. Swinburne

tram is of the 1882 version) because she is represented as having endured the greater sorrow for Tristram's sake and as having been the first cause of Tristram's passion. In *Tristram of Lyonesse* the hero himself is represented as the activator of passionate impulses and, thus, the extension of perennially generative life-forces. He is compared to the sun, and his radiance brings the passions of the two Yseults to blossom. As a result of love's power over them, in the later work all three of the major figures suffer enormously. In the last pages of the 1857 poem Yseult's soliloquy expressing her suffering and her hope for the supreme blessing of fame is really a prelude to the "Prelude" of *Tristram of Lyonesse,* for the mature poet's epic takes up the story where the journeyman poet had put it down.

------

here devises a new version of the episode (from Thomas) in which a trap is laid. Flour is sprinkled on the chamber floor to evidence Tristram's entry and departure. Here snow serves the same function, and Tristram (*Bonchurch,* I, 35–36) is, in fact, reluctant to meet Yseult for fear that the snow will betray him.

5

Tristram of Lyonesse
Visionary and Courtly Epic

Although Swinburne himself considered *Tristram of Lyonesse* his masterwork, this medievalist poetic embodiment of his mature system of beliefs has only recently begun to receive the attention it deserves from both readers and critics.[1] Difficulties with Swinburne's long Arthurian poem have resulted from its philosophical, prosodic, and even grammatical complexities. But a more basic and surprising obstacle to appreciating the poem seems to arise from its formal peculiarities. Unlike most epic poems, this one appears more lyrical than narrative. In fact, many of its special felicities are due to this typically Swinburnean, anti-traditional aspect of the work. Readers seem perpetually unable to define exactly what kind of poem *Tristram* is, and they attempt to evaluate it solely in terms of its adherence to the prerequisites of narrative poetry.[2] Often the best critic of his own work, Swinburne himself did not attempt to classify his magnum opus in

1. The most detailed and useful commentaries are Reed, "Swinburne's *Tristram*," 99–120; McSweeney, "Structure," 691–702; Davis, "Swinburne's Use of His Sources," 96–112; and McGann, *Swinburne,* 137–42, 152–67. See also Francis Jacques Sypher's incisive comparisons in "Swinburne and Wagner," *Victorian Poetry,* IX (1971), 165–83; Benjamin F. Fisher IV, "Swinburne's *Tristram of Lyonesse* in Process," *Texas Studies in Literature and Language,* XIV (1972), 509–28; and Nicolas Tredell, "*Tristram of Lyonesse*: Dangerous Voyage," *Victorian Poetry,* XX (1982), 97–111.
2. John D. Rosenberg notes this imaginative failure on the part of Swinburne's critics (*Swinburne's Selected Poetry and Prose* [New York, 1967], xii–xiii).

conventional terms. Rather, while working on the "Prelude" in December of 1869, he designated the projected poem a "moral history" (*Letters*, II, 78). Later, with *Tristram* nearly completed, Swinburne explained to Burne-Jones that he had tried to write merely a "harmonious narrative" with "as little manipulation as was possible of the different versions of the story" (*Letters*, IV, 287). But Swinburne's definitive statement on the work appears in the Dedicatory Epistle to the 1904 edition of his poems:

> My aim was simply to present that story, not diluted and debased as it had been in our own time by other hands, but undefaced by improvement and undeformed by transformation, as it was known to the age of Dante wherever the chronicles of romance found hearing, from Ercildoune to Florence: and not in the epic or romantic form of sustained or continuous narrative, but mainly through a succession of dramatic scenes or pictures with descriptive settings or backgrounds: the scenes being of the simplest construction, dialogue or monologue, without so much as the classically permissible intervention of a third or fourth person. (*Poems*, I, xvii–xviii)

In spite of Swinburne's explicit emphasis here on the dramatic and lyrical elements of his poem, critics until recently have been unyielding in their refusal to read the work on its own terms. Edmund Gosse insists upon its "total want of energy" as a narrative. There are, he rather inaccurately asserts, "no exploits, no feats of arms; the reader, avid for action, is put off with pages upon pages of amorous hyperbolic conversation between lovers, who howl in melodious couplets to the accompaniment of winds and waves." In his summary view of the work, Gosse castigates Swinburne for producing a long poem, interminably monotonous because of the "strain and effort to make every passage a purple one" (*Bonchurch*, XIX, 240). Most commentators have merely relied and expanded upon Gosse's wrongheaded critique.[3]

Although *Tristram* does not adhere strictly to the conventional criteria for narrative and epic poetry by which early critics evaluated it, and in spite of Swinburne's own disclaimers, his highly wrought masterwork is indeed a species of epic, and as such it is an undeniably

3. For instance, see T. Earle Welby, *A Study of Swinburne* (London, 1926), 217; Chew, *Swinburne*, 170; Humphrey Hare, *Swinburne: A Biographical Approach* (London, 1949), 195; Lafourcade, *Jeunesse*, 292; and Nicolson, *Swinburne*, 179.

successful and unified *tour de force*. Not indeed merely a "sustained or continuous narrative," the poem is formally a complex hybrid, one that brilliantly synthesizes many narrative and dramatic elements of the traditional epic, as well as Romantic lyrical and visionary elements. In addition, its formal and philosophical accomplishments result in part from Swinburne's use of various conventions of courtly love romance and troubadour poetry. Attention to the form as well as the literary and philosophical backgrounds of the poem can provide readers with at least a familiar context in which to approach what is one of Swinburne's greatest achievements and perhaps the most magnificent and truly cohesive "epic" poem of the Victorian age.

That Kerry McSweeney and John Reed have convincingly discussed the structural and thematic integrity of *Tristram*, as well as many of the techniques used to achieve it, attests to the effective artistry of Swinburne's works after 1860.[4] As a self-conscious craftsman, he was incapable of producing a merely episodic rhapsody during his mature period. It is not surprising, then, that *Tristram* does contain numerous qualities that unequivocally define its atmosphere, intent, and final effect as genuinely epic: it begins *in medias res*; an elevated tone dominates the narrative; Swinburne's Tristram and Iseult of Ireland are of epic stature, as is Brittanic Iseult when she becomes Tristram's demonic adversary; many of the verbal devices Swinburne employs are characteristic of the classical epics; and the subject of his narrative is represented as of supreme metaphysical importance.

Tristram is an epic, however, that could have been written only with the formal developments initiated by the Romantic poets well in mind. Karl Kroeber goes far in defining the nature of Swinburne's formal accomplishment in *Tristram* when he describes in general terms the kind of narrative form introduced and sanctioned by the Romantics. Kroeber, like Thomas Vogler after him, terms their use of story "visionary (rather than realistic)" and explains that "in many Romantic poetic tales the naturalistic function of story is minimized or dropped altogether and narrative is employed as a means of expressing a philosophic position, a moral attitude, or a vision of what the poet believes to be genuine reality, a reality which transcends naturalistic appear-

4. McSweeney, "Structure," 691–702; Reed, "Swinburne's *Tristram*," 101.

ance." In Swinburne's "moral history," narrative functions in all these ways. In contrast to Homer, Virgil, Dante, or Spenser, emphasis is not on action, but on expository metaphysical valuation of event and pure lyrical expression within a narrative framework. With Swinburne, as with the Romantic poets, "story is the realization of value. Narrative tension springs not from naturalistic suspense but from the . . . emergence of a system of precious truth, profound insight."[5]

Swinburne's *Tristram* is, however, considerably more than a visionary poem that extends Romantic narrative innovations. All Swinburne's works invoke specific literary traditions, and, to a far greater extent even than most major poets, Swinburne was a superb parodist. His undergraduate lyrics, for example, are remarkable adaptations of the idiom of William Morris. In *Erechtheus* he produces the most starkly brilliant Aeschylean imitation in English. Even his ponderous closest dramas are extraordinary for their fidelity to the form and technique of his favorite Elizabethan and Jacobean playwrights. As we might expect, then, *Tristram of Lyonesse* is a self-consciously epic poem that simultaneously parodies epic tradition and tries to transcend traditional constraints. The poet strives for a formally (and thematically) original work that supersedes its models. Of course, Swinburne is by no means unique in literary history for his attempt. Brian Wilkie in *Romantic Poets and Epic Tradition* convincingly points out that "like the Old Testament prophets, the great poets of the literary epic have always shown . . . both a dedication to the past and a desire to reject or transcend it. No great poet has ever written an epic without radically transforming it or giving to it new dimensions, and often that intention is explicitly declared. . . . The poets observe the fine print in the letter of the law as markedly as they vaunt their independence in the larger matters of subject and heroic theme."[6]

For Swinburne "the anxiety of influence" presented a challenge. In a Blakean spirit, he did not wish his masterwork to be bound by generic definition. Wilkie explains that "the epic poet seldom states generic rules or delimits formal critical categories . . . for the epic poet must use or implicitly claim to use an old form, a tradition that every-

5. Karl Kroeber, *Romantic Narrative Art* (Madison, 1960), 76, 77.
6. Brian Wilkie, *Romantic Poets and Epic Tradition* (Madison, 1965), 11–13.

one already understands, so that the new values he preaches will stand out the more boldly."[7] Swinburne was content with his own ironic designation of *Tristram of Lyonesse* as a "moral history" because the poem's importance to him depended upon the truths self-consciously espoused and the unorthodox values defiantly embodied in it. In large part, these values represent a literal adaptation, a naturalized and sensualized version of the conventions that dominate medieval love poetry and romance. Indeed, *Tristram* can be viewed as an epic transposition of the troubadour love lyric.

In writing *Tristram of Lyonesse*, Swinburne found the perfect opportunity for a complete formulation of the unique synthesis of passion, pantheism, and the courtly love ethos upon which his most important philosophical intuitions were primarily founded. At the same time, however, he felt that the myth needed to be restored to something like its original integrity. Arnold's version (1852) and Tennyson's version (1871) had merely appropriated the legend, ignoring what Swinburne took to be the whole significance of the original myth. To R. H. Horne he wrote on February 13, 1882, "I am working just now as hard as ever I worked towards the completion of a poem in nine parts on the story of Tristram, which is and was always in my eyes the loveliest of mediaeval legends. I do not forget that two eminent contemporaries have been before me in the field, but Arnold has transformed and recast the old legend, and Tennyson—as usual, if I may be permitted to say so—has degraded and debased it" (*Letters*, IV, 260). He suggests the purpose of his own projected poem (and provides a damning critique of Tennyson) in an earlier (1869) letter to Burne-Jones:

> I want my version to be based on notorious facts, and to be acceptable for its orthodoxy and fidelity to the dear old story [and, one might add, its antagonism to current orthodoxies]: so that Tristram may not be mistaken for his late Royal Highness the Duke of Kent, or Iseult for Queen Charlotte, or Palomydes for Mr. Gladstone. I shan't of course include—much less tell at length, saga-fashion—a tithe of the various incidents given in the different old versions; but I want to have in everything *pretty* that is of any importance, and is in keeping with the tone and spirit of the story—not burlesque or dissonant or inconsistent. The thought of your painting and

7. *Ibid.*, 25.

Wagner's music ought to abash but does stimulate me: but my only chance I am aware will be to adhere strongly to Fact and Reality—to shun fiction as perilously akin to lying, and make this piece of sung or spoken History a genuine bit of earnest work in these dim times. Ahem. (*Letters*, II, 51)

The parody of Carlyle here has a double thrust, because this particular "fiction" for Swinburne is something that must be neither transformed nor debased. Like his formulation of the Tannhäuser myth, his rendering of the Tristram legend must be a supreme Reality, a metaphysical one. Tennyson's debasement of the essential truth of the legend constituted for Swinburne the same kind of anathema that Sham and Lying always represented for Carlyle. Although Swinburne emphasizes fidelity to "the dear old story" in describing his intent in *Tristram*, he is clearly concerned with preserving the philosophical precepts he saw embodied in this legend that had deeply moved him since early childhood (*Letters*, III, 332). At least eight centuries of sustained popularity surely seemed for Swinburne adequate validation of the spiritual truths underlying the Tristram myth and sufficient reason for adapting and designating it as the subject for "the very topstone of his poetical monument" (*Bonchurch*, XIX, 239).

The epic dimensions of *Tristram* become clearer from a brief survey of its use of traditional epic devices. Typical are the thematic repetitions and parallelisms already discussed by John Reed and Kerry McSweeney, but just as important is the strategic use of epic similes to transfigure the central characters. The poem's "Prelude" insistently sets the philosophical tone for the rest of the poem and defines the heroic stature of its two ideal lovers. Their story is no merely entertaining tale, but, like the legends of the other lovers cited in the "Prelude," one whose pattern has profound significance for our own lives.[8] In the symbolism of the poem, sun and light represent the irrepressible impulse of Love that governs all people who are totally receptive to the forces of life and therefore in harmony with nature. To the extent that they are always "subject to the sun," these two lovers are "sphery signs" for living generations, just as many of Dante's fig-

8. For the best available discussion of the "Prelude," see McGann, *Swinburne*, 138–41.

ures and Spenser's exempla were intended to be. As such, Tristram and Iseult are frequently exalted, characterized in elevated terms with epic similes.

This is inevitably the case with the descriptions of Tristram's martial exploits. When Tristram assaults Iseult's kidnapper, Palamede, as he flees with Iseult from King Mark, the tumult of the two knights' encounter appears

> As when a bright north-easter, great of heart,
> Scattering the strengths of squadrons, hurls apart
> Ship from ship labouring violently, in such toil
> As earns but ruin. (*Poems*, IV, 47)

Later, after bloody and energetic battle with Mark's noblemen, Tristram is backed onto a pinnacle above the sea where, as he prepares to dive, his excitement culminates in a Hopkinsian intuition of a bird's love of its element:

> And as the sea-gull hovers high, and turns
> With eyes wherein the keen heart glittering yearns
> Down toward the sweet green sea whereon the broad noon burns,
> And suddenly, soul-stricken with delight,
> Drops and the glad wave gladdens, and the light
> Sees wing and wave confuse their fluttering white,
> So Tristram one brief breathing-space apart
> Hung, and gazed down. (*Poems*, IV, 71)

Emphasis on Tristram's heroism in the poem is reinforced not only by his chivalric accomplishments but also by such descriptions as this one, which demonstrate through the use of epic similes his harmony with the passionately receptive spirit of natural objects. His epic stature is further defined by his explicit association with other epic heroes. In "The Last Pilgrimage," for example, Tristram, on the morning of his last battle, is about to consummate his communion with nature by once again plunging into the sea. He stands at its edge,

> Naked, and godlike of his mould as he
> Whose swift foot's sound shook all the towers of Troy,
> So clothed with might, so girt upon with joy
> As, ere the knife had shorn to feed the fire
> His glorious hair before the unkindled pyre
> Whereon the half of his great heart was laid,

Stood, in the light of his live limbs arrayed,
Child of heroic earth and heavenly sea,
The flower of all men: scarce less bright than he,
If any of all men latter-born might stand,
Stood Tristram, silent, on the glimmering strand. (*Poems*, IV, 127)

Like Tristram, Iseult of Brittany, his fatal antagonist, is the object of careful characterization in the poem. If she is to be worthy of her role as an instrument of Fate, this Iseult must be represented first as attractive and innocuous, but as a developing and finally implacable threat to the lovers. Only the crucial stage in her development is depicted at length by Swinburne, and that stage is portrayed in "The Wife's Vigil," primarily a long soliloquy parallel to the forceful monologue of Irish Iseult in "Iseult at Tintagel." Ironically, the soliloquy of Iseult of the White Hands is simultaneous with Tristram and Irish Iseult's last described moments at Joyous Gard, where they enjoy a rapturous sunset communion that includes observations on the fated tragedy of Arthur, Guenevere, and Morgause, as well as ominous speculations on death. "The Wife's Vigil" represents Brittanic Iseult's single night of "passion." Her monologue is adequately prepared for by a narrative introduction that associates her with the natural forces of darkness that are fated to overpower the forces of light. Swinburne's exact observations of nature are reflected here in the description of darkness *ascending* from the depths of earth toward heaven, an apt simile for the birth of evil from within Iseult:

As darkness from deep valleys void and bleak
Climbs till it clothe with night the sunniest peak
Where only of all a mystic mountain-land
Day seems to cling yet with a trembling hand
And yielding heart reluctant to recede,
So, till her soul was clothed with night indeed,
Rose the slow cloud of envious will within
And hardening hate that held itself no sin,
Veiled heads of vision, eyes of evil gleam,
Dim thought on thought, and darkling dream on dream. (*Poems*, IV, 106)

Here, Brittanic Iseult's metamorphosis is accomplished in simple natural images that contain moral resonances gathered as the poem has progressed. This extended simile endows Iseult with the epic qualities needed to make her fatality to Tristram plausible, and it provides a clear, but not facile, counterpoint to the light imagery with which Tristram and Irish Iseult are consistently described and ennobled.

Indeed, the introductory description of Irish Iseult that opens "The Sailing of the Swallow" dazzles us with images of her radiance. She possesses "bright flesh" that appears to be made of "light woven and moonbeam-coloured shade / More fine than moonbeams." Her "eyelids shone / As snow sun-stricken that endures the sun." Eventually, she proves a very incarnation of light, the perfect complement to Tristram, a "man born at sunrise." As light and sun images used to describe them accumulate, Iseult and Tristram develop into beings who possess the highest kind of relationship that exists between omnipotent natural forces and all men. These lovers become symbolic: they are human extensions of the natural world, at once sources and unique receptacles of radiance. On this level Swinburne represents the relationship between each lover and nature as one of reciprocal illumination. For instance, at the conclusion of their first conversation at sea, Iseult looks into the sun and its "face burned against her meeting face / Most like a lover's thrilled with great love's grace / Whose glance takes fire and gives" (*Poems*, IV, 25–26). Earlier, Swinburne had described her "unimaginable eyes":

> As the wave's subtler emerald is pierced through
> With the utmost heaven's inextricable blue,
> And both are woven and molten in one sleight
> Of amorous colour and implicated light
> Under the golden guard and gaze of noon,
> So glowed their awless amorous plenilune,
> Azure and gold and ardent grey, made strange
> With fiery difference and deep interchange
> Inexplicable of glories multiform. (*Poems*, IV, 14)

In this extraordinary instance of synecdoche Iseult's eyes are symbolic of the whole complex of symbiotic relationships that characterize the natural world and without which it cannot be imagined to exist. Iseult's proportions in this epic simile become universal. Like Tristram, she is not merely in harmony with the natural world, she is indistinguishable from it. She contains elemental creation and is contained by it. And since the central power behind that creation is defined throughout the poem and especially in the "Prelude" as love

whose essence is light, Iseult is depicted as the very power of love itself, a power that is compelled to irradiate, to anoint, and to attract all
things.[9]

Strategically placed epic similes, along with a repeated but less conspicuously epic use of images from nature, result in what might best
be described as the pantheistic vision of *Tristram of Lyonesse*. However,
other epic qualities of the poem depend largely on its courtly love elements, its stress on particular values and patterns of behavior derived
from courtly literature, and its explicit setting in the legendary court
of King Arthur.

The Arthurian context has a more significant function in *Tristram*
than commentators have yet acknowledged.[10] In fact, it occupies dia-
logue that dominates two of the three time-periods that Tristram and
Iseult are able to spend freely together, their journey to Tintagel in
"The Sailing of the Swallow" and their sojourn at Joyous Gard. In
these episodes they speak mostly of the Arthurian court, emphasizing the fatal passions of Arthur for his sister Morgause and of Merlin
for Nimue, the enchantress. The first discussion is a prelude to their
drinking the love potion, and serves much the same function as a
foreboding chorus would in a Greek tragedy. Unaware of the ironic
significance of their conversation for their own lives, Tristram and

9. Reed ignores the complex suggestions of Iseult's personal immortality
in descriptions of the intangibles that compose her being. He emphasizes her
transient attributes and claims that she merely "wears the 'fiery raiment' of
Love" ("Swinburne's *Tristram*," 105). But, the "deep interchange / Inexplic-
able of glories multiform" is framed to suggest an expansive merging of the
external infinitude her eyes reflect and the internal infinitude they contain.
For a discussion of the craftsmanship involved in constructing the poem's
"light scheme," see Fisher, "Swinburne's *Tristram*," 517–20.

10. Chew claims that the Arthurian matter is not integral to Swinburne's
narrative purpose. He insists that it obtrudes primarily in order to create "dramatic relief," which "is sought but not very well obtained by introducing one
or two unrelated episodes such as the story of King Arthur's incestuous love.
In itself this passage is interesting as an indirect attack upon the Tennysonian
conception of the 'blameless king' but in the context it forms an irritating in-
terruption of the narrative" (*Swinburne*, 171). The most obvious argument
against Chew's notion is that the longest Arthurian section (five pages of verse
in all) occurs only seven pages into "The Sailing of the Swallow," where dramatic relief is hardly needed.

Iseult openly speculate on the accidental relationship between Arthur and Morgause, whose sin, like that predestined for Tristram and Iseult, was unavoidable and fatal.

Both discussions of Arthurian matter originate from Iseult's preoccupation with two characteristic courtly concerns: "fairness," or beauty viewed from the competitive aspect, and the fidelity of her lover.[11] In these dialogues Iseult appears always ingenuous. She actually begins her relationship with Tristram, in Swinburne's version of the myth, by innocently suggesting a comparison of herself with Guenevere. Tristram's first words to Iseult constitute an apotheosis of her, one that has already been verified in the "Prelude" and that becomes powerfully ironic in retrospect. He praises her with conventional courtly exaggeration: "'As this day raises daylight from the dead / Might not this face the life of a dead man?'" In reply, Iseult cleverly denies any interest in her own beauty, but displays enormous concern for the beauties at Camelot she will be compared with as Mark's Queen. She tells Tristram not to "'Praise me, but tell me there in Camelot, / Saving the queen, who hath most name of fair?'" (*Poems*, IV, 20). She thus initiates a discussion of Morgause and the doom presaged for Arthur and, by extension, for his knights.

This discussion explicitly formulates the visionary fatalism that characterizes the whole body of Arthurian legends and that has become inextricable from the courtly conception of love as expressed by medieval romanceurs and, very often, by the troubadours and trouvère poets. Courtly love implicitly rejects the possibility of any adequate or final consummation to passion. It requires obstruction to perpetuate its ennobling conventions of chivalric praise and virtuous service by the knight on his lady's behalf. In troubadour lyrics the passion involved is inevitably beyond gratification; it is an idealized passion. And, of course, death is exalted as the most profound consolation for the courtly lover. Thus, as I have suggested, in myths that take up the courtly themes, all true love becomes tragic by definition, and it is a natural step to represent a love situation, with all its original courtly values, as predestined to be tragic.

11. See *Poems*, IV, 20, 97. Also note how both Iseults consistently require and are exalted by their lover's praise of their beauty (for example, *Poems*, IV, 65–67, 99–102), as well as the significance to them of fame. Palamede also demonstrates an adherence to courtly courtesies that we would hardly expect.

In *Tristram of Lyonesse*, as in all the major versions of this courtly legend, the presiding deity is Fate. Here that omnipotent power is the source of energy behind all generation, of all unity and diversity, change and changelessness. "The Sailing of the Swan" begins with an invocation to Fate that is comparable to passages that ritually invoke God (or the gods) in the traditional epic, and it is also suggestive of invocations to the poem's acknowledged muse, the active hand of Fate, Love.[12] Unlike such invocations in earlier epics, however, the poet does not figure self-consciously in those of *Tristram*. The rhetoric is that of exposition rather than humility and deference:

> Fate, that was born ere spirit and flesh were made,
> The fire that fills man's life with light and shade;
> The power beyond all godhead which puts on
> All forms of multitudinous unison,
> A raiment of eternal change inwrought
> With shapes and hues more subtly spun than thought,
> Where all things old bear fruit of all things new
> And one deep chord throbs all the music through,
> The chord of change unchanging, shadow and light
> Inseparable as reverberate day from night;
> Fate, that of all things save the soul of man
> Is lord and God since body and soul began. (*Poems*, IV, 133)

In this poem's delineation of Swinburne's mature philosophy, Fate is analogous to the world's presiding monistic life-force, Hertha. In *Tristram*, before the main action begins, the discussion of Arthurian matter in "The Sailing of the Swallow" serves to suggest the two conflicting religious systems in the poem: that of orthodox Christianity, and that presided over by Fate and Love, which have inexorable power over men's lives but are always only half-perceived by men. In this iconoclastic epic, whatever suspense the stories of Arthur, Merlin, and Tristram hold for us must depend upon the gradual discrediting of orthodox religion and the realization of an ultimately benevolent visionary destiny for these legendary victims of Fate, one that is inevitable but only partially discerned by them.

12. The two major invocations to the muse of Love include, of course, the entire "Prelude" and, in the body of the poem, a passage in "Joyous Gard" where Love is addressed as an Apollonian "Lord," "Bard," and "Seer" (see *Poems*, IV, 92).

Because of its fatal implications for Tristram and Iseult, their initial discussion of the Arthurian court is full of irony. At the mention of Morgause's beauty, for instance, Iseult asks in typical courtly fashion, "'is she more tall than I? / Look, I am tall.'" Indeed, if Arthur's sister is so tall and fair, she insists, then "God" must have "'made her for a godlike sign to men.'" In response, Tristram explains at length the disconcerting significance of this "godlike sign": the prospects for Arthur's kingdom that result from his affair with Morgause. In fact, Arthur's sister is both a woman and the vehicle of destiny's self-fulfillment and self-knowledge; she reveals a "fearful forecast of men's fate" in Arthur's realm. To Tristram's explanation Iseult again reacts innocently, and her response would be comical, were it not ironic: "'The happier hap for me, / With no such face to bring men no such fate'" (*Poems*, IV, 21). But the entire discussion is a pedagogical experience for Iseult. When she learns what events resulted from Morgause's beauty and what they foreshadow, her faith in the orthodox deity begins to be undermined. The conversation ends with her (once again innocent and ironic) observation:

> "Great pity it is and strange it seems to me
> God could not do them so much right as we,
> Who slay not men for witless evil done;
> And these the noblest under God's glad sun
> For sin they knew not he that knew shall slay,
> And smite blind men for stumbling in fair day,
> What good is it to God that such should die?
> Shall the sun's light grow sunnier in the sky
> Because their light of spirit is clean put out?" (*Poems*, IV, 25)

The obvious answer to Iseult's first question is that the lovers sinned and therefore should die in order to vindicate the Christian God's repressive laws. However, in terms set out by the "Prelude" and by the recurrent use of sun and light imagery, the answer to her second question is an unequivocal yes, a response that underscores one of the central motifs of the work. We are told in the "Prelude" that the sungod, Love, is fed by the fame of tragic lovers. It is "One fiery raiment with all lives inwrought / And lights of sunny and starry deed and thought" (*Poems*, IV, 5). Moreover, its radiance is enhanced at second hand by those who celebrate the tragedies it presides over. The orthodox God, by contrast, is discredited by the apparently unjust doom of tragic lovers. The fate of Tristram and Iseult themselves, who commit less culpable a sin than that of Arthur and Morgause, proves finally (in "The Sailing of the Swan") that God is a fiction devised by men to rationalize their insipid inhibitions, their fear of opening themselves to life's primal passions.

Iseult's ingenuous questions in "The Sailing of the Swallow" suggest the opposition maintained throughout the poem between the orthodox God and the sun-god. The latter is continually and expansively defined as the poem's images of light and day accumulate. The former is characterized in appeals by the central figures, especially the two Iseults, and in an iconoclastic denunciation of God following the apostrophe to Fate near the end of the poem. There, as a prelude to Tristram's delirious monologue in which the absolute value of guiltless passion is revealed to him, the narrative describes in Blakean metaphors men's vision of God as

> That sovereign shadow cast of souls that dwell
> In darkness and the prison-house of hell
> Whose walls are built of deadly dread, and bound
> The gates thereof with dreams as iron round.
> . . . .
> That shade accursed and worshipped, which hath made
> The soul of man that brought it forth a shade
> Black as the womb of darkness, void and vain,
> A throne for fear, a pasturage for pain,
> Impotent, abject, clothed upon with lies. (*Poems*, IV, 136)

Fate in the end is a far more benevolent deity than man's God or than men can understand. It bestows death and promises no punishment for joy; rather, it assures an "undivided night" that is "More sweet to savour and more clear to sight" than life itself. Fate alone, in fact, promises the traditionally desired consummation to courtly passion: release.

Yet the poem's narrative vision, which keeps us continually conscious of this fact, is always far in advance of Tristram's and the two Iseults' limited personal vision. The most that Tristram is able to hope for on his deathbed is the gift of a courtly *consolamentum* to undercut the threat of God's punishment. Only Irish Iseult can cure his wound, heal him of life, and bestow a blessing that irradiates the dimness of death and transcends even the radiance of life:

                                        "Ay, this were
How much more than the sun and sunbright air,
How much more than the springtide, how much more
Than sweet strong sea-wind quickening wave and shore
With one divine pulse of continuous breath,
If she might kiss me with the kiss of death,
And make the light of life by death's look dim!" (*Poems*, IV, 143)

At this moment, as at other moments of epiphany in the poem, Tristram's voice seems to merge with that of the omniscient narrator. Yet, although the narrative voice validates Tristram's sentiments here, this speech is, ironically, mere courtly rhetoric. Throughout his experiences with Iseult, he never really learns what the poem makes explicit—that his posthumous destiny will not consist in hellish torments but will be the same as that envisioned for Merlin in this work and for Meleager in *Atalanta in Calydon*: perfect peace in harmonious union with the elements. Thus, in spite of Tristram's more typical insistence that only "unrest hath our long love given," Fate is throughout the poem a force of goodness, a deity whose benevolence, however, is never permanently believed in by Tristram or Iseult. The fact is that the courtly ethos, literally subscribed to, defines passion as a source of pain and prevents a full vision of the inevitable and beneficial interaction of Love, Fate, and natural creation that Swinburne in his mature years intuited as fundamental to all life. The joy of passion is always mitigated (as it is in *Rosamond, Atalanta in Calydon, Chastelard* and "Laus Veneris") by fears of transience, concern for fidelity, or a sense of sin. The courtly lovers' vision is tragically limited to the sorrow that attaches to their love, but that becomes a value in itself because it is a consequence of the supreme spiritual experience.

Thus, in "The Queen's Pleasance" and "Joyous Gard" the lovers dwell in part on the dolorous aspects of their passion—its transience, its sinfulness—or the inevitability of death. Similarly, in "The Sailing of the Swallow" the vision that Morgause's passionate moments with Arthur precipitate is wholly dark. It is a vision informed by orthodox taboos rather than by natural sanctions:

                                        "then there came
On that blind sin swift eyesight like a flame
Touching the dark to death, and made her mad
With helpless knowledge that too late forbade

What was before the bidding: and she knew
How sore a life dead love should lead her through
To what sure end how fearful." (*Poems*, IV, 23)

This description, we must remember, is Tristram's and characterizes only his perception of the event. In spite of the joy that has transfigured his own sin with Iseult, he is not able to transcend the limitations of his courtly and Christian perspective, even by the time he dies. He sees in death only the perpetuation of his life's unrest and still perceives Merlin as "Exempt alone of all predestinate" (*Poems*, IV, 98). He is unable even to imagine the truth that Swinburne repeatedly prepares for and explicitly states at the poem's end: that the rest to which Tristram and Iseult are delivered is much the same as the "strange rest at the heart of slumberland" that occupies Merlin's spirit in Broceliande. Tristram is saved by following his passions, as Merlin is by Nimue, whose "'feet . . . move not save by love's own laws'" (*Poems*, IV, 100), according to Swinburne's interpretation of the myth. Tristram and Iseult instinctively perceive their passion as a supreme good, but their joy is burdened by guilt. At the end of "Joyous Gard," Iseult confesses to Tristram the destiny she desires:

> "To die not of division and a heart
> Rent or with sword of severance cloven apart,
> But only when thou diest and only where thou art,
> O thou my soul and spirit and breath to me,
> O light, life, love! yea, let this only be,
> That dying I may praise God who gave me thee,
> Let hap what will thereafter." (*Poems*, IV, 102)

Despite her partial defiance of threatening Christian laws here, Iseult's devotion to passion is finally requited precisely as she wishes. She kisses Tristram just after he has died, and "their four lips" become "one silent mouth." Similarly, although at the end of her soliloquy in "Iseult at Tintagel" she rejects abstinence and disdains the hell promised by God as punishment for her sin, her final prayer for reunion with Tristram is granted. In explicit opposition to what we would expect of the orthodox God, whose efficacy in the world the poem is at pains to disprove, the lovers are allowed a respite from sorrow at Joyous Gard.

Nonetheless, neither Iseult nor Tristram ever feels worthy of the posthumous blessing they know Merlin and Nimue have "earned." In their discussion of death at the end of "Joyous Gard," Iseult, with only momentary belief in the possibility of her own worthiness, rhetorically asks Tristram,

> "am I—nay, my lover, am I one
> To take such part in heaven's enkindling sun
> And in the inviolate air and sacred sea
> As clothes with grace that wondrous Nimue?" (*Poems*, IV, 100)

But both are worthy of such an organic apotheosis because

> This many a year they have served [Love], and deserved,
> If ever man might yet of all that served,
> Since the first heartbeat bade the first man's knee
> Bend, and his mouth take music, praising thee,
> Some comfort. (*Poems*, IV, 92)

Indeed, Tristram and Iseult have been devoted, faithful, and long-suffering courtly lovers, examples to the world, whose sensual indulgences are vindicated by the power of the symbolic love-draught that first united them. And in typical courtly fashion, their indulgences never dissipate, but rather intensify, their passion.

In spite of the epic qualities of *Tristram*, Swinburne's first description of the poem as a "moral history" may be the most useful, because he believed that the Tristram legend and the courtly mythology that inspired it embody the highest laws that govern men's lives, those of Love and Fate. His primary intent was to communicate and glorify that belief. Like Carlyle, Swinburne knew that the supreme spiritual truths constantly realize themselves in history and thus in individual lives, which are governed by a unitary and presiding impulse in the world. For him, Fate was no intelligent, supernatural force, but rather a sort of natural necessity whose active essence was Love. All vital men and women succumb to its power and are tormented by the obstacles to its full consummation until death bestows fulfillment, and the greatest of these men and women function as immortal exempla for the rest of us.

As early as 1857, Swinburne appears to have perceived this philosophy intuitively. In writing *Queen Yseult*, he harbored an aesthetic purpose that grew and nourished him through much of his career. In the final pages of that work, Yseult, mourning Tristram, consoles herself with the knowledge that her love "'Shall not perish though I die,'" because "'men shall praise [Tristram] dead,'" and thus, "'All my story shall be said'" (*Bonchurch*, I, 59). Swinburne is the perennial bestower of such praise. Long before writing *Tristram*, of course, Swinburne had enrolled himself in the small class of Sapphic poets devoted to preserving in song the high reality of insatiable and doomed love, whose fatality ensured that its participants' immortality would be sustained by poets like himself. Swinburne literally gives "Out of my life to make their dead life live" (*Poems*, IV, 12). His relentless devotion to the stories of tragic lovers evidences his feeling of kinship with them, a kinship more strongly attested, perhaps, by the incorporation of a legend of tragic love into his own life. Swinburne's concept of the appropriate functions of great poetry, along with that sense of spiritual kinship, inspired him to treat in a unique but predominantly epic manner the greatest medieval myth of tragic love in order to preserve his intuition of the ultimate philosophical truths behind the legend. As he confides at the end of the "Prelude" to *Tristram of Lyonesse*,

> So many and many of old have given my twain
> Love and live song and honey-hearted pain,
> Whose root is sweetness and whose fruit is sweet,
> So many and with such joy have tracked their feet,
> What should I do to follow? yet I too,
> I have the heart to follow, many or few
> Be the feet gone before me. (*Poems*, IV, 12)

The philosophical perceptions that Swinburne's epic rendering of the Tristram legend enabled him to articulate depend for their validity upon his aesthetic vision. Only the true poet, finally, has the capacity to recreate and thus transmit the profound beauty of amatory tragedies. Doing so, he provides images, in the form of "historical" examples, of that "deep truth" that Shelley—in his own epic, dramatic, philosophical poem, *Prometheus Unbound*—insisted was "imageless."

6

Receptivity and Organicism in *Tristram*

The central human value in *Tristram* is total receptivity to experience. Throughout the poem Swinburne emphasizes the need for self-abandonment, for the unrestrained indulgence of all energies and desires.[1] By 1869 the radically libertarian values that inform his early works, including those fundamental to the poems of his 1866 volume, had matured into a coherent and systematic monistic philosophy, and Swinburne successfully embodied that philosophy in *Tristram*, as well as in such major late poems as "A Nympholept" (1894), "The Lake of Gaube" (1899), and his "brief epic," *The Tale of Balen* (1896). A Blakean openness not only to the power of love but also to experience whose vital, generative, or sensory qualities become associated with love is the most important value in these works, and such openness is a crucial aspect of Swinburne's mature philosophy. Nonetheless, he perceived that, in his version of the Tristram myth, the emphasis upon passion to express his supreme metaphysic was at once a danger and a virtue. An ability to love without inhibition constituted for Swinburne one reflection of the total receptivity to all human physical and

1. Of course, an openness to vital and passionate experience, no matter how unorthodox, was notoriously characteristic of Swinburne himself in his younger days. His well-known interest in perverse sexuality and his ebullient activities with Rossetti and company, as well as with such eccentrics as Richard Burton and Lord Houghton, amply demonstrate Swinburne's eclectic delight in adventure for its own sake. Clearly, even after his placid "retirement" to Putney in 1879, Swinburne did not discard his fundamental belief in the need for total openness to all passionate experience.

spiritual experience that he prized so highly. But his characters' openness to passion—the source of man's harmony with the world of organic nature—might be construed as mere "fleshliness" by readers familiar with his early, sexually charged poetic extravaganzas such as "Dolores," "Faustine," and "Anactoria." Throughout his epic, therefore, Swinburne took care to sustain a spiritual emphasis and philosophical tone while producing some of the most vivid, indeed, spectacular love poetry in the language.

In this respect *Tristram* supersedes such earlier works as *Rosamond, Chastelard,* "Anactoria," "Laus Veneris," and even *Atalanta in Calydon.* But in another, Swinburne's epic resembles these works. Tristram's passion, like Rosamond's, Chastelard's, Meleager's, and even Sappho's, is peculiarly selfless and compelled. Although it is actively received, it is not actively willed. As the symbol of the potion that united them insists, the love between Tristram and Irish Iseult is fated and fateful—one result of the laws that inexorably govern human (as well as natural) behavior. Resignation to those laws and thus persistent receptivity to passionate experience, in spite of the inhibitions of orthodoxy or physical obstacles to its fulfillment, are adequate reasons for salvation in the religion of love that *Tristram of Lyonesse* formulates and propagates.

The poem's purpose is, in every respect, unorthodox and, as Nicolas Tredell correctly insists, powerfully subversive.[2] "Joyous Gard" begins with an invocation to Love. Swinburne will need Love's power to help him demonstrate the quintessential value to human history of Tristram and Iseult's passion—and the myth that perpetuates it:

> Sweet Love, that art so bitter; foolish Love,
> Whom wise men know for wiser, and thy dove
> More subtle than the serpent; for thy sake
> These [two lovers] pray thee for a little beam to break,
> A little grace to help them, lest men think
> Thy servants have but hours like tears to drink.
> O Love, a little comfort, lest they fear
> To serve as these have served thee who stand here. (*Poems*, IV, 87)

Tristram, like many of Swinburne's poems, works most often by an inversion of traditional values. And here, as in *Chastelard, Rosamond,*

2. This is the thrust of Tredell's argument throughout "*Tristram,*" 97–111.

and many of the pieces in *Poems and Ballads, First Series,* an aggressive openness to the passionate encounter, no matter what laws it defies, is the supreme value. Adulterous passion is idealized and all behavior that helps or augments it is sanctioned. As a result, the poem's conclusion and all the passages that emphasize Tristram's and Iseult's harmony with nature make it clear that they do not merely have "hours like tears to drink." By virtue of their passion, they earn an eternity of organic integration with the universe and of spiritual integration with living generations who inherit the value system that is embodied in their myth and that is enhanced by their fame. Their immortality is the subject of the "Prelude," and the vision presented there is contradicted in no part of the poem.

Most commentators observe that the end of Tristram's story is explicit in its beginning, that death is simply the tragic culmination of a compelled but unwilled love affair, attractive largely because of the lovers' impassioned fidelity to each other in the face of numerous obstacles. Death is the simple conclusion to their tragedy, and even Swinburne's critics cite his ostensibly straightforward observation that the lovers "quaffed / Death" when they drank the love potion. In fact, we know from the "Prelude" and from evidence throughout the poem that, for Swinburne, the opposite is true. In *Tristram* he employs precisely the strategy that Shelley and Blake suspected was Milton's in *Paradise Lost.* He uses traditionally loaded terms, especially *death* and *sin,* on two levels at once. For the reader informed by the poem's narrative commentary on events, they mean "immortality" and "virtue." For the personae of the poem and for the orthodox reader who refuses to accept the poem's explicit system of values, they are understood in the conventional way and act as an ironic commentary on the reader's or persona's lack of vision, his inability to participate without reservation in the vital life, the only true life, which the poem exalts. The "Prelude" makes these inverse values clear, and they are explicit throughout the poem. For instance, when Tristram and Iseult drink the potion, "all their life changed in them, for they quaffed / Death; if it be death so to drink and fare / As men who change and are what these twain were" (*Poems,* IV, 37). Obviously it is not death, but life, that they drink. The potion serves as a catalyst, allowing their "sinful" propensities to become dominant and compelling. The love-draught liberates their potential for real passion,

117

for love that includes and extends the courtly love values to which Tristram and Iseult adhere from the start. Early in the narrative we are told that "love upon them like a shadow sate" (*Poems,* IV, 14). The potion, drunk afterwards, is a symbol of the necessity, in Swinburne's doctrine of vitality, to dissolve the formalities and reticence of courtliness so that the tumultuous passions it veils and rechannels can become "naturalized." Their power uncovered, the effect of these passions is immediate:

> And shuddering with eyes full of fear and fire
> And heart-stung with a serpentine desire
> He turned and saw the terror in her eyes
> That yearned upon him shining.
> . . . .
> Nor other hand there needed, nor sweet speech
> To lure their lips together. (*Poems,* IV, 37)

The desire of these lovers is "serpentine," just as was Adam and Eve's. It transgresses all arbitrary inhibitions and impels them to eat all natural fruits.[3] They need no "other hand," no sanctions other than passion, to bring them together; nor do they need any "sweet speech" of courtly rhetoric. The natural "sin" of Tristram and Iseult in this poem is defined unequivocally as virtue, as is all activity depicted as harmonious with nature's powers for generation and integration.

The naturalness of the poem's central figures is measured by their openness to experience and by the passionate energy and enthusiasm

---

3. Kerry McSweeney is correct in noting the Miltonic echoes in Swinburne's description of the drinking of the potion, but he does not detect the irony in them. He claims that "it is doubtless because Swinburne wished to invest this moment of his poem with a gravity and resonance that he alludes so deliberately to the Miltonic description of the fall. . . . But a comparison of the two situations suggests no theological or moral similarities. In this regard 'serpentine desire' is unfortunate; for Swinburne—as the rest of the poem manifests—hardly means to suggest that Tristram and Iseult become creatures of sin and evil or lose their place in the scheme of creation and descend to a bestial level. There is no suggestion in the poem that they are guilty of anything, nor that they have fallen at all" ("Structure," 695). Regarding this second point, we must keep in mind that most of the time the Christian ethos dominates the two principal characters' self-awareness and acts as an ironic counterpoint to the narrative perspective.

with which they meet it.[4] Significantly, sexual passion is expressed only infrequently in human terms and more often in metaphors from nature, the most common source of objective correlatives in this poem. Swinburne's obsession with the pervasive and consuming condition of passion, his extension of courtly love preoccupations, is frequently described here in musical terms suggestive of nature. Song, as usual with Swinburne, proves the only adequate vehicle for expressing the ineffable. He is able most forcefully to communicate an impression of pure passion purely expressed when describing the qualities of song. When Brittanic Iseult and Tristram first yield to their different but equally compelling desires for each other, for instance,

> Something she would and would not fain have said,
> And wist not what the word would be,
> But rose and reached forth to him her hand: and he
> Heart-stricken, bowed his head and dropped his knee,
> And on her fragrant hand his lips were fire;
> And their two hearts were as one trembling lyre
> Touched by the keen wind's kiss with brief desire
> And music shuddering at its own delight. (*Poems*, IV, 67)

Tristram himself has just finished singing his song that "yearns" upon the name of Iseult and serves to reinforce his passion for the absent Irish Queen. "Music shuddering at its own delight" captures both the sensual and intangible qualities of this true passion, which is always, like the wind-touched lyre, spontaneous and uninhibited.

Elsewhere Swinburne chooses only to emphasize either the sensuality or the spirituality of passion, and he does so again by means of imagery from nature. For the latter he selects the most expansive images, those associated with light. By their continual use, these become symbolic of the presiding power of Love in the world. That power finally supersedes the laws normally governing natural objects:

> The spring's breath blew through all [the lovers'] summer time,
> And in their skies would sunlike Love confuse
> Clear April colours with hot August hues,

---

4. McSweeney unfortunately does not expand much on his useful observation that "Swinburne does not invite the reader to judge the lovers in any way except by measuring the fullness of their response to each other and to the natural world" ("Structure," 696).

And in their hearts one light of sun and moon
Reigned, and the morning died not of the noon:
Such might of life was in them, and so high
Their heart of love rose higher than fate could fly. (*Poems,* IV, 94)

Ultimately the natural world is not large enough to contain the ever-expanding "might of life" that characterizes the passion of Tristram and Iseult. Sexual indulgence merely results in "delight that feeds desire," which culminates in speculations on death or even an explicit yearning for it. "The Queen's Pleasance" imitates the *alba* when Iseult implores, "Hast thou no sword? I would not live till day." And earlier the narrative has characterized their passion as one that impels the lovers to yearn for ever more profound realms of expression and experience, to "reach / Beyond all bourne of time or trembling sense" (*Poems,* IV, 50). Natural gratifications of their energetic and expansive passion, though always sought, are always inadequate.

Occasionally, however, their moments of sensual indulgence are described at length, though they perpetually feel "a yearning ardour without scope or name." The paradoxical effect of momentarily gratified passion is sensory disorientation for Iseult, and—for both of them, finally—an absolute coalescence and spiritualization of the senses:

She had nor sight nor voice; her swooning eyes
Knew not if night or light were in the skies.
. . . .
Only with stress of soft fierce hands she prest
Between the throbbing blossoms of her breast
His ardent face, and through his hair her breath
Went quivering as when life is hard on death;
And with strong trembling fingers she strained fast
His head into her bosom; till at last,
Satiate with sweetness of that burning bed,
His eyes afire with tears, he raised his head
And laughed into her lips; and all his heart
Filled hers; then face from face fell, and apart
Each hung on each with panting lips, and felt
Sense into sense and spirit into spirit melt. (*Poems,* IV, 50–51)

A transfiguring receptivity analogous to that which death requires and bestows is, for Swinburne, the quintessence of the "quivering," "trembling," "throbbing" sensations that characterize the supreme ecstasy of passion. The end of the experience is literally "consummation"; each lover is consumed by the other in spiritual exaltation, just as the veil of life is devoured by death. The unity these lovers achieve corresponds to the organic unity that, as the poem frequently observes, is attained finally by all separate objects and phenomena in nature. These "die" into each other so that they can be reborn or transformed. At the beginning of "Tristram in Brittany," Tristram reflects upon the "passionate" behavior of all natural occurrences, which present analogues to the lovers' experience:

> "as the worn-out noon
> Loves twilight, and as twilight loves the moon
> That on its grave a silver seal shall set—
> We have loved and slain each other and love yet.
> Slain; for we live not surely, being in twain." (*Poems,* IV, 54)

Here dying into unity becomes the only source of real life for separate creatures. Indeed, immediately afterwards this dialectical pattern is described as the source of all continued cosmic generation. Tristram asserts that he and Iseult, like "all the streams on earth and all fresh springs . . . Even with one heart's love seek one bitter grave." Similarly,

> "So strive all lives for death which all lives win;
> So sought her soul to my soul, and therein
> Was poured and perished: O my love, and mine
> Sought to thee and died of thee and died as thine.
> As the dawn loves the sunlight that must cease
> Ere dawn again may rise and pass in peace;
> Must die that she being dead may live again,
> To be by his new rising nearly slain.
> So rolls the great wheel of the great world round,
> And no change in it and no fault is found,
> And no true life of perdurable breath,
> And surely no irrevocable death." (*Poems,* IV, 55)

Openness to the passionate encounter is finally a necessity if the world is to continue, and in Swinburne's metaphysic of love, death becomes merely a metaphor for the process of integration and transformation.

Such openness, however, implies enthusiastic receptivity to all experience, not only to love, which Swinburne's hero and heroine exhibit continually. For instance, in "The Sailing of the Swallow," Iseult's characteristic receptivity is imagined in her passionate confrontation with the newly risen sun, which virtually quickens her to womanhood:

> And [the sun's] face burned against her meeting face
> Most like a lover's thrilled with great love's grace
> Whose glance takes fire and gives.
> . . . .
> So as a fire the mighty morning smote
> Throughout her, and incensed with the influent hour
> Her whole soul's one great mystical red flower
> Burst, and the bud of her sweet spirit broke
> Rose-fashion, and the strong spring at a stroke
> Thrilled, and was cloven, and from the full sheath came
> The whole rose of the woman red as flame. (*Poems,* IV, 25–27)

The effect of the sun's passionate anointing power is the generation not merely of Iseult as a sexual entity, the "woman red as flame," but also of the inseparable spiritual counterpart of her sexual being. Iseult's blossoming can be adequately described only in a vivid and sexually charged metaphor from nature because she possesses the same components and is subject to precisely the same forces as natural objects are. Her human spiritual potential is not projected onto a rose; rather, this natural object is conceived as a symbol of the essential soul that all things partake of and that here is merely being realized in Iseult as her own "great mystical red flower." Only after this experience can she perceive within herself the yearning for that love-accomplished unity that inspires Tristram after he leaves her and goes to Brittany, and that for him is simply an echo of the impassioned feeling all natural things have toward the power that will kill and ultimately regenerate them. The total significance of the presiding power of Love is suggested in both versions of Tristram's first song aboard the *Swallow,* which precipitates Iseult's perception of her passion for unity:

> "Ah, who knows yet if one be twain or one,
> And sunlight separable again from sun,
>   And I from thee with all my lifesprings dry,
> And thou from me with all thine heartbeats done?" (*Poems,* IV, 33)

Throughout Swinburne's epic, Iseult opens herself totally to Tristram and to all unitary experience. Paradoxically indicative of Iseult's passion for life is her desire even to explore "love's last possible eminence" in death. In addition, upon Tristram's reappearance in Cornwall with Ganhardine, she is the one to suggest they flee to Camelot and seek Guenevere's assistance, "'Which love shall be full fain to lend, nor loth / Shall my love be to take it'" (*Poems*, IV, 91). Afterwards, at Joyous Gard, Iseult eagerly communes with nature at Tristram's side, open to its multiform phenomena in the same way that she is "subject to the sun": "They took the moorland's or the bright sea's boon / With all their hearts into their spirit of sense, / Rejoicing" (*Poems*, IV, 95).[5] But for Iseult passionate enjoyment of nature requires the company of her personal sun-god, Tristram. Like the sun itself in "The Sailing of the Swallow," Tristram's love is an influent force that opens, sensitizes, and transfigures Iseult. Under his caresses,

> her bright limbs palpitated and shrank
> And rose and fluctuated as flowers in rain
> That bends them and they tremble and rise again
> And heave and straighten and quiver all through with bliss
> And turn afresh their mouths up for a kiss,
> Amorous, athirst. (*Poems*, IV, 51–52)

Descriptions of Iseult's thirst for passionate natural experiences are necessarily less frequent and more limited than are descriptions of Tristram's, for she is represented as and conceives herself to be primarily an adjunct of his fate.[6] Although the virtue of their love assures both Tristram and Iseult immortality in myth, as well as an organically envisioned afterlife similar to that of Merlin and Nimue, the crucial events of the legend result primarily from Tristram's actions. Moreover, in spite of his uncharacteristic attention to Christian pro-

5. McSweeney defines this difficult and recurrent phrase as "man's most spiritual quality, but something that is inseparable from his sense, his perception of other human beings and of the external world. Without sense, spirit cannot exist; without spirit, sense perceives merely a drab otherness" ("Structure," 696).

6. That fact is especially patent in her monologue at Tintagel, but she also acknowledges it in private conversations with Tristram. At Joyous Gard she questions her lover:

> "what am I,
> Love, that have strength but to desire and die,
> That have but grace to love and do thee wrong,
> What am I that my name should live so long,
> With hers whose life was light to Launcelot?" (*Poems*, IV, 100)

nouncements while dying, Tristram is in closer touch with man's spiritual source in nature than is Iseult or are any of the other central figures of the poem. Thus, his experience is the work's philosophical focus and the means to depict man's place in relation to all parts of the cosmic organism. Although he possesses more limited vision than does Merlin, nature's high priest in the poem, Tristram consistently precipitates and frequently formulates the pantheistic insights that are repeatedly associated with the wizard. Tristram is intermittently able to achieve real vision, however, not by any superhuman powers, but by virtue of his dominant trait, total rceptivity to all types of passionate experience. Love is certainly the most important of those types; the energy and enthusiasm with which he greets his love for Iseult are also exhibited in battle and in impassioned encounters with the sea.

Except for his fight against Iseult's kidnapper, Palamede (in "The Queen's Pleasance"), Tristram's major battles occur in "The Last Pilgrimage," as do two of his major encounters with the sea—one passive and philosophical, the other active and rapturous. Because of a summons from Arthur to assist his Welsh vassal against Urgan, "an iron bulk of giant mold," Tristram and Iseult are forced to abandon Joyous Gard and their luxurious intimacy. Consequently, Iseult, nearly in despair, appears as "a cloud full-charged with storm and shower." Tristram's blithe and energetic mood, however, contrasts significantly with hers.[7] He is

> High-hearted with desire of happy fight
> And strong in soul with merrier sense of might
> Than since the fair first years that hailed him knight. (*Poems*, IV, 115)

Tristram's appetite for glory equals his appetite for adventure. He quests for "Fame, the broad flower whose breath makes death more sweet / Than roses crushed by love's receding feet" (*Poems*, IV, 115). The immortality that chivalric fame promises, however, is always subordinate to that bestowed by love. Battle becomes a fiery alternative to love when the possibility of love is denied. It is merely one more

7. Yet Tristram by no means forgets Iseult. When apart from her, "his heart mourned within him, knowing how she / Whose heart with his was fatefully made fast / Sat now fast bound . . . such a brief space eastward thence" (*Poems*, IV, 118).

manifestation of the passionate vital spirit in men that is finally responsible for all fame, whether achieved through love, heroism, or wizardry.

In Wales, Tristram triumphs over Urgan, and the country finds itself "by Tristram's grace . . . free." Renewed by success and the "high laud and honour" it bestows, Tristram sets out in a meditative frame of mind for Brittany. There he is intercepted by a namesake who asks his commitment once again to love's cause by battling the kidnappers of this new Tristram's lady. The poem's hero, for the sake of his fame and in order to "do the unrighteous griefs of good men right" (*Poems*, IV, 123), feels bound to assist, and he does so with spirit. The night before the encounter finds him "With heart of hope triumphant as the sun / Dreaming asleep of love and fame and fight," the triune virtues. Then at dawn, "with joy / full-souled and perfect passion," he awakens feeling the "rapture of the hour / That brought his spirit and all the world to flower" (*Poems*, I, 125). For Tristram, that moment of delight is inseparable from the sensation of his own birth and an awareness of regeneration as nature's perpetual process. His earlier reveries on natural objects emphasize the freedom with which they give themselves continually to compelling life-forces, just as he himself and Iseult have given themselves openly and totally to Love and Fate. Tristram's sense of harmony with the world drives him now to the sea, into which he impetuously plunges and from which he emerges "Strong-spirited for the chance and cheer of fight" (*Poems*, IV, 128). His yearning for passionate interaction with the world is indomitable, and it is nearly always rewarded by physical pleasure or self-fulfilling reverie. For instance, while swimming, Tristram discovers a supreme sensation that characterizes many of his impassioned moments. The narrative insists upon its sublimity:

> No song, no sound of clarions that rejoice,
> Can set that glory forth which fills with fire
> The body and soul that have their whole desire
> Silent, and freer than birds or dreams are free
> Take all their will of all the encountering sea. (*Poems*, IV, 127)

Tristram, in fact, takes all his will of all experience, and the battle that follows his ecstatic union with the sea is no exception. In the tumultuous confrontation Tristram is descried "exalting like a flame":

"his heart bounded in him, and was fain / As fire or wind that takes its fill by night / Of tempest and of triumph" (*Poems*, IV, 130). The analogy depicts Tristram as one natural force harmoniously and exultantly interacting with others.

Although Tristram does not explicitly acknowledge the fact, it is the spirit that impels these composite forces (Love) and the laws that govern them (Fate) that also inform his own receptivity to experience and inspire his passions. Tristram is always resigned to these mysterious powers that control his life and that he consistently associates with the sun and sea. Even after three years of painful separation from Irish Iseult, he fervently acknowledges his subjection:

> "O strong sun! O sea!
> I bid not you, divine things! comfort me,
> I stand not up to match you in your sight—
> Who hath said ye have mercy toward us, ye who have might?
> And though ye had mercy, I think I would not pray
> That ye should change your counsel or your way
> To make our life less bitter." (*Poems*, IV, 57–58)

In Kierkegaardian terms, Tristram is a knight of infinite resignation. Not always content, as Swinburne declared himself to be, accepting the "absolute mystery" of destiny, he nonetheless rejoices in the experiences and visions of nature's unity that his fate allows him.[8] Although he alternates between triumph and grief, even at his worst moments this "changefully forlorn" knight is regenerated by an instinct of hope, whose symbol and sanction in the natural world is the planet Venus and in Arthurian society is Merlin.

According to Tristram, Merlin, who succumbed inexorably to his love of Nimue, exists "at the heart of slumberland" in perfect harmony with the consoling and magnanimous generative forces of the world, as Tristram himself is in moments of impassioned confrontation with nature and as he would like to be in death. Merlin, in his

---

8. For one of Swinburne's most explicit statements on religious matters, see his letter to D. G. Rossetti in 1869 (*Letters*, II, 43). This letter, of course, reflects the frame of mind Swinburne was in when he was writing *Tristram's* "Prelude." The later parts of the poem do not contradict but, rather, sanction and explicate his conception of an "absolute mystery," emphasizing its ultimate beneficence.

integral union with the elemental world, embodies the paradox of organicism that all creatures manifest. Being at once discreet and incorporate, he

> "knows the soul that was his soul at one
> With the ardent world's, and in the spirit of earth
> His spirit of life reborn to mightier birth
> And mixed with things of elder life than ours." (*Poems*, IV, 98)

Merlin lives perpetually in a state of extended existence, of "deathless life and death," that is attained by grace of Nimue's passion for him. Unrestrained passionate interaction between individuals in life results after death in rapturous integration with all living things and the dominant spirit infusing them. Thus Nimue and Merlin have been absorbed into the presiding procreative life-force without sacrificing their individuality. The wizard "hears in spirit a song" that is "shed" from "the mystic mouth of Nimue / . . . like a consecration." That song is reminiscent of the courtly songs of love that Tristram sings and that beatify both the singer and his beloved. At the sound of Nimue's ethereal lyric, Merlin's heart

> "is made for love's sake as a part
> Of that far singing, and the life thereof
> Part of that life that feeds the world with love:
> Yea, heart in heart is molten, hers and his,
> Into the world's heart and the soul that is
> Beyond or sense or vision; and their breath
> Stirs the soft springs of deathless life and death,
> Death that bears life, and change that brings forth seed
> Of life to death and death to life indeed,
> As blood recircling through the unsounded veins
> Of earth and heaven with all their joys and pains." (*Poems*, IV, 99)

Change, as it is consistently feared by living creatures and especially those in love, thus becomes the unique and beneficent source of the world's constant regeneration and of its multitudinous unity. Tristram and Iseult usually conceive of death incorrectly as an ending and a time for punishment. Death is, however, what permanently allows the unity that they have experienced transiently in their lovemaking and that Tristram perceives as the dominant fact of nature. Indeed, Tristram displays enough visionary instinct by the poem's end to reconcile himself to the facts of Fate, to change and death, though he is unable to perceive them as beneficent aspects of the world-force, Love. His peculiarly eager resignation resembles Iseult's impulse to explore love's "last possible eminence," death, as a potential source of consummate joy.

Both characters thus feel intimations of the impalpable "Truth" always associated with love, which the narrative finally proclaims (in "The Sailing of the Swan") as the "Fountain of all things living, source and seed" (*Poems*, IV, 135). In the pantheistic vision that the poem projects, this quintessential Truth involves the benevolent dominance of Fate over all the world's objects and laws, and defines Love as the universal unifying force. That Tristram partially perceives this ultimate Truth throughout the narrative is suggested in his first song. Although he is forced to sing a second, simplified version of "these wrought riddles made of night and day," the irreducible complexity of the first song becomes less enigmatic as the poem advances. The song contains the monistic philosophical vision that *Tristram* as a whole embodies and explicates:

> "O which is elder, night or light, who knows?
> And life or love, which first of these twain grows?
>   For life is born of love to wail and cry,
> And love is born of life to heal his woes,
>   And light of night, that day should live and die.
>
> "O sun of heaven above the worldly sea,
> O very love, what light is this of thee!
>   My sea of soul is deep as thou art high,
> But all thy light is shed through all of me,
>   As love's through love, while day shall live and die." (*Poems*, IV, 31)

As *Tristram* progresses, what appear here to be paradoxes and tautologies gradually are perceived as self-fulfilling Blakean cycles. Day and night, life and death, permanence and change, darkness and light, all opposed phenomena and all contrarious concepts are reciprocally dependent: "Each into each dies, each of each is born" (*Poems*, IV, 55). *Love*, which normally describes sensation, in *Tristram* also describes the set of forces by which all the world becomes dialectical process. That which is usually viewed as static must be perceived as being in a state of constant transformation. Such perception of Love's activity in the world requires conscious and eager subjection to its power. Human love therefore produces a visionary state whose sensory aspect can be adequately expressed only in conventional terms of passion.

Thus, descriptions of natural and sexual interaction become interchangeable, because all activity ultimately reflects the same transformational laws that govern all phenomena and every object that exists. The primary manifestations of these laws are dissolution and rebirth precipitated by intense sensation. Every object or activity is merely one aspect of a cosmic and organic unity whose functions are described by these laws. Appropriately, therefore, sunrise aboard the *Swallow* is depicted in explicitly sexual terms:

> swift the moon
> Withered to westward as a face in swoon
> Death-stricken by glad tidings: and the height
> Throbbed and the centre quivered with delight
> And the depth quailed with passion as of love,
> Till like the heart of some new-mated dove
> Air, light, and wave seemed full of burning rest,
> With motion as of one God's beating breast. (*Poems*, IV, 26)

One hundred pages later, when Tristram takes his final sunrise swim, the interaction of sun and sea at the sun's birth is similarly described. His soul drank in

> the free
> Limitless love that lifts the stirring sea
> When on her bare bright bosom as a bride
> She takes the young sun, perfect in his pride,
> Home to his place with passion. (*Poems*, IV, 126)

Such descriptions help to determine *Tristram*'s dominant lyrical quality, for they are frequent in the work. These repeated descriptions are, however, not merely projections of human spirit and activity onto objects in nature. Rather, they attempt to elicit a recognition of the all-pervasive "sovereign conscience of the spirit of life," in which man merely participates. Whereas in Wordsworth or Keats the poet's psyche informs a receptive natural world, here the spirited and unitary natural world informs man's limited vision of its beneficent and self-conscious omnipotence. Early in "The Last Pilgrimage" the narrative reveals the "very bay whence very love, / . . . might have risen" as Aphrodite. The waters therefore become a symbol of all joyfully interacting forces and creatures:

who sets eye thereon soever knows
How since these rocks and waves first rolled and rose
The marvel of their many-coloured might
Hath borne this record sensible to sight,
The witness and the symbol of their own delight,
The gospel graven of life's most heavenly law,
Joy, brooding on its own still soul with awe,
A sense of godlike rest in godlike strife,
The sovereign conscience of the spirit of life. (*Poems,* IV, 119)

The Wordsworthian (and Miltonic) atmosphere here is unmistakable, especially in the last five lines. It suggests the extent to which this vision of Tristram's, though unaccompanied by a perception of his own and his love's part in it, is epic in scope and revolutionary. Indeed, he receives solace from this vision of self-fulfilling and complementary activites in the world. He is comforted to see "The strong deep joy of living sun and sea, / The large deep love of living sea and land" (*Poems,* IV, 118).

Tristram often participates in this joyous and loving unity.[9] He does so most energetically in his amorous union with the sea at dawn just before his last battle, having been inspired by the example of the sun borne by the "bare bright bosom" of the sea. His heart

Trembled for joy within the man whose part
Was here not least in living; and his mind
Was rapt abroad beyond man's meaner kind
And pierced with love of all things and with mirth
Moved to make one with heaven and heavenlike earth
And with the light live water. (*Poems,* IV, 126)

Ironically, in this scene Tristram is only temporarily able to achieve that sense of his unity with the rest of the world that always subtends his conscious life. Among the waves, "all the life that moved him seemed to aspire, / As all the sea's life toward the sun," until "each glad limb became / A note of rapture in the tune of life" (*Poems,* IV, 128). Finally his sense of unity is fulfilled by a sensation of new birth, as is every transformation that reveals an underlying unity:

And like the sun his heart rejoiced in him,
And brightened with a broadening flame of mirth:

9. In addition to the present example, see *Poems,* IV, 56–57, 61, 62, 121–22, 140.

> And hardly seemed its life a part of earth,
> But the life kindled of a fiery birth
> And passion of a new-begotten son
> Between the live sea and the living sun. (*Poems*, IV, 128)

Tristram's experience here imitates the cycles of all natural life. Much earlier he had perceived that " 'full sure / All [things] and we are parts of one same end'" (*Poems*, IV, 56), but never before has sensation so graphically proven how all things are parts of one same life. His experience has been limited to intimations of spiritual harmony: "the heart of the ancient hills and his were one" (*Poems*, IV, 61). Only now does he perceive in full the dynamic cosmic unity of which he is a physical, as well as a spiritual, part.

Tristram's epiphany in his final swim is one among many that are central to Swinburne's early and late poems, from *Atalanta in Calydon* through "A Nympholept" and "The Lake of Gaube." Unfortunately, critics until now have not taken his mystical, organicist philosophy with adequate seriousness, largely because they have not been able to perceive the complex strains of meaning within his deceptively musical verse. The crucial message of most of Swinburne's philosophical poetry is the same, though it is embedded in strikingly different contexts and expressed in a startling variety of forms. These diverse forms serve finally to reveal not only Swinburne's artistic versatility but also the essential monistic faith that informs his whole body of song: that Fate

> smites and soothes with heavy and healing hand
> All joys and sorrows born in life's dim land,
> Till joy be found a shadow and sorrow a breath
> And life no discord in the tune with death,
> But all things fain alike to die and live
> In pulse and lapse of tides alternative,
> Through silence and through sound of peace and strife,
> Till birth and death be one in sight of life. (*Poems*, IV, 133)

The central idea here—albeit in a highly generalized form—is akin to that of Keats's "Ode on Melancholy." In Swinburne's philosophy the world is depicted as a single organism where all objects, all phenomena, and all contraries are inseparably interrelated in the paradoxical, beneficent tragedy we call mutability. The human spirit yearns passionately but vainly for absolute and permanent union with the be-

131

loved and with the world in order to be fulfilled. Realizing the impossibility of this quest, man turns either to death or to the nurture of spiritual states in order to attain transcendence. This world view is characteristic not just of nineteenth-century Romanticism; it has its roots in the varieties of medieval mysticism upon which much romance and troubadour poetry is constructed. For example, in Rudel's poems, Jean de Meun's section of the *Roman de la Rose,* as well as Dante's *Vita Nuova* and the *Divine Comedy,* absolute love of one's lady integrates the lover with the universe. Moreover, love simultaneously allows for the transcendence—no matter how temporary—of a world whose human component appears irrevocably corrupt. Thus, no matter how much suffering love compels and no matter how tragic its end, love becomes the ultimate source of all redemption. However, for Swinburne and the Romantics, as for Malory, Chaucer, and medieval French romanceurs (as well as for such theologians as Saint Benedict and Cassian, who were indispensable to medieval writers on the subject of love), erotic passion was only one expression of the redemptive impulse basic to spirited and spiritual men. Brotherly love, *caritas,* also served to ennoble man and reveal humanity's potential for transcendence through integration with others and with the world.[10]

10. As John C. Moore suggests, the constellation of attitudes toward love discussed here derives originally from classical tradition, which "provided [the Middle Ages] with several main themes of love. It was a spiritual longing for the Good which could not be satisfied in the material world; it was a passionate and erotic desire to possess the beloved; it was simple erotic pleasure, which should not be taken too seriously, lest it cease to be pleasurable; it was a reciprocal bond of good will and affection, possible between men of high character; on a cosmic scale, it was a mysterious force or power which generated all life in the universe and maintained harmony among its disparate parts" (*Love in Twelfth-Century France* [Philadelphia, 1972], 27).

7

The Tale of Balen
Medievalism and Tragedy

While bringing Irish Iseult to King Mark at the beginning of *Tristram of Lyonesse,* Swinburne's hero introduces Iseult (and the unfamiliar reader as well) to the whole body of Arthurian myth that surrounds Tristram and Iseult's story. The two are sailing aboard the *Swallow* when

> the soft speech between them grew again
> With questionings and records of what men
> Rose mightiest, and what names of love or fight
> Shone starriest overhead of queen or knight. (*Poems,* IV, 27)

Among these "records," Tristram recounts the experiences of the knight Balen, whose legend Swinburne took up thirteen years after the publication of *Tristram* in his second grand poem on Arthurian themes, *The Tale of Balen* (published in 1896). *Tristram's* brief description of Balen's life serves as a virtual précis of the later work, revealing how little Swinburne's essential conception of the heroic character and fate of Balen changed during almost two decades. Swinburne summarizes Tristram's view of "the toil of Balen," who, for all his labor and virtue and for "all his days," reaped

> but thorns for fruit and tears for praise,
> Whose hap was evil as his heart was good,
> And all his works and ways by wold and wood
> Led through much pain to one last labouring day
> When blood for tears washed grief with life away. (*Poems,* IV, 29)

133

The emphasis here, as in the *Tale* itself, is upon Balen's deeds and his innocence. In this last truly important Victorian medievalist poem, the good knight's various attempts to cleanse and regenerate an irretrievably corrupt world are ineffectual.

The omission of *Balen* from most critical considerations of Swinburne's accomplishment is surprising since his *Tale* is a dense and extraordinarily energetic work.[1] As is typical of Swinburne, this long narrative poem is self-consciously innovative, if not revolutionary. Indeed, because of its unique form and unusual prosody as well as its energy and poignancy, the work was much admired by its initial reviewers and early critics. As Clyde Hyder recalls, "*The Times* suggests that [Balen] is not 'unworthy of comparison with the efforts of the late Poet Laureate.' *The Saturday Review* more justly reflects that Swinburne's version is truer to the spirit of the old story." Hyder reinforces such commentaries, insisting that "the skillful use of the nine-line stanza for narrative purposes could not fail to excite admiration." Comments by significant early ciritics support his contention. T. Earle Welby describes *Balen* as "the freshest, most human, most lucid, least straining long poem of Swinburne's last twenty years . . . full of its own youth and of the clean sharp air of his native Northumberland." The poem is, for Welby, one of Swinburne's "masterpieces on the great scale." Georges Lafourcade insists that *Balen* is a "subtle and powerful" poem. Even more forcefully, Samuel Chew asserts that it "is certainly the finest achievement of Swinburne's later life, an extraordinarily fresh evocation of the spirit of adventure, of chivalry, and of the wild northern country." Regarding Swinburne's "metrical feat," Chew observes, "the stanza is varied in tone and color to suit the sense, now light and dancing, now swift, trenchant and severe."[2]

However, the only recent critic to concur with these early evaluations is Jerome McGann, who argues that *Balen* "is graced with a

1. The best discussions of the poem appear in Chew, *Swinburne*, 179–84; McGann, *Swinburne*, 258–68; McSweeney, *Tennyson and Swinburne*, 191–97; and Staines, "Swinburne's Arthurian World," 64–70. None of these treatments of the poem, however, is adequate to deal with its complexity and its diverse virtues.

2. Hyder, *Swinburne's Literary Career and Fame*, 224–25; Welby, *A Study of Swinburne*, 152, 115; Lafourcade, *Swinburne*, 225; Chew, *Swinburne*, 183–84.

richness and artistic ease which only come when a poet's mind and craft have reached maturity" (McGann, 258).[3] Despite McGann's often incisive discussion of the poem and despite the visibly rapid growth of interest in Swinburne's works and their remarkable influence on his contemporaries as well as on subsequent generations of writers, however, no thorough and sympathetic analysis of *Balen* has yet appeared. Such an analysis not only helps to refute the gradually dissolving commonplace among Victorianists that Swinburne entered his dotage after 1879. It also demonstrates the extent to which the poet continued until the end of the century to be a major force in the extremely complex and persistent developments of Victorian medievalism.

In *The Tale of Balen,* Swinburne once again confronts and overturns the typically Victorian idealization of medieval times, particularly the "Golden Age" of Arthur. In his conception of history as essentially cyclical, this age, like any other, is characterized by the agonies of disappointed love, by travail and Empedoclean strife, by the futile battle against evil, by dissimulation of all kinds and, perhaps most significantly, by a hopeless tangle of moral uncertainties and ambiguities that always frustrate and eventually destroy the stalwart and ingenuous heart. As McGann carefully points out in his treatment of the *Tale,* the world of Camelot is thoroughly corrupt. Unlike its depiction in the early books of Tennyson's *Idylls of the King,* the image of Arthur's realm and the forces that control it in Swinburne's poem is a morally bleak one: "In the world ruled by Arthur nothing is innocent or even what it seems: all pleasures are delusive joys or entirely illusory, while all pain is cruelty and viciousness developed through forms of deception or cowardice or self-indulgence" (McGann, 260). Through his inversion of Victorian preconceptions about the medieval world, but also by means of other radically innovative procedures and techniques, Swinburne constructs a remarkable poem, one whose central thematic concerns are Love and Fate, as is the case with his other major works set in medieval times. But here Swinburne extends his previous uses of medieval sources and a medieval atmosphere by thoroughly Hellenizing his subject matter. Although much of the poem's

3. McSweeney's enthusiasm for *Balen* is, for example, minimal (*Tennyson and Swinburne,* 192).

starkly compressed narrative is taken up with intense descriptions of chivalric warfare, the events described are not fundamentally romantic. Balen's martial successes (like Oedipus' apparent accomplishments) only lead Balen closer to the malignant fate that Merlin continually reminds us is inevitable for him. Similarly, the love focused on here is always fraternal or filial (appropriate to the feudal context) rather than erotic, and Balen's dedication to his fellow man always turns out badly, if not tragically, for those he seeks to aid and for himself. As a result, the poem is fraught with dramatic ironies and with highly realistic moral ambiguities. Both depend, in large part, upon Swinburne's careful depiction of his hero as an ingenuous, exuberant, and stoical knight. Swinburne's "Balen the Wild" is not, like the antihero of Tennyson's idyll, an irrepressibly savage man. He is, instead, a vital and morally pure primitive. He is quintessential Romantic man, but his energies and admirable moral inclinations serve only tragic and therefore dolorously unromantic ends.

Essential to Swinburne's endeavor in *Balen* are its form, its prosody, and its image patterns, all of which prove to be obstacles to readers' enjoyment of the *Tale* but which themselves constitute crucial archaisms reinforcing the poem's medieval atmosphere as well as its tragic view of the human condition. In the Dedicatory Epistle to his collected *Poems,* Swinburne explains:

> The form . . . was chosen as a test of the truth of my conviction that such a work could be done better on the straitest and strictest principles of verse than on the looser and more slippery lines of mediaeval or modern improvisation. The impulsive and irregular verse which had been held sufficient for the stanza selected or accepted by Thornton and by Tennyson seemed capable of improvement and invigoration as a vehicle or a medium for poetic narrative. And I think it has not been found unfit to give something of the dignity as well as facility to a narrative which recasts in modern English verse one of the noblest and loveliest old English legends.[4]

Yet Swinburne himself at first had reservations about the poem's form and prosody, as he implies in a letter to Theodore Watts six months before *Balen's* publication. Visiting his ailing mother, Swinburne recounts that "I have just had a very pleasant interview with her and

---

4. Hyder (ed.), *Swinburne Replies,* 105.

read her part of the tale of Balen in Mallory [*sic*] and the first fytte of my poem, which she seems much pleased with—metre and all" (*Letters*, VI, 85).

Like Swinburne's mother, early readers of *The Tale of Balen* seemed to find its prosody no barrier to enjoyment, though modern critics seem daunted by the highly alliterative and densely rhymed nine-line stanzas. Philip Henderson observes that "the poem has been highly praised, but a metre resembling 'The Lady of Shalott' becomes almost unendurable when spun out to such a length."[5] The resemblance between Swinburne's iambic tetrameter stanzas and those of Tennyson's poem is immediately apparent to every reader and seems with the same immediacy to be appropriately "medieval." Although few readers pursue the reasons for this nearly subliminal perception, they are quite clear. The use of frequent repetition, of short lines, and of predominantly monosyllabic words results in the appearance of an almost balladic simplicity that, because of entrenched literary prejudices, we at once associate with the "primitive" past, *i.e.*, with medieval times. Yet for Swinburne, as for Tennyson, these deceptively unsophisticated stanzas that evoke a medieval atmosphere can be used to achieve complex, sometimes sublime effects. In *Balen* they do suggest a return to natural primitivism, which is reinforced by abundant nature imagery; they allow for the extremely compressed depiction of intense action (especially in battle scenes); and they enable the poet repeatedly to underscore his tragic world view by means of simple understatement and frequent ironies.

In his attempt to generate a medieval atmosphere, Swinburne employs nature imagery copiously. Like Tennyson's *Idylls*, *The Tale of Balen* is organized seasonally. Its seven sections begin with an evocative description of springtime, and its final "fytte" starts with a philosophical depiction of winter, which for "northern men" inspires "Music that bids the spirit sing / And day give thanks for night." Between the seasonal frames, the poem is dense with similes and metaphors from nature, reinforcing our identification of Balen as primitive man. Much like Tristram, he is a virtuous extension of nature, which is throughout the poem a benevolent force, though it has no control over any heroic individual's inevitably tragic fate.

5. Henderson, *Swinburne*, 273.

Stanza one of the first section typifies Swinburne's use of nature imagery and simple langauge to create an exuberant mood and to achieve transcendental thematic effects.

> In hawthorn-time the heart grows light,
> The world is sweet in sound and sight,
> Glad thoughts and birds take flower and flight,
> The heather kindles toward the light,
>   The whin is frankincense and flame.
> And be it for strife or be it for love
> The falcon quickens as the dove
> When earth is touched from heaven above
>   With joy that knows no name. (*Poems*, IV, 157)

Swinburne presents us here with the Empedoclean world of his poem governed by Mars and Venus, the falcon and the dove, strife and love. It is a world that is nonetheless innocent—indeed, intractably regenerate (perpetually quickened "When . . . touched from heaven"), at least as far as nature (and Balen) are concerned. In the next stanza we find that the "northern child" Balen

> glad in spirit and sad in soul
> With dream and doubt of days that roll
> As waves that race and find no goal
> Rode on by bush and brake and bole. (*Poems*, IV, 157)

The simple diction and imagery in this passage underscore Balen's oneness with the seminal benevolent and destructive forces of nature. He is a medieval brother, not only to Balan, but also to Swinburne's Chastelard, Meleager, Thalassius, and Tristram.

Throughout *Balen,* Swinburne uses these images to suggest a return to nature that Victorians such as Ruskin and Morris continually associated with medieval times.[6] He also employs images from nature to enhance the medieval atmosphere. Pre-Raphaelite effects periodically suspend the poem's intense action and provide tableaux, as in a Gothic tapestry. Our eyes are drawn from the activity of man to the significant stasis of nature, which reflects the benevolent generative forces always at work in the world:

6. For instance, the pun on the word *nature* in Ruskin's famous chapter "The Nature of Gothic" has to my knowledge not yet been mentioned by his critics.

And down a dim deep woodland way
They rode between the boughs asway
With flickering winds whose flash and play
Made sunlight sunnier where the day
    Laughed, leapt, and fluttered like a bird
Caught in a light loose leafy net
That earth for amorous heaven had set
To hold and see the sundawn yet
    And hear what morning heard. (*Poems,* IV, 201)

This is a striking example of a Pre-Raphaelite "special moment" in which, as Jeffrey Prince has observed, characters "often half mad with the acute deliquescence of their world . . . tend to dwell on isolated moments of intense sensation which lend meaning to their thwarted lives."[7]

Beyond the nature imagery that evokes a primitive atmosphere and the static qualities typical of medieval art, the versification in *Balen* enables Swinburne to compress action in balladic fashion. The most expert and prolific of Victorian ballad writers, Swinburne enunciates in his essay "The Poems of Dante Gabriel Rossetti" his central ideas about the ballad as a literary form:

> The highest form of ballad requires from a poet at once narrative power, lyrical, and dramatic; it must hold in fusion these three faculties at once, or fail of its mark: it must condense the large loose fluency of romantic tale-telling into tight and intense brevity; it must give as in summary the result and extract of events and emotions, without the exhibition of their gradual change and growth which a romance of the older type or the newer must lay open to us in order; it must be swifter to step and sharper of stroke than any other form of poetry. The writer of a first-rate tragic ballad must be yet more select in his matter and terse in his treatment of what he selects from the heap of possible incident, than Chaucer in the compilation of his "Knight's Tale" from the epic romance of Boccaccio, or Morris in the sculpture of his noble master-poem, "The Lovers of Gudrun," from the unhewn rock of a half-formed history or a half-grown legend. Ballads have been cut out of such poems as these, even as they were carven out of shapeless chronicles. There can be no pause in a ballad, and no excess; nothing that flags, nothing that overflows; there must be no waste of a word or a minute in the course of its rapid and fiery motion. (*Bonchurch,* IV, 27)

7. Jeffrey Prince, "D. G. Rossetti and the Pre-Raphaelite Conception of the Special Moment," *Modern Language Quarterly,* XXXVII (1976), 350.

Two passages in which Swinburne exploits the potential effects of balladic compression are especially instructive. For instance, when Balen and his brother successfully confront the forces of King Ryons, Arthur's Welsh foe, they

> smote their strong king down, ere yet
> His hurrying horde of spears might get
> Fierce vantage of them. Then the fight
> Grew great and joyous as it grew,
> For left and right those brethren slew,
> Till all the lawn waxed red with dew
> More deep than dews of night. (*Poems*, IV, 187)

The extreme telescoping of action here contributes to the medieval atmosphere by suggesting a historical distance that Swinburne confirms in the next stanza: "And ere the full fierce tale was read / Full forty lay before them dead." The tumultuous events just described have immediately become petrified as a tale.

Events and the hero's response to them are similarly compressed early in the fourth section of the poem when Balen confronts Launceor. He pursued Balen with Arthur's sanction after Balen had rashly beheaded his own enemy but Arthur's friend, the Lady of the Lake, and fled Camelot (fytte three).

> Balen's spear through Launceor's shield
> Clove as a ploughshare cleaves the field
> And pierced the hauberk triple-steeled,
> That horse with horseman stricken reeled,
> And as a storm-breached rock falls, fell,
> And Balen turned his horse again
> And wist not yet his foe lay slain,
> And saw him dead that sought his bane
> And wrought and fared not well. (*Poems*, IV, 177)

Here, besides achieving remarkable compression and explosive energy, we find Swinburne making careful use of his stanza's ninth, trimeter line to force upon us, through the kind of ironic understatement typical of Malory and Chaucer, an awareness of *Balen*'s pervasively tragic world view. Immediately afterwards, musing "in many-minded mood / If life or death were evil or good," Balen watches helplessly as Launceor's distraught "maiden flower-like white" appears suddenly from the woods and kills herself—she "struck one swift and bitter stroke / That healed her, and she died." Such unanticipated tragedies punctuate the *Tale* and reinforce its fatalism. Swinburne in fact throughout the poem associates his medieval subject and the work's medievalist form and atmosphere with specifically Greek conceptions of the tragic human condition, a procedure that is neither illogical nor unprecedented.

Associations of the medieval with the Hellenic and specifically with Homer, though lost to most of Swinburne's contemporaries, have their roots in the eighteenth century. Alice Chandler cites such an association in the works of both Richard Hurd (who published *Letters on Chivalry and Romance* in 1760) and Thomas Warton: "Hurd wrote in a passage that seems to mark the ending of an exclusively neoclassic ideal that Homer would have preferred the Middle Ages to his own times '*for the improved gallantry of the feudal times and the superior solemnity of their superstitions.*' This idea was echoed in *The History of English Poetry* (1774–81) by Thomas Warton who claimed that medieval manners had 'the same common merit with the pictures in Homer, that of being founded in truth and reality.'" That Arthurian and Trojan themes are two of the central sources of subject matter for medieval romanceurs reveals how natural the connection between them is, but it was one seldom made during the nineteenth century. However, Swinburne, conscious in his usual scholarly fashion of his place in literary tradition, revives the historical association between Greek and Arthurian mythology. Discussing *The Tale of Balen* in the Dedicatory Epistle to his collected *Poems*, Swinburne observes:

> The age when these [Arthurian] romances actually lived side by side with the reviving legends of Thebes and Troy, not in the crude and bloodless forms of Celtic and archaic fancy but in the ampler and manlier developments of Teutonic and medieval imagination, was the age of Dante and Chaucer. . . .
>
> There is no episode in the cycle of Arthurian romance more genuinely Homeric in its sublime simplicity of submission to the masterdom of fate than that which I have rather reproduced than recast in "The Tale of Balen": and impossible as it is to render the text or express the spirit of the Iliad in prose or rhyme—above all, in English blank verse—it is possible in such a metre as was chosen and refashioned for this poem, to give some sense of the rage and rapture of battle for which Homer himself could only find fit and full expression by similitudes drawn like mine from . . . the sea.

The identification of the Hellenic and the medieval depends, of course, on the intense fatalism Swinburne perceives at the heart of both cultures' mythologies. Significantly, it is a perception that only a few of his contemporaries, including Hardy and Arnold, would have shared, but it is one with which Georges Lafourcade concurs. He explains that in *Balen,* Swinburne has "returned to the more sober style and monotonous metre of his early poems; with unfailing instinct he has recaptured the essential features of the medieval theme—the sense of unjust oppressive doom heroically endured." Appropriately, Lafourcade concludes his discussion of the poem with a deft observation: "*Balen* is to *Tristram* what *Erechtheus* is to *Atalanta.*"[8] Swinburne would certainly have approved this juxtaposition of medieval narrative and Greek tragedy.

The tragic implications of Balen's life and the fatalistic world view that this poem propounds are monitored throughout the *Tale* by the narrator as well as by Merlin, who functions virtually as a symbol of Fate. The narrator, too, continually reminds us that his hero's "hap was evil as his heart was good." In the course of the poem's events Balen is motivated principally by filial and feudal ties—by his remarkable, entirely democratic loyalty to all men and women who are not clearly enemies and by his unshakable loyalty to Arthur, who in Swinburne's poem lacks both wisdom and vision. Like nearly all of *Balen*'s characters including the hero himself, Arthur repeatedly acts in rash, uninformed ways. Surrounding every event in the tale, moreover, is an atmosphere of moral ambiguity that, as in all tragedies, lends force to the poem's fatalism.

The omnipresence of "doom" is articulated in the first stanzas of each section of the poem, and it is always described with metaphors from nature. These descriptions help to define the poem's symmetrical structure and emphasize its fundamental concern with mutability and with the inseparability of all contraries in the cycles of nature, history, and every man's life—generation and destruction, triumph and defeat, joy and grief. In the poem's third stanza we are introduced to a constitutionally ebullient Balen, whose "blood and breath / Sang out within him" and for whom "time and death / Were even as words

8. Chandler, *A Dream of Order,* 17; Hyder (ed.), *Swinburne Replies,* 100–106; Lafourcade, *Swinburne,* 225.

a dreamer saith." Balen is a monist, a pantheist, and a stoic, as are all Swinburne's unequivocal heroes. For him

> light and life and spring were one.
> The steed between his knees that sprang,
> The moors and woods that shone and sang,
> The hours where through the spring's breath rang,
> Seemed ageless as the sun.

But we learn immediately that despite his exultant, Wordsworthian communion with the objects and spirit of nature,

> His soul forfelt a shadow of doom,
> His heart foreknew a gloomier gloom
> > Than closes all men's equal ways. (*Poems,* IV, 157–58)

At every turn in the poem we are reminded of that "shadow of doom," sometimes with a heavy-handedness that becomes oppressive. The narrator serves, in one role, as a fatalistic choral voice, as does Merlin throughout the poem. At the beginning of section seven, parallel to the opening of every other section, the entirely sympathetic narrator repeats that

> Aloud and dark as hell or hate
> Round Balen's head the wind of fate
> Blew storm and cloud from death's wide gate:
> But joy as grief in him was great
> > To face God's doom and live or die,
> Sorrowing for ill wrought unaware,
> Rejoicing in desire to dare
> All ill that innocence might bear
> > With changeless heart and eye. (*Poems,* IV, 214)

Despite alarming prophecies and events that confirm them, Balen maintains an irrepressible spirit. His autonomy, stoicism, and tenacity are subtly but ingeniously defined in this passage by Swinburne's pun on *bear.* Balen simultaneously endures evil, unwittingly conveys it to others, and exposes it in the Arthurian world.

One evil that Balen quite literally bears throughout the poem is the sword Malison, which he wins from the distressed maiden captive to it in the first fytte. As the central symbol of fate, it is the vehicle for all Balen's unwitting "evil" deeds, which include his killing the Lady of the Lake, Launceor, Garlon, and his own brother Balan. Each sword stroke for Balen is increasingly dolorous. But two additional and subordinate emblems of fate's malignancy also appear, each presiding over approximately half the poem. The first is Arthur; the second, Balen's foe Garlon.

Arthur is himself a victim of inscrutable forces but also the indirect cause of Balen's fate, insofar as Balen is continually trying either to placate or to please his monarch. Digressing from the legend as it appears in Malory, Swinburne periodically in the first half of his narrative allows the forbidding shadow of Arthur's incestuous relationship with Morgause and its fatal consequence (Mordred) to interrupt and dominate his hero's own experiences. Morgause appears first at Camelot, just before Balen releases the maiden from Malison's spell, and then at the funeral of her husband, King Lot, who unsuccessfully attempts to rescue King Ryons, his brother whom Balen has captured. During both of Morgause's appearances Swinburne makes ironic use of eye imagery to remind us of fate's inevitability and to suggest the ominous interaction throughout the Arthurian saga between Arthur's blind rashness and Merlin's futile vision.

At Camelot in the poem's second fytte, Morgause is described, significantly, sitting between two other ill-fated Arthurian beauties, Iseult and Guenevere, but Morgause is "darklier doomed than they whose cheer / Foreshadowed not yet the deadlier year / That bids the queenliest head bow down" (*Poems*, IV, 163). As Morgause views vain attempts by various knights to liberate the maiden from the power of Malison, her "eyes / That dwelt on days afar," alternating "bright and dark, . . . / Shone strange as fate" (*Poems*, IV, 166). Shortly, in a striking instance of foreshadowing after Lamoracke fails to draw the mysterious sword, Morgause's eyes meet Arthur's,

> And one in blood and one in sin
> Their hearts caught fire of pain within
> And knew no goal for them to sin
>   But death that guerdons guilt. (*Poems*, IV, 164)

The inevitability of continued suffering and corruption, of ruined dreams, and of evil's ultimate dominion in the world is affirmed once more with eye imagery at the end of the poem's fifth section when Morgause mourns Lot's death:

> The splendour of her sovereign eyes
> Flashed darkness deeper than the skies

> Feel or fear when the sunset dies
> On his that felt as midnight rise
>   Their doom upon them, there undone
> By faith in fear ere thought could yield
> A shadowy sense of days revealed,
> The ravin of the final field,
>   The terror of their son.
>
> For Arthur's, as they caught the light
> That sought and durst not seek his sight,
> Darkened, and all his spirit's might
> Withered within him even as night
>   Withers when sunrise thrills the sea.
> But Mordred's lightened as with fire
> That smote his mother and his sire
> With darkling doom and deep desire
>   That bade its darkness be. (*Poems*, IV, 195)

Deftly, Swinburne here reveals that Arthur and the ideals he represents are not sovereign in the world of Camelot. In league with Mordred, Morgause presides over events while her ruthlessly destructive son by Arthur is a functionary of "darkling doom." Thus, both occasions on which the larger Arthurian myth is introduced during the first half of *Balen* serve to reinforce the poem's tragedy and to enhance the significance of Balen's traditionally subordinate tale and our response to it.

Through much of the second half of the narrative, Garlon, King Pellam's brother who is repeatedly described as "the invisible evil," symbolizes Fate, just as Arthur is an emblem of its power in the world during the first half. Early in the sixth section (the poem's last two fyttes are half the work), Balen encounters the first of Garlon's victims that we hear of, an anonymous wayfaring knight accompanied by a maiden. At Arthur's request, Balen pursues him. In his usual fraternal manner Balen, knowing nothing at all of the knight's background, spontaneously agrees to be his protector: "I / Will be your warrant or will die" (*Poems*, IV, 200). Then at Arthur's very doorstep a symbolic challenge to the establishment of any dreams of order or the survival of goodness in the world unexpectedly occurs:

> Suddenly fell the strange knight, slain
> By one that came and went again
>   And none might see him; but his spear
> Clove through the body, swift as fire. (*Poems*, IV, 200)

This victim of Garlon is significantly like Balen in being "one that death held dear," a "man whose doom" is "forefelt as dire." But he is unlike Balen because his premonitions "Had darkened all his life's desire." Balen never fears Garlon while pursuing him after this event, nor ultimately does he fear death itself. In the *Tale's* last scene, unknowingly about to fight his own brother, Balen demonstrates the stoic resignation that is, throughout the narrative, the counterpart of his indefatigable zest for life. He says,

> "Be it life or death, my change I take,
> Be it life's to build or death's to break:
> And fall what may, me lists not make
> Moan for sad life's or death's sad sake."
>   Then looked he on his armour, glad
> And high of heart, and found it strong. (*Poems*, IV, 224–25)

It is finally this irrepressible gusto and Balen's impulsive determination to combat all apparent evils that result in his own and Balan's destruction. But all this is predetermined, as Merlin continually reminds us and as the symbol of Garlon suggests.

Balen and the maiden encounter the third victim of "the invisible evil" in section six when they come upon the grief-stricken father of a boy seriously wounded by Garlon. The father's description of Garlon makes clear the extent to which he symbolizes all men's doom. Almost an allegorical figure, Garlon resembles Death in Chaucer's "Pardoner's Tale":

> "Invisible as the spirit of night
> That heaven and earth in depth and height
> May see not by the mild moon's light
> Nor even when the star would grant them sight,
>   He walks and slays as plague's blind breath
> Slays." (*Poems*, IV, 206)

The Chaucerian atmosphere is blatant in this passage, with its allusions to astrology and the plague. But unlike Chaucer's Death, which is the traditional wages of sin, death in *Balen* overshadows the lives of all heroic men. It threatens to and always does undermine good works and ideals. Moreover, premonitions of its inevitability darken "all [the] life's desire" of those singled out as special targets of Fate. By means of these emblematic victims whose tragedies are grand and poignant, Fate's power is revealed to the world. Balen and Arthur are, of course, two such victims, and Merlin is the monitory spokesman against Fate in the case of each hero. But, as in all tragedies, Merlin's prophetic wisdom ironically brings on "all the latter woe" (*Poems*, IV, 197) rather than retarding it. Early in section six of the *Tale* we learn that, just before the first appearance of Garlon, Merlin had "shown the king / The doom that songs unborn should sing." As a result, "on the king for fear's sake fell / Sickness, and sorrow deep as hell." Like the role of the seer in many Greek tragedies, the role of Merlin as an unwilling functionary of Fate in *The Tale of Balen* intensifies the poem's ironies and our emotional responses to them.

Throughout the poem Merlin serves as a self-appointed liaison between Arthur and Balen. Formally, he mediates between the *Tale's* Arthurian materials and those concerned exclusively with Balen. He thus becomes an extension of the narrator but, like the chorus in a Greek tragedy, remains indirectly involved in events and emotionally engaged with them. Thus, after explaining to Arthur why the king was wrong to banish Balen for slaying the Lady of the Lake, and after recounting the conspiracy between Lady Lyle and the maiden who bore Malison to Camelot, he can lament,

> "grief it is to think how he
> That won it, being of heart so free
> And perfect found in chivalry,
> Shall by that sword be slain." (*Poems*, IV, 173)

Similarly, after Launceor's death at Balen's hands and the suicide of Launceor's beloved, Merlin addresses Balen despairingly:

> "My heart is wrung for this deed's sake,
> To know thee therefore doomed to take
> Upon thine hand a curse, and make
> Three kingdoms pine through twelve years' change,
> In want and woe: for thou shalt smite
> The man most noble and truest knight
> That looks upon the live world's light
> A dolorous stroke and strange." (*Poems*, IV, 184)

The whole world of *Balen* is indeed dolorous and strange not only because of the catastrophic fate its heroes suffer but also because the morality of actions taken by them is persistently indeterminate. Although Balen's filial values and heroic virtues never become suspect in the course of the poem, his impetuous behavior does. Like the greatest heroes in Homer and in Greek tragedy, Balen suffers from both *hamartia* and *hubris*. The poem's first fytte recounts Balen's origins and his first rash actions that tarnished the honor his knightly deeds had brought to "the strange north strand / That sent him south so goodly a knight" (*Poems*, IV, 159). Insulted by one of Arthur's kinsmen, Balen "Swift from his place leapt" and "wrote / His wrath in blood upon the bloat / Brute cheek" of the "king-born knave" (*Poems*, IV, 160). In this encounter Balen is defending Northumberland as well as his own pride, but the morality of his actions and the justification for them remain equivocal. For his rash violence in killing the slanderous knight, Balen is imprisoned by Arthur for six months, and the present action of the poem begins in its second fytte with the arrival of the maiden captive to Malison's spell. She appears just as Balen's own captivity ends.

In almost all Balen's subsequent deeds the morality of his behavior is similarly indeterminate, because in the world of Camelot as realistically depicted by Swinburne, moral certainties are impossible, and even the most apparently virtuous actions affect Balen and his world in unanticipated, adverse ways. As Balen himself realizes at his death, "here / Light is as darkness, hope as fear / And love as hate" (*Poems*, IV, 230). Ultimately, the reader is led to sympathize with every character in the *Tale* who is not totally flat. No matter how ostensibly "evil," each is, like Balen and like Arthur, a victim of Fate in a perversely amoral world. Such is the case with King Lot and King Pellam, each of whom in his assault upon Balen (or Arthur) acts from filial motives. As a result, we do not know, for instance, how to construe Balen's sudden murder of the Lady of the Lake in fytte two, even though the narrator informs us that by "her fell craft his mother died." Our first response to Balen's impetuous deed is like Arthur's:

> "Alas for shame," the high king said,
> "That one found once my friend lies dead;
> Alas for all our shame!" (*Poems*, IV, 169)

The implication of Arthur's last words here is, significantly, that any of us might have done precisely as Balen did, but our actions, like his, would have been misguided. Despite all monitions, impulse tragically governs all men's behavior, as it has done in Arthur's relations with Morgause and as it does Balen's throughout his *Tale.*

Balen's character itself therefore often seems only equivocally virtuous. His usually admirable ebullience and vitality appear as mere unwarranted capriciousness when he refuses to return Malison to the maiden who bore it to Camelot. Despite her clear warning that

> "with it thou shalt surely slay
> Of all that look upon the day
> The man best loved of thee, and lay
> Thine own life down for his,"

Balen perversely responds, "God's will . . . it is, we know, / Wherewith our lives are bound" (*Poems*, IV, 166). What in other circumstances we would describe as tenacity, here seems to be simple stubbornness. Later in the poem, commenting on the martial valor of Balen and his brother during the battle between Arthur's forces and those of King Lot, the narrator reinforces the moral uncertainties that pervade the *Tale* when he observes that

> Strong wonder smote the souls of men
> If heaven's own host or hell's deep den
> Had sent them forth to slay. (*Poems*, IV, 191)

But as in Blake's *Marriage of Heaven and Hell*, facile moral tags are in this poem mere stultifying fictions. In Swinburne's pessimistic adaptation of Blake's optimistic epistemology, such terms as *heaven* and *hell* are inadequate to the tragic conception of human experience projected by this poem.

Throughout *The Tale of Balen* moral ambiguity alternates with transparent irony in conveying Swinburne's world view. No matter how virtuous Balen's motives initially appear, his actions inevitably generate suffering, if not calamity. His keeping Malison, of course, provides the vehicle for the poem's framing tragedy, but many subordinate tragedies intervene. His killing of Launceor in self-defense results in the suicide of that knight's beloved. His capture of King Ryons and Lot's attempt to rescue his brother end with Lot's death and the slaughter of "many a mother's son" (*Poems*, IV, 194). Balen's killing of Garlon, as prophesied, "Brought sorrow down for many a year / On many a man in many a land" (*Poems*, IV, 211). After Pellam's death and the de-

149

struction of his castle, Balen travels aimlessly, seeing that "on either hand" in

> Bright fields and cities built to stand
> Till time should break them, dead men lay;
> And loud and long from all their folk
> Living, one cry that cursed him broke;
> Three countries had his dolorous stroke
> Slain, or should surely slay. (*Poems*, IV, 213)

And, in his penultimate adventure, Balen is responsible for three other deaths. Bringing the knight Garnysshe to a garden in which his adulterous beloved lies with another, Balen watches Garnysshe impetuously behead the false lovers. When Garnysshe repents, he rebukes Balen: "ere this my life was glad. / Thou hast done this deed." He explains: "I had lived my sorrow down, hadst thou / Not shown me what I saw but now" (*Poems*, IV, 219). Balen's well-intentioned strategy has failed, but he enunciates it nonetheless:

> "God knows,
> I did, to set a bondman free,
> But as I would thou hadst done by me,
> That seeing what love must die to see
> Love's end might well be woe's." (*Poems*, IV, 220)

With the suicide of Garnysshe, Balen himself is ready for death. Soon hearing merrymakers in the neighborhood blowing a horn, he says, "That blast is blown for me . . . / The prize am I who am yet not dead" (*Poems*, IV, 221).

Balen, of course, dies, ironically, at the hands (and virtually in the arms) of his brother, an appropriate culmination to a moving legend. Swinburne surely chose this subject for his last major Arthurian work because of its tragic poignancy and because it allowed him to extend and complete his poetic discussion of Love. In previous works his focus had been primarily on the tragedy of erotic love and the comedy of pantheistic spiritual passion that serves throughout Swinburne's poems as a consolatory counterpoint to *eros*.[9] Also, in works such as

---

9. Among the optimistic poems that dwell on joyous intercourse with nature, see, for example, "Thalassius," "On the Cliffs," "A Nympholept," "The Lake of Gaube," and "The Garden of Cymodoce."

Atalanta in Calydon, "Phaedra," and his novels he had dealt with perverse examples of filial love. However, in *The Tale of Balen,* Swinburne
is able to represent in tragic fashion the whole spectrum of filial and
fraternal love relationships. The medieval setting of *Balen* is especially
appropriate because the poet can make use of nineteenth-century
idealizations of medieval society as pervasively altruistic and harmonious. Such portrayals appear from Scott through Carlyle, Ruskin,
Arnold, Marx, and Morris. Alice Chandler correctly observes that
"feudalism was seen as fatherhood, and the medieval world—to adopt
Carlyle's phrase—was thought to be 'godlike and my Father's.'"[10] The
extended implication here is that all God's children are bound by un-
breakable filial ties. Such is unequivocally the case in Swinburne's
poem (though populated by several feudal families hostile to one another), and he fully exploits the tragic ironies that arise because of
these ties. The work is, significantly, dedicated to his mother and recounts events in the lives of at least three pairs of actual brothers.

In his dedication Swinburne alerts us to the emphasis upon filial
"Love that holds life and death in fee, / Deep as the clear unsounded
sea" (*Poems,* IV, 155), and in the *Tale* itself we are repeatedly reminded
that familial ties, like erotic ones, are sublime but inevitably tragic.
Apart from continual narrative reminders that Balen and Balan are
doomed, we are given the examples of King Lot's devotion to his
brother, Ryons, and of Pellam's fatal dedication—"For love of this my
brother slain" (*Poems,* IV, 210)—to avenging Garlon's death. Such
blood ties between brothers exemplify but are ultimately subsumed
under larger secular, religious, and aesthetic systems of reciprocal filial allegiance appropriate to the feudal context. In the poem, brothers
who vainly sacrifice themselves for one another become types, re-
spectively, of Arthur, the worldly king whose filial dedication to humanity is doomed; of Christ, the spiritual king whose symbols are
preserved in Pellam's castle and whose self-sacrifice for mankind
(from the evidence of the radically fallen world of this poem) was
equally futile; and of the poet whose attempt in verse at least to memorialize tragedies of human allegiance is fated to enjoy at best only
cyclical and therefore limited success. The poem "needs must live a
springtide space, / While April suns grow strong" (*Poems,* IV, 155).

10. Chandler, *A Dream of Order,* 1.

These larger exemplars of sublime devotion to the human community serve as a chronological frame and thematic groundwork for the more extended particular treatments of doomed brotherly love in the poem.

Among the framing filial relationships the most significant and the one treated in the greatest detail is Balen's with Arthur. In a passage from the poem's sixth fytte, immediately after Arthur defeats Lot's forces, Swinburne's proverbial hero worship appears in service to the poem's essential theme. Balen alights from his horse before the king

> In reverence made for love's sake bright
> With joy that set his face alight
>   As theirs who see, alive, above,
> The sovereign of their souls, whose name
> To them is even as love's own flame
> To enkindle hope that heeds not fame
>   And knows no lord but love. (*Poems,* IV, 198)

Arthur's paternalism inspires in Balen transcendent emotions that generate selfless behavior.

The same is also true of all relationships in the poem that are characterized by brotherly love. Selfless generosity and devotion, even to others who have no familial claims, appear repeatedly. For instance, just after the deaths of Launceor and his beloved, King Mark appears, "whose name the sweet south-west / Held high in honour" (*Poems,* IV, 181). Resembling the poet dedicated to memoralizing tragic lovers in *Tristram of Lyonesse* and in this poem, Mark "made moan to hear their doom," and

>   for their sorrow's sake he sware
> To seek in all the marches there
> The church that man might find most fair
>   And build therein their tomb. (*Poems,* IV, 182)

Like those who survive the victims of fraternal or erotic love in this poem (at least those not immediately bent on revenge), Mark is sorrowful but resigned to events, rather than rancorous toward Balen, who is directly responsible for the lovers' deaths. Acceptance like Mark's reflects the fatalistic world view held by almost all the characters in the poem.

An episode in the sixth fytte also reveals the extent to which spontaneous love of one's fellows (along with its contrary, strife between feudal camps) governs the world of *Balen*. Accompanied by his maiden,

Balen discovers a castle occupied by a "lady stricken" who, to be healed, requires a bowl of blood from "a maiden clean and whole / In virgin body and virgin soul / Whose name was writ on Royal roll." Spontaneously, the maiden insists upon making whatever sacrifice is necessary: "'Good knight of mine, good will have I / To help this healing though I die.'" Predictably, Balen adds, "'Nay . . . but love may try / What help in living love may lie'" (*Poems*, IV, 203–205). Although this attempt fails, the lady *is* later saved by sisterly self-sacrifice. "Another maid in later Mays / Won with her life" the "woful praise" of healing her.

The numerous instances of self-sacrificial devotion to one's fellows that are recounted in *The Tale of Balen* serve primarily to enhance the tragic example of Balen himself, who is the model of brotherly love (except, of course, in his behavior to those who directly threaten him, his family, and his king). As in the case of the "lady stricken," Balen at every turn devotes himself spontaneously to the welfare of others. He does so with the first of Garlon's victims and the father of the third, whose son Garlon has unexpectedly assaulted and wounded, "even ere love might fear / That hate were strong as death" (*Poems*, IV, 206). Balen commiserates, explaining that Garlon has already killed "'two knights of mine, / Two comrades, sealed by faith's bright sign'" (*Poems*, IV, 206). When Balen soon finds and impetuously kills Garlon, however, the repercussions are catastrophic, just as they are almost every time Balen tries to serve his king, protect the reputation of his homeland, or assist a fellow knight. As I have observed, such is the case with Garnysshe, whom Balen strives to aid immediately after he has killed Garlon along with his brother, Pellam, and realized the dreadful truth of Merlin's prophecies concerning the dolorous stroke. Balen is renewed at first by his encounter with Garnysshe—his "face as dawn's grew bright, / For hope to help a happier man" (*Poems*, IV, 218). But Garnysshe falls on his own sword after killing his faithless beloved and the knight beside her.

The culmination of all Balen's frustrated, misguided, and doomed exercises in fraternal devotion is, of course, his fatal encounter with his real brother, an encounter steeped in dramatic irony. Balen does battle with the "good knight" guarding the island simply because of external circumstances and pressures, not because of any significant internal motivation. The extent to which the *Tale's* final calamity is inevitable and compulsory becomes clear when the merrymakers instruct Balen that "all for whom these halls make cheer" must fight the knight on the island who "guards . . . / Against all swords that chance brings near." Tragically disheartened by the dolorous results of all his previous experiences, Balen proceeds to the island, even though he decries the "evil custom" that allows "none whom chance hath led / Hither, if knighthood crown his head, / To pass unstirred to strife" (*Poems*, IV, 222). Apparently Balen, like the reader, by now sees the "evil custom" as a symbol of the whole tragic and fatal enterprise of life itself. He is therefore resigned to the inevitability of his participation.

The tragedy of the heroic brothers' combat at the end of the *Tale* is fully prepared for early on. In fact, all Balen's fraternal overtures, his doomed attempts to assist fellow knights, reflect Balen's determination to extend to the rest of the world his sublime relationship with Balan, which is detailed early in the narrative. The extraordinary sense of identity between the brothers encompasses more than their names. Balan is first described as the

> Twin flower of bright Northumberland,
> Twin sea-bird of their loud sea-strand,
> Twin song-bird of their morn. (*Poems*, IV, 179)

The narrator celebrates "The likeness graven of face and face" when the two "kissed and wept upon each other / For joy and pity . . . / And love engraffed by sire and mother" (*Poems*, IV, 180). The striking term *engraffed* suggests the extent to which Balen and Balen are virtually twin parts of a single organism. Alone each is, by implication, deficient and the world disharmonious. Balen's exuberance and nostalgia at their reunion is, thus, in every sense natural:

> the might of joy in love
> Brake forth within him as a fire,
> And deep delight in deep desire
> Of far-flown days whose full-souled quire
> Rang round from the air above. (*Poems*, IV, 179)

After the two knights part, it is understandable that Balen tries repeatedly but without success to complete and fulfill himself in relationships based upon the fraternal pattern that must be the basis of all wholesome social intercourse and of any potentially ideal human community in the world of this poem. Unique to Swinburne's version of the legend, this fact geometrically amplifies the ironic significance of Balen's final battle.

As in all great tragedies, fate in *Balen* operates as a force that is both internal and external, impelling and compelling. No external threats alone—including the Lady of the Lake, King Ryons' soldiers, Garlon, Pellam, or even the atmosphere of Christian sanctification that protects Pellam—can destroy Balen. This monarch among knights, heroic in his strength, his filial virtues, his tenacity, endurance, and stoicism, can succumb only to his own best powers symbolized by his brother, Balan. At the same time, however, in his last fight Balen finally liberates himself from an irretrievably corrupt and grievous world, one for which his heart is too high, his spirit too pure. Swinburne describes the last moments of the brothers' battle in appropriately ironic terms. By the end of it, "With blood that either spilt and bled / Was all the ground they fought on red." Each knight "unmailed and marked" from the fight "poured and drank the draught of death, / Till fate was full at last" (*Poems*, IV, 227) in a parody communion, a metaphorical celebration of the supreme tragedy of fraternal love. At the end they make "a mutual moan" that defines their tragedy:

> "Both we came out of one tomb,
> One star-crossed mother's woful womb,
> And so within one grave pit's gloom
> Untimely shall we lie." (*Poems*, IV, 230)

Thus, "the last blind battle broke / The consummated spell" that has surrounded the lives of these brothers. But using the mode of correspondences, in the way Swinburne has by now taught us to read his narrative, we realize that more is revealed here than the tragedy of two heroic medieval knights. Balen's career, based on thwarted filial and fraternal ideals, is by extension the tragedy of mankind whose pitiable fate it is to strive for fulfillment through filial, erotic, and fraternal love, but, in doing so, to generate only strife and be freed from frustration and suffering only in death.

Epilogue

In 1868, Walter Pater published a review of William Morris's first three volumes of poetry. Five years later a revised version of his essay became the famous "Conclusion" to *The Renaissance*. In its original version the review focuses not only on Morris' poems but also on a constellation of literary, historical, and philosophical issues as relevant to any serious discussion of Swinburne's medievalist poetry as to analyses of Morris' *Defence of Guenevere* volume, *The Life and Death of Jason,* and *The Earthly Paradise.*[1] Pater sees Morris as a model of significant new developments in contemporary literary practice; these encourage Pater finally to propound the aestheticist values that conclude his review essay and *The Renaissance*. His initial concern here is the emergence in his own day of "a higher degree of passion in literature," which is one crucial aspect of "the sudden pre-occupation with things mediaeval." He is especialy intrigued by the mystic "mood of the cloister" first displayed by Dante and Saint Louis, who formulate a "stricter, imaginative mediaevalism which recreates the mind of the middle age." In Pater's own era the mood has become a "profounder

---

1. All quotations from Pater's essay are cited from James Sambrook's edition of it in *Pre-Raphaelitism: A Collection of Critical Essays* (Chicago, 1974), 105–17. Sambrook reprints the original text from *Westminister Review,* n.s., xxxiv (1868), 300–312, rather than the abridged version that appeared in Pater's *Appreciations* (1889). Page numbers will appear in parentheses after quotations.

mediaevalism," in which "religion shades into sensuous love and sensuous love into religion" (104–105).

Like Swinburne in his early medievalist poems and essays, as well as in the medievalist works of 1866, Pater returns to twelfth-century France to discuss the topoi, the atmosphere, and the effects of the new "medievalist" love poetry.

> As before in the cloister, so now in the [medieval] chateau . . . earthly love enters, and becomes a prolonged somnambulism. Of religion it learns the art of directing towards an imaginary object sentiments whose natural direction is toward objects of sense. Hence a love defined by the absence of the beloved, choosing to be without hope, protesting against all lower uses of love, barren, extravagant, antinomian. It is the love which is incompatible with marriage, for the chevalier who never comes, of the serf for the chatelaine, the rose for the nightingale, of Rudel for the lady of Tripoli. Another element of extravagance came in with the feudal spirit: Provençal love is full of the very forms of vassalage. To be the servant of love, to have offended, to taste the subtle luxury of chastisement, of reconciliation—the religious spirit, too, knows that, and meets just there . . . the delicacies of earthly love. Here, under this strange complex of conditions, as in some medicated air, exotic flowers of sentiment expand, among people of a remote and unaccustomed beauty, somnambulistic, frail, androgynous, the light almost shining through them. (106–107)

Derivative in diction, tone, and effect from Swinburne's 1862 review of Baudelaire, this passage could well serve to describe in catalog form, the frequent situations, moods, and concerns of *Queen Yseult, Rosamond, Chastelard,* "Laus Veneris," "The Leper," "St. Dorothy," and *Tristram of Lyonesse,* as well as many of Swinburne's non-medievalist love poems, such as *Atalanta in Calydon,* "The Triumph of Time," "Anactoria," and "Hermaphroditus." Pater even extends his discussion to include remarks on the solipsistic relationship between man and the world of external nature, an issue of special importance, as we have seen, in Swinburne's later medievalist (and non-medievalist) poetry.[2] In these works nature appears to be governed by the same fatal but ultimately beneficent laws and to be compelled by the same

2. Preparing to review *The Renaissance* for the *Fortnightly Review,* which he edited, John Morley apparently wrote to ask Swinburne his opinion of Pater's work. On April 11, Swinburne responded: "I admire and enjoy Pater's work so heartily that I am somewhat shy of saying how much, ever since on my

inescapable passions that dominate men and women. Pater remarks upon the "wild, convulsed sensuousness in the poetry of the middle age . . . in which the things of nature begin to play a delirious part. Of the things of nature the mediaeval mind had a deep sense; but its sense of them was not objective, no real escape to the world without one. The aspects and motions of nature only reinforced its prevailing mood, and were in conspiracy with one's own brain. . . . A single sentiment invaded the world; everything was infused with a motive drawn from the soul" (108).

Such observations suggest not only the solipsism but also, by their tone, the fatalism of the medieval world view as Pater understood it, and, of course, as Swinburne interpreted it repeatedly in his poetry, but with special emphasis in *Tristram* and *The Tale of Balen*. As Pater insists later in his essay, "the bloom of the world . . . gives new seduction" to an emphasis on mutability: "the sense of death and the desire of beauty; the desire of beauty quickened by the sense of death" (113).

Thus, the general characteristics of Pre-Raphaelite medievalist love poetry, which Pater announces in his deliberately expansive and philosophical review of Morris, also consistently apply to Swinburne's—and much of Rossetti's—medievalist poetry. Despite the frequent similarities in subject matter, mood, tone, and technique, however, Swinburne must finally be seen as more coherently, systematically, and overtly philosophical in his medievalist poems than is either Morris or Rossetti. Morris' emphasis in his early medievalist poems is often brutally realistic; in his later medievalist works it is, equally often, self-consciously escapist. Rossetti's use of medieval settings and topoi is, throughout his career, largely ornamental and tangential to the communication of philosophical ideas. The fundamental purpose of Swinburne's "medievalizing"—to communicate a coherent and firmly held vision of the world, a system of historical, social, moral, and spiritual values—more closely resembles the purpose of his non-Pre-Raphaelite medievalizing contemporaries. But the vision and val-

---

telling him once at Oxford how highly Rossetti (D.G.) as well as myself estimated his first papers in the *Fortnightly,* he replied to the effect that he considered them as owing their inspiration entirely to my own work in the same line" (*Letters,* II, 240–41).

ues embodied in medievalist works by Tennyson, Arnold, Carlyle, Ruskin, and writers of the Oxford movement, for instance, are entirely antithetical to Swinburne's in their essential conservatism. The unyielding and radical Romantic libertarianism (and humanitarianism) of Swinburne's medievalist poems is one characteristic that distinguishes his works.

An equally pervasive and equally distinctive characteristic is what Pater calls the "desire of beauty." The wisest men, according to Pater's concluding words, spend their lives "in art and song," generating "high passions" that evoke a "quickened sense of life, ecstacy and sorrow of love, political or religious enthusiasm, or the 'enthusiasm of humanity'" (116). Such passions characterize the origins and effects, the substance and the style of Swinburne's medievalist poems, the function of whose historical settings and topoi are also helpfully explained by Pater:

> The composite experience of all the ages is part of each one of us; to deduct from that experience, to obliterate any part of it, to come face to face with the people of a past age . . . is as impossible as to become a little child, or enter again into the womb and be born. But though it is not possible to repress a single phase of that humanity, which, because we live and move and have our being in the life of humanity, makes us what we are; it is possible to isolate such a phase, to throw it into relief. . . . We cannot conceive the age; we can conceive the element it has contributed to our culture; we can treat the subjects of the age bringing that into relief. (111)

For Swinburne the element that the medieval age contributed to our culture was rich and complex. But, as we have seen, the late Middle Ages especially served Swinburne as a historical paradigm, a premodern period of relatively simple though conflicting political, social, religious, and amatory values that gave birth to great myths of love. Such myths and the art that embodies them powerfully expose all important aspects of the tragic human condition and its ultimate beauty.

Late in his career Swinburne's emphasis, as in *The Tale of Balen,* is on the essential brotherhood of mankind. Such brotherhood results from all men's tragic, because inevitably frustrated, experience of life's potential for spiritual fulfillment through love relationships and communion with nature. As Swinburne matured, his important poetry became less erotic and sadomasochistic, less iconoclastic, and concerned less with the divisions between men than with the common experiences that unite them. The movement of his love poetry's dominant philosophical concerns—from *eros* to *caritas*—reflects that development. His initial sympathies with the special individual in conflict with society and tortured by frustrated passion, expanded to include all individuals in society who blindly suffer erotic unfulfillment and inevitably endure impassioned political, religious, and amatory conflict. Increasingly, too, in all his poems sympathy and communion with nature (which is in harmony with the ostensible disharmony of men's lives) provide temporary solace and fulfillment, as does art that memorializes human tragedies of love and conflict. Yet, throughout his career, more consistently and successfully than any other distinct group of works by Swinburne, his medievalist poems demonstrate his irrepressible desire to memorialize and beatify the tragic life of humanity, in which we all live and move and have our being.

Appendix I
Swinburne's Medievalist Works

The dates of composition are taken from Lafourcade, *Jeunesse*, II; *Bonchurch*, XX (Wise's bibliography), 588–92; Gosse's *Life* (*Bonchurch*, XIX); or derived from the evidence of letters.

1857   "King Ban"

1857–58   *Queen Yseult*
            "The Leper" (earlier, "The White Hind")
            "Southwards"

1858   "Lancelot"
            "The Death of Rudel"
            The Albigenses (lost)
            "A Lay of Lilies"

1858–59   "Second Love"
            "The Dream by the River"

1858–62   *Rosamond*
            "The Two Dreams"
            "The Sea-Swallows"
            "A Christmas Carol"
            "After Death"
            "May Janet"

| 1859 | *The Queen's Tragedy* |
| | "Joyeuse Garde" |

1859–61	Border Ballads
	Ballads by a Borderer
	Chastelard

1859–62	"Dead Love"
	"Triameron"
	"The Portrait"
	"The Marriage of the Monna Lisa"
	Chronicle of Queen Fredegond

1860	"St. Dorothy"
	Balliol essays (see Appendix II)
	"April: (from the French of the Vidame de Chartres, 12–?)"
	"August"
	"Madonna Mia"
	"The Bloody Son"
	"The King's Daughter"
	"In the Orchard"

| 1861–63 | Villonaries |

1862	"Lord Soulis"
	"Lord Scales"
	"The Two Knights"
	"The Complaint of Lisa"
	"The Masque of Queen Bersabe"
	"Laus Veneris"
	"A Ballad of Burdens"

| 1869–82 | *Tristram of Lyonesse* |
| | "The Weary Wedding" |

| 1885 | *Marino Faliero* |

| 1895–96 | *The Tale of Balen* |

Appendix II
Balliol College Essays
and Notes, 1860

The British Library's Ashley manuscript 5069 is a hardcover notebook
with sewn binding that contains a series of previously unpublished
essays written by Swinburne probably in his final year at Balliol College (see *Letters*, I, 35). Upon forty-nine of the notebook's fifty-nine
pages Swinburne has written five essays on historical subjects: (1)
"Notes on Roman and Feudal Law" (pp. 2−4); (2) one on Charlemagne (pp. 5−9); (3) "Crusades" (pp. 10−14); (4) one on Saint Louis
(pp. 15−37); and (5) "Joinville" (pp. 38−49). In addition, starting
from the back of the notebook and written upside down are ten pages
occupied fully or in part by notes on Henry Hallam's *Middle Ages*. The
emphasis in all five essays is on medieval subjects, most of which deal
with the history surrounding the development of courtly literature.
Swinburne's knowledge of his subject here demonstrates not only his
preoccupation with the medieval period but also a self-confidence
lacking in his undergraduate essays on Greek literature, logic, philosophy, and the other standard subjects of the Balliol "Greats" curricu-
lum in 1860.[1] In these essays on medieval history, Swinburne's most
important sources are Hallam's *Middle Ages*; Michelet's *Saint Louis*;

1. Such essays are to be found both in the Ashley collection and elsewhere.
Ashley manuscript 4349 contains brief essays with the following titles: "Source
of Greek History"; "On Deductive and Inductive Re⸺ning": "Of Analogy";
"Origin of Moral Ideas"; "The Period of Mythical F   sophy"; "The Constitutional Influence of Small Republics"; "Use of Logic"; "Analogy of the Arts

and a biography of Joinville. Swinburne's fidelity to Michelet's text is often so great that his paragraphs appear to be virtual translations of that source.

In general, Swinburne revised these essays very little, and what changes he did make seem to have been immediate. The manuscript pages are therefore quite clean, and, of the approximately 8,500 words, only about 10 remain indecipherable. I have placed cancellations in angle brackets, and indecipherable words are indicated thus [*illegible*]. All such matter in italics is supplied by me. In spelling, grammar, and capitalization, I have normally followed the rule of literal presentation. Misspellings should not be viewed as typographical errors; the words are as they appear in the original text. Throughout, I have retained Swinburne's punctuation, but I have always spelled in full the following abbreviations he often used: & (and); agst (against); Cmagne (Charlemagne); kg. (king); bp. (bishop); wh: (which or who); w^d (would); Gk: (Greek); altho' (although); c^d (could); y^t (that); am^g (among); acc^t (account); w^h (with); k^{nts} (knights). In Swinburne's notes, which are redactions of Hallam's introductory comments on the period from A.D. 486 to 1300, I have attempted to retain Swinburne's spelling, punctuation, and symbols exactly, as well as to approach as closely as possible the format he used.

Obviously, encyclopedic notes could be provided to comment on the people, places, and events in these essays. I have, however, tried to dispense almost entirely with such notes except in cases where a reference is particularly obscure and not easily found in Swinburne's sources, in other easily accessible historical studies, in encyclopedias, or in dictionaries.

In most respects these essays speak for themselves. They tell us much about Swinburne's background in historical studies of the me-

---

and Virtues"; "Influence of Greek Philosophy at Rome in the Time of Cicero"; and "Consciousness." All these essays are between three and five pages long. In the Eton College Library are two unpublished college essays donated by T. J. Wise on December 10, 1924. One, in Latin, is entitled "De Morte Mariie Scotorum Regina" (On the death of Mary Queen of Scots), and the other, "On the Character of Mahomet." Both are brief. Finally, in the library of Worcester College at Oxford are the essays edited by Ed Schuldt that appeared as "Three Unpublished Balliol Essays of A. C. Swinburne" in *Review of English Studies,* XXVII (1976).

dieval period; they display his impressive ability to master facts and details, which lasted till his death; and they give us some sense of Swinburne's developing prose style.

Notes on Roman and Feudal Law

The idea of nations is a later one than that of races.[2] This latter is the idea which, prior to the feudal system, occupied historians and patriots: the former is a product simply of the feudal system. In the tenth century, law, which had previously been individual,—a matter of persons—became local,—a matter of tribes and governments. The earlier laws which obtained weight after the virtual destruction of the Roman empire touched in several points on the previous jurisdiction of classical periods; and in many diverged from it. An early Teutonic law was that which in Homer appears as ποινη. This system of personal reprisals and physical retribution was an established and legal custom among the Rissciarian tribe of the Franks.

An opposite instance—an instance of the broad difference made between the barbarian conquerors and those who had once enjoyed the privilege and now endured the disadvantage of Roman citizenship—is as follows. While it is matter of doubt among antiquarians whether this stigma could be removed at the will of the citizen suffering from it, it is certain that this was the scale of charges at which men were valued by the laws. A bishop was worth 100 pieces of gold, a Frank noble 600, a Roman noble 300—a Frank plebeian 200—a Roman plebeian 100 or even 50. Judicial proceedings had two separate bases: first—conpurgators, men who bore witness as to the general repute and standing of the person accused and to their own opinion of his character—secondly, the famous institution of combat or ordeal known as the Judgement of God, against whose unfairness a Towbard chieftain, a man of such clear and strong intellect as also to comprehend the perilous injustice of charges of witchcraft, was the first to

2. "Notes on Roman and Feudal Law" at best lives up to its title. The brief remarks are very disjointed. They do, however, reveal Swinburne's concern with connections between the classical and the medieval, two poles between which his entire value system seems to alternate, always in search of a reconciliation.

appeal. The very notion of evidence as to the actual facts of the case is entirely a late invention. Of the two kinds of Judgement the ordeal was classical, the combat purely feudal.

[*On Charlemagne*]

The name of Charlemagne is one of those names which history acknowledges as great, while as a rule it abstains from defining the component parts which go to make up its greatness.[3] And in fact the position of Charlemagne is one altogether anomalous and unlike that of other conquerors or other statesmen. He is in French history a sort of compound of the legendary Arthur and the Alfred of the chronicles. He is the central figure of a wide and various body of legends. The "emporeur à la barbe [*illegible*]"—of innumerable traditions, the constantly reappearing Deus e machinâ of mediaeval poetry at least as far as the 13th century. Witness the legends, to take only two instances out of many,[4] of Amis and Amiloun and Floris and Blancheflor. From these and such as these his name passed over into England and assumed a similar prestige there. Even late and grave historians have not thoroughly disengaged the idea of the historical warrior and reformer from that of the man who had been made by anticipation a model of chivalrous action, a centre of chivalrous tradition. The deep and wide anachronism, afterwards taken up by the Italians, which made of Charlemagne an Amadis or a Lancelot has to this day confused and impaired the appreciation of his real position and influence on his time. Again, writers who were most anxious to escape any such confusion as that above referred to, have under the influence of such a reaction missed understanding the actual reason and gist of his wars and his legislation. He was undoubtedly a politician and lawgiver of the most clear intuition and profound skill: but as undoubtedly he was liable to be guided and misguided by the religion of the time in which he lived and acted. Hallam for example professes him-

3. Swinburne's remarks on Charlemagne are random and general. He approaches Charlemagne through the vast medieval literature on him and then tries in an admittedly short space to move beyond it.

4. *Bullfinch's Mythology,* for instance, contains nearly two hundred pages of commentary on these legends.

self unable to apprehend the reason which induced the emperor to waste thirty years of his turbulent reign on the ungrateful task of subduing Saxony and Wesphalia, when Italy and Spain might far more easily have been melded into the imperial structure. The reason is surely plain, the Saxon war, with its irrational earnestness and straightforward fanaticism, was as much a religious enterprise as the crusades which it anticipated and prefigured. Such also was the Saxon war, which was (as Hallam has previously stated) Charlemagne's first great success. It is simply to assert an anachronism, to assert that Charlemagne, in taking the pope's part against the insurgent Lombards and supplanting as the champion of the church the iconoclastic emperors of the east, was actuated by principles of mere policy. That he was a statesman, and a great statesman, his capitularies and the institution of the "missi dominici" would of themselves suffice to bear witness. But to overlook the religious element of his reign is to overlook at least as vital and important an element of his character. In popular tradition, evidently, Charlemagne was for centuries the representative of the Catholic monarchy, as Desiderius the Lombard of <the> heretical usurpation.

In representing his personal character, history and legend agree. Even Hallam and Gibbon can on this ground be conciliated with the account of mediaeval poets and romances. The vigorous and passionate nature of the man comes out in all details. Those extravagant accusations as to his private life upon which Gibbon touches (not without exposing his usual facile enjoyment and subdued relish of indecent traditions) were probably enough only the exaggerations of <a> conduct not likely to have been a model of ascetic virtue. His time was coarse and fierce; and Charlemagne was not <likely> the man to anticipate it in such points. In the shedding of blood—especially with a view to conversion—he was certainly as liberal as other conquerors and practical prophets of a new faith—and certainly not more so. In spite of which we may add that Hallam's summary—totally omitting as it does the peculiar religious position and belief of Charlemagne and solely considering his intellectual power as lawgiver ruler and restorer of the empire—is so unfair, that altering the names and dates it would do almost as well for the man who, without conscience honesty or faith, attempted to give the fifteenth century a second edition of Charlemagne—for Caesar Borgia.

Crusades

It was 20 years before the first crusade that Hildebrand imagined the possibility of an European expedition against Asia. The Greek empire was even then imperilled by the events of Turkish power. Under Urban II, this danger had become more pressing. But this, as Hallam remarks, was not even a secondary consideration to the men who undertook the first crusade under the stimulus solely of the religious sentiment. It is hard to realize the spiritual position of Europe at the time of this first attempt. Undoubtedly there grew up afterwards many personal and interested reasons, to further and to second the devotional impulse which first set the enterprise on foot. Immunity from the punishment of crime—from the payment of debts contracted, from liability to taxes—from the jurisdiction of civil courts in ordinary cases—all these advantages must of course have mingled their influence with that of faith and devotion. But these were the growth of a later development of the crusading impulse. In the first crusade many of the advantages above recounted must have been wanting—for this reason: that it was a mere expedition of priests, peasants and the lesser nobility. It was not the kings and emperors who dignified by their success and failure the last crusades, whose support swelled the ranks aroused by Peter the Hermit or led to destruction by Walter the Penniless. That unhappy "rabble" as historians term it which perished fruitlessly in Hungary was not only a mere caricature of the weakness, heat and haste which misguided the expedition in so many ways; it was a convincing test how thoroughly the religious passion had pervaded the lower ranks of society before it practically touched the higher.

Except in open battle the loss of the first crusaders was vast and their failure almost constant. Their final success was but the achievement of subduing the maritime parts of Syria. Bohemond, indeed obtained Antioch as a principality, and Godfrey Jerusalem as a kingdom: but the Syrian Latins, even after Tyre and Ascalon had fallen into their hands, remained liable to Mohometan aggression. From this first the second crusade failed to deliver them; and the principalities, although better protected by European volunteers than by their own insufficient military guard, and in spite of the splendid successes of their unequal force against the Moslems in repeated battles—Jerusalem fell into the power of Saladin 40 years after the second crusade. Two years later the most renowned attempt of all—the third crusade—was undertaken by the greatest of European princes, to result in practical failure.

Passing over for the present the mistimed <attempt> endeavor of St. Louis to renew a war and rekindle enthusiasm for a cause which had already fallen out of date, we may try lastly to sum up the main causes of the crusades as follows. Fanaticism is the easiest and slightest reason to give in their explanation. To this we may add that these wars did certainly afford an outlet and diversion for the surplus of warlike and political excitement which might otherwise have been employed on European dissension. Again, as before hinted, it is no less certain that they afforded a requisite or a convenient security to men otherwise embarrassed by civil causes or criminal charges. They were also an instrument of penance and expiation suitable alike to inflict and to undergo. Men like Foulques Nerra, laden with the guilt of perjury and massacre, in a period when even the most treacherous and violent of men could not escape the consciousness of sin, and had not as yet learnt the trick of modern traitors and tyrants to shift off the blame upon their "mission" or their "star," went, doubtless with at least as much conviction as policy, to fight and to be scourged in the streets of Jerusalem or before the Sepulchre itself, accepting the labour, the peril and the humiliation as the natural price to pay for success at home—sometimes even, one may conjecture, as a cost on which they had counted from the first and found the prize worth the payment. Out of all these harmonious or conflicting reasons it is hopeless to extract the pure and simple impulse which would comment on and explain them all. To understand the crusades, we now think, we should be able to go back to their time: and when that was done, the loss of all later experience and of all analogy would perhaps have the fact actually occurring before our eyes as hard as ever to explain fully. It was not merely rational, and cannot be rationally accounted for. It was not purely religious, and cannot be submitted to purely religious appreciation. Somewhere the balance must be struck between the scepticism of the last century and the neo-Catholicism of this—between Gibbon and the school of believers in the "Ages of

Faith": and we know of no historian who has done <the> this with thorough fairness. In fact, to give a fair weight and value to both sides, a man would have to combine such utterly opposite qualities that we may almost as soon expect a historian of inspired candour and insight beyond the insight of all common men.

[*On Saint Louis*]

A reign that was to leave upon the popular mind an impression the more favourable for the contrast it presented to those before and after it, opened in the midst of contention and danger. Blanche of Castille, the King's mother, had to fight for her regency. The papal legate supported her with his counsel, and it was the common report that he was requited by her affection. Against them were ranged, among others, Pierre de Dreux, Count of Brittany, and Philippe Hurepel, Count of Boulogne: the first had earned the name Mauclerc by his opposition to that clerical policy supported by the religious character of the queen-regent; the latter a son of Philippe Auguste, and uncle to the king, though by a marriage which the Church refused to admit as legal. These nobles and their party claimed a restitution of the political rights of their order: security against loss of property and rank unless after judgement of their 12 peers; the grant of a year's notice before anyone could be legally denounced as a public enemy; and finally they demanded the liberty of those noblemen imprisoned by the late king's father.

Blanche did not await their leave or their resistance. At Scissons her son was made knight, at Rheims anointed king. Philippe of Boulogne she conciliated by the grant of two castles which his father had [held under] occupied with royal garrisons; his father-in-law, the ex-count, she retained in prison, lest he might interfere with Philippe's claims; and a timely suicide removed him out of the way. Ferrand Count of Flanders she also liberated on payment of a ransom. Thus the coronation of a boy of eleven was made a less hazardous step. The 29 Nov. 1226 was the day on which his reign began.

Meantime however the league remained strong. In it were Richard of Aquitaine and the Countess of Angoulême, brother and mother to Henry III of England, whom they regarded as its head. Hugues de Lusignan, re-married to the English ex-queen whom he had ceded to

King John during the reign of that monarch (he had carried off Isabelle in 1200 and married her), received <for> from his wife and her son in return for this pliant forgiveness the county of Angoulême and other valuable fiefs. The English king had also claims on Anjou, Poitou, Normandy and Maine. The French nobles would have sided with him, if only to keep their own king in dependance; but his mismanagement of home affairs threw out his chance. The chance was taken up by a more illustrious hand. Thibaud Count of Champagne, the real inventor of the league, hateful to the royal house by his support of the feudal rights of his order, hateful to the priests by his Albigensian sympathies and regrets, came forward to take up arms against the queen-mother, to whom he had paid court at least in his poems, and probably by personal suit. Blanche had resolved to forestall her lover's purpose, and had summoned the crown vassals to Tours for a levy of the army, when Thibaud appeared to do homage for his fiefs and was cordially received. This some attribute to the queen's negociations, supposing her desirous to get rid of Philippe Hurepel—Thibaud's hereditary and deadly enemy—at all costs, before his friendship became too dangerous: others to an untimely outbreak of the count's poetical affection for Blanche. After this the League melted away by degrees— at last in March the counts of Brittany and LaMarche rescinded their oaths to the king of England at Vendôme. Hereupon Philippe Hurepel, seeing his rival's influence increase, accused him of adultery with the queen-mother and of the murder by witchcraft of the late king. To revenge this he convoked the disaffected nobles; and so nearly was the League renewed in full power that the queen, flying from <Orel> Orleans[5] with her son, had to be escorted, by a detachment of citizens summoned from Paris, past the enemy's army at MontChéri and so into the city; a timely aid, accompanied with expressions of loyalty and devotion, which the king in after life mentioned with grateful pleasure <in his> to Joinville.

At this time Blanche had other enemies to contend with. The popes Honorius III and Gregory IX took part against her for the king of England. The regent conciliated them by a renewal of the Albigensian war, which ended in the ruin of Raymond VII after a few recesses

5. On the blank page that appears at this point between pages 17 and 18 are found the following notes: "Summary"; "Louis IX at Montcheri"; "Papal Opposition"; and "End of Albigensian War."

whose effect was impaired by his cruelties. Arles fell to the popes for a time—Languedoc to the French crown. The daughter of Raymond was ransomed for a marriage with the king's third brother. In carrying out this crusade Folquet bishop of Toulouse took a main part; he lived till 1231, strenthening the inquisition by all his influence and intrigue. The final cession had been made by Raymond in April 1229.

Thibaud of Champagne, after the war in Brittany in which Henry III took part <after> in spite of a winter's delay caused by the French leaving of Hubert de Burgh his favourite, was obliged by the league, which had already raised up against him the claims of his cousin, Alice queen of Cyprus, was <now> obliged to undertake a crusade which he could not accomplish for years. The same year a disturbance fell out between the students of Paris and the citizens; the soldiers intervened at Blanche's order: blood was shed, and the university dispersed in other towns for a period of more than a year, when a papal rebuke to the regent and the bishop of Paris settled the dispute.

In <April> May the King of England came to the aid of the barons in Brittany; after the peace made with Thibaud and the <King> <the> queen he went back; and soon after Mauclerc came to terms. After this treaty had been signed July 1231, the civil war of the regency ended.

There were however disputes with the bishop of Beauvais, the rights of whose town were infringed by the appointment of a foreign mayor and its resistance cruelly punished, and with the bishop of Rouen, in both which the Pope and the ecclesiastical power of interdict got the better of the regent. Another slight attempt was made by Henry III on the expiration of a three years' truce; on its failure, Mauclerc broke with England definitively. Reconciled to France, he took part in the unfortunate crusade of 1235 with Thibaud, now king of Navarre on the death of Sancho, his father-in-law; who had agreed to leave it to the king of Arragon; but the king of Arragon was occupied in a war against the Moors in Majorca for which he had recruited Provence: and Thibaud, Philippe Hurepel having died (not without suspicions of poison) while urging the claims of the queen of Cyprus, bought off her claim with money received from Blanche in return for the cession of certain fiefs.

At this period (1236) Louis IX attained his majority. We have seen that the courageous and active intellect of the queen-mother had brought him through great and various perils to a prosperous security. Two years before she had made him accept the hand of Margaret daughter of Raymond Beranger IV, Count of Provence. The king's mind was already, it is probable, turned towards the chances of a crusade. It may not be out of place to give here such brief summary as we can of his character and position. Hitherto he has done nothing: from this point his becomes the principal figure, and that of Blanche recedes.

Nature had made him constitutionally reverent and gentle; education had developed these qualities to a point almost morbidly sensitive. His submission to his mother was so much a matter of conscience that for years after his marriage he complied with her desire that he should scarcely ever see his wife; or the wife and husband would meet by a secret passage and part hastily when a signal warned them of the queen's coming. We say the queen advisedly, for Margaret was thwarted in every way by Blanche. Again, the king was come into a fair and full inheritance: but even if his claim to Normandy, Poitou and the other provinces wrested from England was a small one, the southern provinces had been won at the cost of that Albigensian crusade which to this day remains a portent of cruelty among <the> European wars. It was perhaps not without an idea of expiation that the Eastern war presented itself to his mind. The main qualities of Louis IX seem to have been a perfect purity, an unspotted singleness of purpose, a gentle courage mixed with a tenderness for the lives of his followers which explains their devotion to a king in whose views the wisest of them were often unable to join—Joinville for instance on the occasion of the second crusade in which he flatly refused to take part. His religion was coloured and moulded by these qualities; it was also tainted by the want of candour, justice and courage which distinguished the belief of <the> an age which had to choose between Frederick II and Gregory IX—a sceptical emperor and a pope memorable mainly for treachery, self-interest, and his share in the last cruelties inflicted on the already overthrown Albigeois. Ready to lay down his life for the Cross at all instants, the king was also ready to tear out with hot irons the tongues that spoke against the lightest article of faith. And in this <t>he was behind others of his period. Repeatedly he has to repress or answer as he best can—and his forte does not lie in argument—the objections or doubts of Joinville—an orthodox man too, but disposed to approve of arguing with Jews (for example) where it was his duty to put them to the edge of the sword at once.

The crusade could not begin at once. Raymond of Toulouse after 14 years of a humiliated peace was up again in the South. He would have married Beatrice of Provence and united that province with <Toulouse> Languedoc in defiance of the Parisian treaty of <1225> 1227. Trencavel, the dispossed[6] heir of Nimes and Carcassonne, also reappeared. Henry III was to help him: Navarre Castille and Arragon were his allies. But Henry III was again too late. But for his brother Richard's intercession, his army would have perished at <Ni> Taillebourg: at Taintes he was routed and fled to Bordeaux. Louis used his success with a wise leniency. He even left to Raymond the old terms of the treaty of 1229.

At length the seizure of Gaza and Jerusalem and the treacherous massacre of their inhabitants by the Mongol tribes determined the king to that action by which he is yet most widely remembered. A vow made at the point of death and renewed in health in spite for once of the opposition of Blanche and even of the priest, was the ostensible and immediate cause. Gregory IX, by this time expelled[7] Italy and forced to extort by soliciation leave to enter Lyons, threw every hindrance possible in his way, to divert his arms against the emperor or the King of England, with both of whom he was then at enmity. But Louis gave no heed to this. He even restored to England some of the French conquests. He gave money to Trencavel in payment of his lands and attached him to the crusade. He prepared all things necessary for the foundation, as a groundwork to the holy war, of a strong Egyptian colony. To have a harbour of his own, as the Provençal harbours belonged to Charles of Anjou, he <built> dug that of Aiguesmortes.

His first point was Cyprus. There the army waited for Charles and his reinforcements till it became thoroughly enervated and depraved. Ambassadors came to do the king honour from Constantinople, Syria,

6. Probably "dispossessed" was intended.
7. Swinburne probably left out "from."

the Assassins, the Mongols themselves. But there were profligate resorts established about the very tent of the king and queen. At last they set sail for Egypt and <a> the wind decided their course for Damietta, which was easily taken. But from that point the misfortunes of the ruinous enterprise began. By slow marches, harassed and decimated by the Greek fire of the Saracens, they reached Mansourah, getting through ten leagues in a month. At Mansourah, after many dangerous and vain attempts to force a passage of the Nile by a dam, they were guided to a ford.

First Robert d'Artois brother to the king crossed, and scorning the advice of the Templars to wait for the rest of the army, broke into the city with the vanguard. The Templars followed, but without hope. The Mamelukes (overpow[2]ered them) in a[1] short (time);[8] the streets were barricaded and the windows emptied stones<,> wood etc. on the heads of the French.

Meantime the king had crossed and met the Saracens. Here it was that Joinville saw him "coming with all his battle, with great noise and great clamour of trumpets, and he paused on a raised way; but so fair a man at arms I never saw, for he showed above all his men shoulder-high, a gold helmet upon his head, a German sword in his hand." Till the evening the battle was bravely kept up; and then came the news of his brother's death. Then, Joinville says, the king answered that God should be praised for that which he had sent him; and then there fell from his eyes full great tears. Again when one asked him for news of the Count of Artois; "All I know" said he "is that he is in Paradise."

On the road to Cairo there were further encounters; the Count of Anjou was nearly captured and only rescued by Louis at his extreme personal risk. The entrenchments were notwithstanding saved: and the king could not resolve to fall back at once on Damietta. Hideous diseases broke out in the army, from impure food and damp mainly: the corpses were too loathsome to touch, although the king set the example of burying them with his own hands. At last the retreat began; but Louis was too ill himself to travel far: the Saracens enclosed them by land and water; all were massacred who would not renounce

8. The numbers are Swinburne's and apparently indicate his desire to rearrange the phrases.

their faith; only the king and the prisoners of note were spared. Louis, who could not grant the cession of Jerusalem which belonged to the German emperor, had agreed to give up Damietta and pay 600,000 gold bezants, when the Sultan was murdered in a revolt of the Mamelukes.

At Damietta, three days after Margaret had heard of her husband's capture, she bore a child named Jean, surnamed Tristan.

Complete as was the overthrow of Louis IX, he remained a year after this in Palestine, fortified the main cities, and remained as long as his presence was thought useful; <when> at length the sudden death of the queen-mother recalled him to Europe.

The failure of his expedition had been utter: and such was his despondency. All Christendom, he said, was disgraced in him and by him. <There was never an completer instance of the growth of a man's greatest glory from a noble failure.> Nevertheless it was from this mistimed and mismanaged attempt that the chief reputation of St. Louis was to grow. Admitting all the impolicy and aimless misconduct which have to be deducted from the sum of his glory, yet the true valour and purity of purpose, the heroism and the patience he displayed in battle and in worse than battle—his faithful care of his people—his pity of their lost lives—his tenderness for their dishonoured bodies— all these things, even for those who need not regard him as saint or martyr, make his name and his memory among the most pure, noble, worthy of love and loving honour, in all history.

In France a fresh danger awaited <him> Louis; the insurrection, as it was called, of the Pastoureaux. This singular rising, of which any complete and judicious account would be a great help to our comprehension of the period, was for the most part religious. It broke out among the lowest of the people; shepherds chiefly, whence its name. These men, on the first news of the king's imprisonment, banded themselves together under the plea of marching to his rescue. How far this was a pretext, and how far they really saw in Louis IX their best chance of escape from oppression, we cannot determine. At all events, their main animosity fell (by an instinct which probably was not far wrong) upon the priests. These they put to the sword; but the most remarkable point is that they at once proceeded to establish a Church of their own—complete with a clergy, pope, cardinals and bishops: which according to early accounts gave them some elements of stability and resistance. Their chief was a mysterious prophet who professed to carry always in his closed hand an autograph letter from the Virgin summoning Pastoureaux to the holy land. Paris and Orleans allowed their passage; but with time they were killed out "like mad dogs, dispersedly" as Michelet quotes from Matthew Paris. —It is easy to recognize the first ostensible and superficial reasons for the anti-clerical movement of these unfortunate Pastoreaux. At no time yet had the priestly power been so fatal, so treacherous, so merciless, as it had been during the last reigns. Even the miserable plea of private purity of life and individual regularity of devotion—that plea so often set up without sense or reason, so often bested and overthrown, only to be again seized upon and clung to with the irrational force of fear—even this they could hardly then fall back upon. If Folquet of Toulouse was steeped in innocent blood, there were brother prelates of his not less deeply dyed with falsehood and impurity: the cardinal-legate Romano, e.g. was accused of adultery with Queen Blanche. Everywhere the intellectual revolt was begun or beginning. The Albigeois [*illegible*] was burnt out; but the very university of Paris had incurred, although it promptly bowed to, a warning against secular teaching and tenets that attempted to prove revealed religion the equivalent of natural. St. Louis himself—and this Michelet most acutely points out as a test of the wide spread and deep root of scepticism—has to contemplate the possibility of doubt and the duty of stifling it; a duty which an earlier believer of the same purity and zeal—say for instance King Robert—would never have thought of. Oriental studies were in full growth among the great and wise—Frederic II for one, and his court; democratic leanings were visible among the populace—as this very outbreak of the Pastoureaux. And <as> to counterbalance all this, the Inquisition, with all its worst and most shameful ingredients already matured, was in full establishment and regular work. Torture indeed was not yet a system—a physical infliction at least was not: but all the elements of lying, fraudulent admissions, false promises, false pretensions, false sympathy, false charity, and the whole arsenal of moral forgeries were in play. Lismondi gives a prolonged list of the instructions drawn up for the use of inquisitors, their officials, and their converts: and a more repulsive catalogue of lies of all colours and shapes it would be hard to find and painful to read.

To St. Louis either side of the question must have been painful to investigate. On his return, the main facts we hear of his conduct are his devotions, his disciplines, his sensitive dread of any fresh wrong-doing. To England he delivered up the Limousin, the Pirigord and other provinces on condition that the English claim on the conquered lands of Poitou Normandy etc. should be legally and definitely abandoned. This cession made for conscience' sake cost him much opposition from his brother, from the nobles, and all France; also the lasting rancour of the provinces given up, which refused to take part in the festival of his canonization. But on the other hand Louis allowed his brother Charles to accept, what for himself he steadily refused, the papal offer of a share in the Italian spoils of the German empire: and that unjust and pitiless policy, the reaction from which was the sicilian Vespers, was partly due to the same king whose tender conscience despoiled him of his own inherited lands. St. Louis was decidedly not the man to manage a home policy. For the rest, Charles of Anjou had on him that influence which opposite characters often mutually exercise. "The dark man who took little sleep"—hard, unjust, hot and quick to take offence—was as complete an antithesis to St. Louis as one could well conceive.

The king's interference, solicited and reclaimed as it was by both sides, in English polities, had not a much happier result. Indeed no power could have extricated Henry III at the point he had come to. Perplexed between the Church (which he supported by introducing Italian priests into English benefices) and the barons and people (in whom a society had sprung up to check this <It>[9] foreign overgrowth by the direct and simple method of murdering the papal messengers), he had fallen back on his Poitevin favourites. Against these there was a fresh rising; Simon de Montfort, the hereditary enemy of Southern France, turned suddenly against the king: the Oxford parliament had confirmed the charter; and after six years' war they agreed to refer to the French king. Louis, on the authority of the text concerning "submission to the powers" etc., annulled the Oxford resolutions; and war at once recommenced.

We have mentioned above the influence mutually exercized by Louis and Charles. This influence by itself makes it probable that Louis cannot be with justice exempted from the charge of sharing in

9. Swinburne probably began to write "Italian."

the Italian campaign, of the king of Sicily. Into the detail of those wars this is not the place to enter: we will simply refer in passing to the observation of Michelet that to St. Louis they might have appeared almost in the light of a new species of crusade. For the Church was thoroughly with them; and the Imperial house which they went to destroy was taxed, not simply with licence and rebellion, but also with actual disbelief. Manfred, the bastard successor of Frederic II, was challenged by Charles as the Sultan of Nocera in which place as in Luceria he had posted the Saracen troups on which, like his father, he mainly relied for Italian support. [*illegible*] That the concord between the brothers was a real and complete one, a contemporary anecdote proves. Louis had chosen to take personal part in the building of a monastery at Roiaumont—wheeling barrows-full of stones, for one thing; he pressed his brothers into the same service. If they wished in the intervals of hod-carrying to indulge in [*illegible*] merriment or conversation, the king said to them: "the monks at work here keep silence, and so ought we to keep it." If they wished to sit down and rest while wheeling their hand barrows—"The monks" said the king "take no rest, neither should you take any."

They were soon to take part with him in an enterprise more weighty than mason's work, and less guilty if less hopeful than an Italian war. In Syria, the Mamelukes who had come to supplant the Mongols were carrying on a persecution more terrible even than theirs. In Antioch alone seventeen thousand Christians were massacred, <20,000> 10,000 sold into slavery. On May 25th 1267 the king of France entered the great hall of the Louvre, weakened with austerities, carrying in his hand the crown of thorns which he had purchased from the Greek Emperor as a relic beyond price. He resumed the cross and compelled his three sons to do likewise. His brothers Alphonse and Charles, with many nobles, followed their example. Louis left no stone unturned to attach to his enterprise the neighbouring princes. He paid 70,000 livres to the English princes; he offered to furnish equipages, reconcile disputes, anything to get livres. To the Southern assemblies of Carcassonne <and> Beaucaire he gave <the licence of> leave to have representatives of the citizens—the first germ of the States of Languedoc. In spite of all, when the army was gathered together, there remained great opposition without and great despondency within. For two months it loitered at Aigues-Mortes, in an unhealthy neighbourhood; with its direction undetermined. Egypt was alarmed. A mouth of the Nile was stopped up. The Greek emperor, dreading (says Michelet) <C> the ambition of Charles of Anjou, sent to offer a reconciliation between the Eastern and Western Churches. The passage was very slow; Pisa <refused leave to> closed her harbours against the Genoese ships <to land>; Louis could hardly get leave to land his numerous sick. At this rate they could never get as far as Palestine or Egypt. Tunis was suggested as a substitute: to reduce Tunis was the interest of the king of Sicily. It was thought that the Sultan, who was on friendly terms with France, might be converted rather by a mild intimidation than by force. Louis had formerly made the Tunis ambassadors witnesses of the baptism of a converted Jew and had then sent by them the following message of their Sultan: "That I desire so earnestly the <salvation> wellbeing of his soul that I would choose to be in the Saracen prisons all my life through and not see the light of day again, if at such cost I might make your king and his people Xtians, even as this man is made."

But such was not the outlook for the Genoese. Plunder was their aim, and Tunis was reported to be worth the sacking. They seized the ships that fell in their way off Carthage. On landing, the Moors drew them on by <means> feigned attacks and sudden retreats.[10] The Genoese seized the fort of Carthage, its Saracen garrison of 200 men were slaughtered, or perished in the fire. Their corpses had to be cleared out before Louis and his army could get lodging among the ruins. Here they were to wait for Charles of Anjou. The very name of that king seemed to bring ill fortune to his brother; this <w> <same> was a repetition of the reverse which had maimed the Egyptian expedition on first setting out. In eight days the plague broke out. It was no wonder: they had no vegetable food; the air was hot and foul; shelterless sand and the stench of corpses completed the bad work. Many nobles perished; also the youngest and favourite son of the king. <Ten> Eight days later, when Louis himself was near death, his confessor saw fit to give him the news. After this he quietly went through such ceremonies of religion as there remained for him; he received the Greek ambassadors who came to ask his intercession and help

10. Swinburne's original intention was probably to say "on by means of feigned attacks and sudden retreats."

against the designs of Charles; spoke justly to them, promised his aid and goodwill should he live; but it never availed them. He made them take him out of bed and lay him in ashes. Then he spread out his arms cross-wise, and prayed, with his hands lifted, saying: "Fair lord God, take pity on this people that abides here, and bring my men back to their own land that they fall not into the hand of their enemies and be not driven to deny the holy name." They thought he might get to sleep and so die; but he sighed and said <in a low> twice under his breath: "O Jerusalem: O Jerusalem." And so died by the break of day.

That was the end of the last crusade, or crusades either. It seems to us that Joinville had no such great reason to thank God (as he does) that he for one took no part in it. He might have done worse than go. It was a very fair and perfect end; this at least was not <untimely> mistimed, not misplaced if Louis' work in life had been so. Old words, which are become bywords, <w> phrases used out, which are come to have no sense or merely a sense of ceremony and false worship—seem still the only fit phrases and words for it. In his life any man now [*illegible*] may see flaws and gaps—as many then did, only let him treat even these, as the men about <him> Louis did, not without some reverence. The world has had many men greater; no man ever won more love. And to this day he has kept it, in a vague irrational <man> sort. It is not a name that many men to whom it is known at all would like to hear slighted or reviled. And then in his life he had surely failure and trouble enough. It may be best to leave him and his period—the age of which he was, so to speak, the crown and the con-clusion,—even as they stand, to give in their own account. Those are not wise who would reproduce it for profit of some modern cause or party; neither are those who would cast stones at it for our satisfac-tion. It is gone for good, and neither regret nor contempt can alter that. As little can either alter one whit of its good or evil. <There> Let us leave it, even as it went out with the life of Louis—saying as little as need be of praise or sorrow or blame; the one will not help it; for the other we have no heart, were it as just as is unjust and dull. But as to regretting such an end for it, no man need think of that. Louis had no regret for it or for himself; he <did> had nothing to repent of for his share. That he could not enter Jerusalem to purify it—could not earn the right to give thanks for leave given to complete his good service—this may have been a sorrowful thing to him; there was much more to wish done, but little surely to wish undone. <We will [*illegible*] with the [*illegible*].> His last words he said were the words of this prayer: words fit to wind up his life: "Lord God, give us heart that we may despise the bitterness of this world, so that we may have no fear of any adversity."

Joinville

The debateable ground between history and biography is a ground attractive to all men for all reasons. It seems likely to give us a true and clear notion of all that lies choked in an overgrowth of statistics or wanders before modern eyes in the mist of speculation. It is also dangerous ground. A thoroughly bad historical memoir is about the most thoroughly bad book that can well be written. It has claims beyond the classics of romance, and duties less strict than the duties of history. If it abuse this prestige and this privilege, the dullest <history> chronicle, the loosest historical novel, is far preferable. We in England have been of late years much plagued with an infectious and illegitimate growth of this kind. The best mode of bringing to the test such a swarm of counterfeits is to confront them for an instant with a really great work of the same class.

M. Caboclu in his late work on the historical memoirs of France has done, we think, bare justice to Joinville. There is a taint, a twang of modernism about his references and citations, which <seems> does not seem to promise well for his handling of the matter. He has a cold candour, a placid sense of judgement, which is apt to turn irritating after a few sentences. Clearly the duc de Saint-Simon is more in his line than Froissart or than Joinville. Now Joinville was undoubtedly not a great man. To say that he has not the grace, the brilliant strength, the facile beauty, the perfect dramatic power and the superb enjoyment of Froissart, is simply to say that Froissart, not Joinville, was the greatest of all historians. It is here, as M. Caboclu remarks, that Joinville did not enjoy the crusade. He was drawn—rather, haled—into it by St. Louis. Evidently the seneschal of Champagne and Brie was lost, in his own opinion, at home. He was in many ways what <men> we might now call a cool man of hard and healthy common sense. The zest with which he throws the whole weight of his mind and the whole interest of his daily life into the regulations of life and behav-

iour at his castle is the reverse of Froissart's changeable, active, in-
quisitive life as the guest now of one knight or queen, now of another.
The Canon of Chimay, had he been the head of a knightly household,
would by no means have thought of the following domestic ordinance.

"Never heard I him (St. Louis) name the devil unless it were in
some book where he must of necessity be named, or in the life of the
saints of whom the book spoke. And it is great shame to the kingdom
of France (and the king when he suffers it) that one can scarce speak
but he shall say "the devil take it!" And it is a great fault in language
of discourse when one <shall> makes over to the devil the man or
the woman who were given to God at their baptism. In the castle of
Joinville he that says such a word <owes the> incurs a blow on his
cheek or a box on his ear, whereby this evil langauge is there almost
wholly beaten down."

Joinville is distinctively a respectable man—not in the worst sense
of the word. For he has a sufficient independence of his own when
you come at it. At times he will hold his own against St. Louis himself.
Take these examples following:

"He asked me, did I wash the feet of poor men on Holy Thursday.
Sir, said I, in an evil hour should I do it; the feet of these unclean
villains will I <wash> never wash. —Truly, said he, that was ill said."

But Joinville held to his own aristocratic taste, for the conversation
is repeated with additions towards the end of the book. Neither did he
spare the king by proxy, in the persons of his favourites: witness this
word-combat with Robert de Cerbou:

"He said to me (this was at Pentecost feast) You are greatly to blame
in that you are clad more nobly than the king: for you clothe yourself
with vair and green which the king does not. And I answered him;
Master Robert, saving our favour, I do nought to blame if I wear green
and vair, for this coat my father and mother left me; but you are to
blame, for you are <a peasant and a peasant's son> son of a low father and a low mother (fils de vilain et de vilainne) and are clothed
with richer stuff than the king is. And then I took the skirt of his sur-
coat and the skirt of the king's and <held> said to him; Now look
whether or no I speak truth. And then the king undertook to defend
Maitre Robert with words to the best of his power." Afterwards in private the king took Joinville's part and allowed that he had only come
to the rescue because the founder of the Sorbonne was so utterly dis-

comfited. This independence Joinville always retained. Having occasion to cite a saying of Louis IX on God's justice, he adds; "Therefore let the king that now is take heed, for he has escaped as great peril or more than did we: so let him amend himself of his misdeeds <but> in such manner that God smite not heavily on him or his." A warning of which Philip the Fair stood in as much need as most men, but which in a memoir addressed to his son is at least a singular instance of plain speaking.

Joinville himself divides his work into two distinct parts—the collection of <various> sayings and doings of the king; and the account of that war in which the writer took a personal part. In such rough and scanty notice as we here give, it may be well to follow this division. We shall then treat first, and separately, of what may be called the miscellaneous half of the book. Careful analysis might perhaps, were it worth while, range under various heads the various anecdotes strewn over the opening passages: might for instance part off one branch of stories as illustrative of the king's religious views, another as illustrative of his opinions on policy, morals, social duties and conduct, and so on. We will be content to select from the <vari> different groups, at first, such points as may serve to illustrate the subject in hand—that is, the quality and worth that is in this book.

And first, then, there is this one merit which no reader who dips upon any stray page can fail to catch; the merit of a noble and reasonable loyalty; a loyalty as far as man can imagine from the servility which is engrained in a courtier or the affected union—confusion rather—of rapture and recurence which is in the nature of a sentimental theorist. Secondly, allowing for the changes of belief and expression since the 13th century, we may say that what Joinville admires in St. Louis is what makes him really admirable. It is not his blind tenacity of devotion to a cause which most men even then saw to be a delusion; it was not, we believe, the submission of <the> his intellect to religious tenets and religious teachers; but his lofty theories of general right and universal duty, his noble care for his people, his loving and sincere nature.

Of the second quality sighted take this instance: Joinville mentions with a just applause the words of Louis to his son "Fair son, I pray thee that thou wilt make thyself beloved by the people of kingdom for truly I would rather that a Scot came out of Scotland to rule the people of the kingdom well and loyally, than that thou shouldst govern it amiss."

Of his high theories of moral worth the following is a witness: "He asked me would I be honoured in this world and win <honour> heaven at my death. And I said yes. Then he said to me: Take heed then that you do or say nothing to your knowledge, which if it were known to all the world, you could not acknowledge, saying this have I said; this have I done."

It is not till Joinville is fairly launched into the Crusade that the main interest of the book begins. Hitherto we have had only detached remarks and miscellaneous anecdotes, each severally of interest and value: from this point we attain a coherent narrative. The style seems to kindle and quicken; the narrator seizes on those points only which have had a personal relation if not to himself yet to his immediate neighbours: there was little taken on trust before, but now there is nothing. The war with Henry III is dismissed almost as briefly as the baronial feuds which disturbed the regency of Blanche. For the summons given by the king after his illness, Joinville at once passes to the adoption of the cross by himself. We see him distributing among those to whom he had done any wrong the value of their claims; we see him passing out of his castle to visit the relics at Blechicourt and St. Urbain, when "I would not all the while turn back my head towards Joinville lest my heart should be moved for the fair castle I was leaving and for my two children." The action marches rapidly, encumbered only by a few rare and quaint reflections. Everywhere we can observe in Joinville a man of keen sight and cool head, quick to decide and sharp-witted in the execution of his designs. What happened is told with a clear simplicity and a direct choice of matter which bring out every [*illegible*] point <with> worth knowing at once and vividly.

Between France and Cyprus nothing occurs worth mention, except the phenomenon of a round-shaped mountain off Barbary, <at> before which after a whole night's sailing they again found themselves in the morning; an inconvenience from which they were only delivered by the spiritual offices of a priest on board.

At Cyprus the main facts recorded are the embassy from the "great king of Tartary"—supposed to mean the <Vatican's> Khan's lieutenant in Asia-Minor,—which came to offer <the> his assistance in

185

wresting Jerusalem from the keeping of the Saracens: the tent made in fashion of a chapel which St. Louis sent in return, with the Annunciation and other miracles wrought therein as an instrument of conversion: the rumours of war between the <sultan> king of Armenia and sultan of Iconium which drew away some of the French army to join on the chance of success—these <of> naturally were not heard of again: and the arrival of the Greek Empress to seek help for her husband; <who> her courteous reception by the king; and the destitution she was in by the miscarriage of her ships, a destitution so complete that Joinville had to provide her with suitable apparel at his own charge. He and others undertook her defence if the king would supply them with 300 knights when they were at liberty; but when the disastrous campaign of Egypt was over St. Louis had no knights to spare.

The landing at Damietta is given in full and spirited detail. The loss for the time of the greater number of the ships (ships were dispersed by a sudden wind)—the difficulty of getting to the shore—the (seemingly) instant malevolence of Jean de Beaumont towards Joinville—the knight who was drowned in trying to leap into a boat as it put off—the two mortal enemies who had "taken each other by the hair" at Cyprus and whom Joinville compelled to a reconciliation before landing. The counsel held in which the rash advice of the Count of Artois to march for Cairo as the capital of Egypt unhappily prevailed over the sounder opinions of the majority—all these matters are recounted one after another with the same straightforward and business-like ease.

St. Louis had a touch of hard discipline in him too. When Gauclier d'Aubreclu charged the Saracens by himself and received wounds of which he died, the king's comment was that he would be sorry to have 1000 such that would not obey his commandment. The passage is no bad instance of Joinville's simple picturesque power.

"Late that evening Mgr. Aubert de Nancy proposed to me to go and see him, as we had not yet had sight of him and he was a man of great name and great worth. We came into his tent, and his chamberlain met us to say that should walk softly and not awake his master. We found him lying under a coverlet of miniver and drew towards him quietly and found that he was dead."

After this came fresh delay; they had to wait for the count of Poitiers. They became weary after some time, but a procession of three consecutive Saturdays suggested by Joinville as the remedy which had delivered him and his in the matter of the Barbary rock restored the absent count to the army just late enough to escape a hurricane that dispersed <many> 12 score ships.

The main errors of the march on Damietta have been previously stated. We will add to them some of the little dramatic touches by which Joinville gives life to the recital.

On St. Nicholas' day the march began; orders were strictly given that there should be no charge made: which the Turks perceiving took advantage of to make an onset in which the Templar (brother Renaud de Bichiers) was overthrown. When he saw this he cried out to his brothers: Now upon them for God's sake, for this can I not suffer. The result of charging with fresh horses the wearied horses of the enemy was that all were destroyed either in the battle or in flight by the river.

Hallam's Middle Ages

Notes

(c. 1 pt. 1)

Division of Empire
Vandals in Africa — Spain = Suevi & Visigoths: Visigoths = part of Gaul:
Burgundians = provinces of Rhone & Saône: Ostrogoths over Italy:
N.W. of Gaul (between Seine & Loire) =? Armorican Republic (federations under bishops)
(486) Soissons (1st victory of Clovis) & received titles of Counsul & Patrician fr: the Emp:
(496) defeated Allemanni (=Suabians) at Zulpich, nr. Cologne; converted (God of Clotilda)
(507) defeated Alaric (Kg. of Visigoths) near Poitiers (Urlick Third) and reduces Goths to Septimania:

Reduces chiefs of his own family abt. <surrounding> the Rhine: Dies
(511): kingdom divided am^g four sons: (three sons of Clotilda's)

Kingdom of Clovis
$^{1)}$France: $^{2)}$western & central Germany: $^{3)}$Bavaria & (?) $^{4)}$Swabia
(under hired: subordinates)
$^{2)}$Austrasia (=German section) falls to Thierry: capital at Metz:
Clodomir at Orleans: Childebert at Paris: Clotaire at Soissons.
(N.B. Aquitaine divided into 3 (or 2? Th: Ch: had shared, but? as
to Clod?^{11} _____:) Then
Paris afterwards capital of Neustria (=Soissons & Paris & Orleans.)
(558) Clotaire inherits & re-divides all am^g his four sons:
(613) Clotaire (his grandson) re-unites all: (Period of Brunehaut &
Fredegonde)
After Dagobert (son of Clotaire II) came the Fools (insensati) 628–
638
Louis the Debonair attempts to perpetuate system of election subordi-
nate to that of primogeniture or virtual superiority of the first born.
Lothaire revolts ——
Elective Mayors of Neustria & Austrasia: Pepin d'Heristal.
(N.B. α) Burgandy (elective government) subordinate to Neustria:
    β) Aquitaine (from Dagobert downwards governed by ducal dy-
        nasty of Aribert (D's brother.)
Pepin Duke of Austrasia allows a Merovingian kg. in Neustria:
(732) Charles Martel (his son) gains Septimania from Saracens aft:
    battle between Tours and Poitiers
((752) Pepin completes the conquest.)
Accession of Pepin (752) (son of Ch: Martel, grandson of Heristal.)

Childeric^{12} III. deposed by Pope Zacharias
Affairs of Italy

Gk. iconoclasts alienate Rome:
Lombards seize exarchate of Ravenna; (752 = date of Pepin's accession)
Accession of Charlemagne 768–772 (=death of Carloman)

11. "Th:" stands for Thierry; "Ch:" for Chilperic; "Clod" for Clodomir.
12. This name should be Chilperic.

Expedition agst Lombardy (774)

Resistance of dukes of Friuli and Benevento:

Conquest of Spanish March fr. Pyrenees to Ebro (kept by France till 12th century) (reduction of [1] Saxon, [2] Sclavonians, [3] Avars)

Emperor (800)

(834) Treaty of Verdun.

Charles the Bald, Louis & Lothaire (sons of Louis le Débonnaire Charlemagne's grandson)

break up the French & German empire. Louis <gets> "the Germanic" gets all beyond the Rhine

Lothaire Italy & Lorraine: Charles France.

Empire dismembered, kgdom. of Arles (Provence & pt of Switzerland)

Charles Fat deposed (887)

Accession of Hugh Capet on death of Louis V. (987)

Incursion of Normans under Carlovingian kgs.

Policy of Charles Simple—Cession of Normandy (918)

Conversion of Rollo. _____

Proofs of Hugh's usurpation & non-election: (p. 23) [13]

Robert — Henry I — Philip I:

Louis VI. reduces the barons: Rivalry of France & England begins:

Louis VII. (1137) repudiates Eleanor:

Normandy & Anjou & Guienne fall to Henry II. of England:

Philip Augustus (1180) summons John before a court of his peers; as Duke of Normandy & his vassal

John loses Anjou. Maine. Normandy;

(1223) Louis VIII. reconquers Guienne: Languedoc turns Albigensian:

Crusade of Simon de Montfort (_____ Ph. Aug:) [14]

Cession by count of Toulouse of part of Languedoc, <u>after</u> Louis VIII. And reversion of the rest to Alphonso, St. Louis; brother: or to the kg. in person.

St. Louis (1259) restores part of conquest to Henry III.

His commissaries appointed for restitution of unjust gains.

---

13. Swinburne here and elsewhere apparently indicates the page number of the edition of Hallam he was using.

14. "Ph. Aug:" stands for Philip Augustus.

Crusades

First idea of Europe attacking Asia started by Hildebrand <(1027)>
1074

Peter the Hermit (1095); councils of Piacenza & Clermont: (Deus
[*illegible*])

Crusaders freed from debts   taxes   . . .

First, Second & Third Crusade.

Crusade of St. Louis in Egypt   ⎤
───────────────── to Tunis: ⎦

Death of St. Louis: Accession of Philip III: under whom

Poitou, Saintonge, Auvergne, & Toulouse fall to the crown: (1270–
1285)

War of Aragon: Champagne falls to Philip IV. (the Fair) by his wife:

Who also outwits Edmund, brother of Edward I., & seizes fortresses
of Guienne

Edward being occupied in Scotch wars overlooks it:

Matters adjusted by marriage of Isabel Philip's daughter to Edward II.

Failures of Philip in Flanders: battle of Courtray. (4000 pair of gilt
spurs taken)

Philip seizes Angoulême & La March: city of Lyons wrested fr: the
archbishop

Louis de Hutin dies after a year's reign:

leaves one daughter, & Margaret of Burgandy pregnant:

Philip V. & Eudes of Burgandy agree that Navarre & Champagne (the
inheritance of Louis de Hutin's mother) shall fall to his daughters
when of age, if Margaret has a daughter:

Further—if the princesses refuse this, their claim to France stands;
but

Philip has the reversion of Navarre and Champagne. (1315–1316)

A son (John I) is born & dies in three or four days: whereupon Philip
    V. proclaims himself king in violation of treaty w^h Eudes ──

conciliates Eudes by promising his daughter's hand (Philip's)

Eudes abandons the cause of his niece Jane (Margaret's daughter) as
well as her claim to Nav: & Cha: as to France. (p. 44–46)

    First establishment of (nominally) Salic Law:

    Philip V. leaves three daughters: his brother Charles succeeds.

    Charles IV. leaves one daughter: Philip VI. count of Valois*
        succeeds. (*grandson of King Ph: III.)

The claim of Edward III. false:

For, put away the Salic Law, & these princesses succeed:

Or, if only <u>male issue of female heirs</u> is to succeed, Jane's son (kg. of Navarre) comes in.

? Did Edward claim France <u>before</u> accession of Ph: VI.?

He does homage <u>for Guienne</u>.

(End of c. 1. pt. 1.)

(Part II)

Expedition of Edwd. III. agst Phi of Valois & John:

Is allied wth emperor Louis, Flanders, & princes of Netherlands & Rhine:

But unsuccessful till the war passes from Flanders to Poitou & Normandy.

Action of States <-> General <u>after</u> battle of Poitiers.

Two pbs.[15] were before established:

(α) No resolution carried without consent of all three orders:

(β) Taxes to be levied & regulated by them)

Charles the Bad kg of Navarre, son of Jane, marries daughter of John:

Assassinated Kg John's favourite:

Allies himself to Edward: his inheritance of Evreux in Normandy.

Pestilence of 1348:

General ravages of the Tree Lawes:

Jacquerie of 1358.

Peace of Bretigni 1360:

Cession of six provinces <to> & Calais to Edwd: within the year, who resigns title of kg of France.

Doubt as to which party failed in making the "renunciations" at Bruges ((1361)) but Edwd: governs the Provinces thenceforward & establishes his son in Aquitaine; who taxes Guienne after his Castile expedition.

(1368) Guienne & Gascony appeal to Chas. V. who had been kg. 6 years: he summons the Prince to answer: war resume<d>s.

1) These became hereditary in 13th cent:

Feudal System (c. 2, pt. 2)

Hallam thinks y^t the feudal system of tenure can be traced no higher than the Merovingian kgs. He distinguishes it fr: dieutage or

---

15. "Pbs." perhaps stands for "principles."

commendatio by the element of landholding, & the essential fact y^t it depended _not on <a> the kg but on a lord. It entered England first after the Conquest - then Scotland Canaque bequeathed it to Aragon. the Lombards of Benevento to Naples.

The chapter is devoted to French-German institutions.

1. Nobility. The beneficiaries becoming a hereditary class added the influence of rank to that of wealth. The Dukes & Counts as they became provincial lords instead of governors, were at the head. After them came the vassals, rich alodialists &c. induced to claim this rank [*illegible*], down to every holder of a fief, the military privileges were above those of the commonalty. In France even those who held at _____ fr. the Emp: or kg: were not ignoble. Surnames, & coats of arms [1] (derived fr: the crusades or fr: tournaments), grew up in the 11th & 12th centuries. Franc-fief was a fine p^d to the crown every 20 yrs by plebeians holding land on a noble tenure.

─────────

A possession of 3 generations - ennobled - after heirs or purchasers had been allowed fiefs.

In france nobility was self-created.

English baronies by tenure were given by the crown.

1271 Philip the Hardy granted letters of nobility without regard to land tenure.

Lawyers got ennobled by official exercise of magistracy∴[16] they reduced all subj to the kg's grant.

Chivalry [increased] multiplied gentlemen, [*illegible*].

Landed aristocracy was weakened.

Orders of nobility (α) Barons: who held directly of the crown: (: Valvassores Majores & Capitanei of the empire.) fought under their own banner:
higher territorial jurisdiction.

(β) Vavassors: of whom the Châtelains (who held fortified houses & had larger rights of justice) were the highest.

A Vavassor knighted = bachelor: unknighted = squire.

60 solidi[17]

16. Therefore
17. Written upside down on the next page, which is otherwise blank.

II. Clergy. The higher clergy (tho' not bound to military service except
   when they held military services as a condition of their benefices) were expected to <do so> give it (instance at Arincourt).
   Cmagne had capitularies <u>against</u> their personal service. Frank-
   almoigne was a tenure dispensing them fr: every service but that
   of masses. Tho they elected advocates am^g the feudal lords in
   their neighborhood.
III. Classes below the gentry. $^{α)}$ Freemen $^{β)}$ Villeins.
   $^{1)}$ Citizens of chartered towns. Socagers in England. Tenants for
   life or yeomen.
   1&2 confounded in French records as <u>gens potestatis</u>. More $α)$ [18]
   in S. France than in N.
   Freedom comes by the mother. Salic law mentions Tributarii,
   Lidi, Coloni, who were bound to reside on or cultivate their lord's
   estate, <u>but</u>, had civil rights. The kgs were called <u>Fiscalini</u>. As private wealth increased men <u>became</u> slaves for the sake of $^{1)}$<u>food</u>
   (Charles Bald permits redemption fr: this) $^{2)}$ protection $^{3)}$ by failure to pay fines for offences or $^{4)}$ <u>Heribann</u> to the kg for non-
   attendance in war: or even $^{5)}$ for superstition, to the church.
A villein must remain on the land; could not sell land: his person was
   bound.
<u>Serfs</u> were without redress, slaves = <u>villeins proper</u> (tho' liable to
   particular oppression) were <u>only</u> bound to fixt payments & duties—<u>not</u> to menial service.

18. "$α$" seems to stand for freemen.

Works Cited

Baird, Julian. "Swinburne, Sade, and Blake: The Pleasure-Pain Paradox." *Victorian Poetry,* IX (1971), 49–75.

Brodwin, Lenora Leet. *Elizabethan Love Tragedy, 1587–1625.* New York, 1971.

Browning Institute Studies, VIII. New York, 1980.

Chandler, Alice. *A Dream of Order: The Medieval Ideal in Nineteenth-Century English Literature.* Lincoln, Neb., 1970.

Charlesworth, Barbara. *Dark Passages: The Decadent Consciousness in Victorian Literature.* Madison, 1965.

Chew, Samuel. *Swinburne.* Boston, 1929.

Connolly, Thomas E. *Swinburne's Theory of Poetry.* Albany, 1964.

Dahl, Curtis. "Swinburne's Mary Stuart: A Reading of Ronsard." *Papers in English Language and Literature,* I (1965), 39–49.

D'Arcy, M. C., S.J. *The Mind and Heart of Love: Lion and Unicorn, A Study in Eros and Agape.* New York, 1947.

Davis, Mary Byrd. "Swinburne's Use of His Sources in *Tristram of Lyonesse.*" *Philological Quarterly,* LV (1977), 96–112.

d'Hangest, Germain. *Walter Pater: L'Homme et l'oeuvre.* 2 vols. Paris, 1961.

Eggers, J. Phillip. *King Arthur's Laureate.* New York, 1971.

Eliot, T. S., ed. *Literary Essays of Ezra Pound.* New York, 1954.

Fass, Barbara. *La Belle Dame Sans Merci and the Aesthetics of Romanticism.* Detroit, 1974.

Ferrante, Joan M. *Woman as Image in Medieval Literature: From the Twelfth Century to Dante.* New York, 1975.

Fisher, Benjamin F., IV. "Swinburne's *Tristram of Lyonesse* in Process." *Texas Studies in Literature and Language,* XIV (1972), 509–28.

Ford, George. *Keats and the Victorians.* New Haven, 1944.

Girouard, Mark. *The Return to Camelot: Chivalry and the English Gentleman.* New Haven, 1981.

Greenberg, Robert A. "Swinburne and the Redefinition of Classical Myth." *Victorian Poetry,* XIV (1976), 175–96.

Hare, Humphrey. *Swinburne: A Biographical Approach.* London, 1949.

Harrison, Antony H. "The Swinburnean Woman." *Philological Quarterly,* LVIII (1979), 90–102.

———. "Swinburne's Losses: The Poetics of Passion." *ELH,* XLIX (1982), 689–706.

Henderson, Philip. *Swinburne: Portrait of a Poet.* New York, 1974.

Hirsch, E. D. *Validity in Interpretation.* New Haven, 1967.

Hughes, Randolph. *Algernon Charles Swinburne: A Centenary Survey.* London, 1937.

Hunt, John Dixon. *The Pre-Raphaelite Imagination, 1848–1900.* Lincoln, Neb., 1968.

Hyder, Clyde K. "The Medieval Backgrounds of Swinburne's *The Leper.*" *Publications of the Modern Language Association,* XLVI (1931), 1280–88.

———. *Swinburne's Literary Career and Fame.* Durham, 1933.

———, ed. *Swinburne Replies.* Syracuse, 1966.

Kinneavy, Gerald. "Character and Action in Swinburne's *Chastelard.*" *Victorian Poetry,* V (1967), 31–36.

Kozicki, Henry. *Tennyson and Clio: History in the Major Poems.* Baltimore, 1979.

Kroeber, Karl. *Romantic Narrative Art.* Madison, 1960.

Lafourcade, Georges. *La Jeunesse de Swinburne.* 2 vols. London, 1928.

———. *Swinburne: A Literary Biography.* New York, 1932.

———. *Swinburne's Hyperion and Other Poems: With an Essay on Swinburne and Keats.* London, 1927.

Lang, Cecil Y. "Swinburne's Lost Love." *Publications of the Modern Language Association,* LXXIV (1959), 123–30.

———, ed. *The Swinburne Letters.* 6 vols. New Haven, 1959–62.

Langbaum, Robert. *The Poetry of Experience.* New York, 1963.

Leavy, Barbara Fass. "Iseult of Brittainy: A New Interpretation of Matthew Arnold's *Tristram and Iseult.*" *Victorian Poetry,* XVIII (1980), 1–22.

Lewis, C. S. *The Allegory of Love.* London, 1936.

Linsey, Edith D. "Medievalism in the Poetry of Swinburne," Ph.D. dissertation, University of Alabama, 1974.

Loomis, Roger Sherman, ed. *The Romance of Tristram and Ysolt by Thomas of Britain.* New York, 1981.

Lowith, Karl. *Meaning in History.* Chicago, 1949.

McGann, Jerome J. "Rossetti's Significant Details." *Victorian Poetry,* VII (1969), 41–54.

———. *Swinburne: An Experiment in Criticism.* Chicago, 1972.

McSweeney, Kerry. "The Structure of Swinburne's 'Tristram of Lyonesse.'" *Queen's Quarterly,* LXXV (1968), 691–702.

———. *Tennyson and Swinburne as Romantic Naturalists.* Toronto, 1981.

Moore, John C. *Love in Twelfth-Century France.* Philadelphia, 1972.

Morgan, Thais E. "Swinburne's Dramatic Monologues: Sex and Ideology." *Victorian Poetry,* XXII (1984), 175–95.

Murfin, Ross C. *Swinburne, Hardy, Lawrence, and the Burden of Belief.* Chicago, 1978.

Newman, Francis X., ed. *The Meaning of Courtly Love.* Albany, 1968.

Nicolson, Harold. *Swinburne.* London, 1926.

Pater, Walter. *The Renaissance.* Edited by Donald Hill. Berkeley, 1980.

Peters, Robert. "The Tannhäuser Theme: Swinburne's 'Laus Veneris.'" *Pre-Raphaelite Review,* III (1979), 12–28.

Pound, Ezra. *The Spirit of Romance.* New York, n.d.

Praz, Mario. *The Romantic Agony.* London, 1933.

Press, Alan R., ed. and trans. *The Anthology of Troubadour Lyric Poetry.* Austin, 1971.

Prince, Jeffrey. "D. G. Rossetti and the Pre-Raphaelite Conception of the Special Moment." *Modern Language Quarterly,* XXXVII (1976), 349–69.

Rader, Ralph W. "Notes on Some Structural Varieties and Variations in Dramatic 'I' Poems and Their Theoretical Implications." *Victorian Poetry,* XXII (1984), 103–20.

Reed, John R. "Swinburne's *Tristram of Lyonesse*: The Poet-Lover's

Song of Love." *Victorian Poetry,* IV (1966), 99–120.

Riede, David G. *Swinburne: A Study in Romantic Mythmaking.* Charlottesville, 1978.

Robinson, James K. "A Neglected Phase of the Aesthetic Movement: English Parnassianism." *Publications of the Modern Language Association,* LXVIII (1953), 733–54.

Rosenberg, John D. *Swinburne's Selected Poetry and Prose.* New York, 1967.

Rougement, Denis de. *Love in the Western World,* trans. Montgomery Belgion. New York, 1956.

Rutland, William. *Swinburne: A Nineteenth-Century Hellene.* Oxford, 1931.

Sambrook, James. *Pre-Raphaelitism: A Collection of Critical Essays.* Chicago, 1974.

Snodgrass, Chris. "Swinburne's Circle of Desire: A Decadent Theme." In *Decadence and the 1890's,* edited by Ian Fletcher. London, 1979.

Staines, David. "Swinburne's Arthurian World: Swinburne's Arthurian Poetry and Its Medieval Sources." *Studia Neophilologica,* L (1978), 53–70.

Stevenson, Lionel. *The Pre-Raphaelite Poets.* New York, 1974.

Stubbs, William. *The Letters of William Stubbs.* Edited by W. H. Hutton. London, 1904.

Swinburne, Algernon Charles. *The Complete Works of Algernon Charles Swinburne.* Bonchurch Edition, edited by Sir Edmund Gosse and Thomas J. Wise. 20 vols. London, 1925–27.

———. *The Poems of Algernon Charles Swinburne.* 6 vols. London, 1904.

———. *Posthumous Poems by Algernon Charles Swinburne.* Edited by Edmund Gosse and T. J. Wise. London, 1917.

———. *The Tragedies of Algernon Charles Swinburne.* 5 vols. New York, 1906.

Sypher, Francis Jacques. "Swinburne and Wagner." *Victorian Poetry,* IX (1971), 165–83.

Tredell, Nicolas. "*Tristram of Lyonesse*: Dangerous Voyage." *Victorian Poetry,* XX (1982), 97–111.

Vogler, Thomas. *Preludes to Vision.* Berkeley, 1971.

Welby, T. Earle. *A Study of Swinburne.* London, 1926.

White, Hayden. *Metahistory: The Historical Imagination in Nineteenth-Century Europe.* Baltimore, 1973.

————. *Tropics of Discourse: Essays in Cultural Criticism.* Baltimore, 1978.

Wilkie, Brian. *Romantic Poets and Epic Tradition.* Madison, 1965.

Wise, T. J. *A Bibliography of the Writings in Prose and Verse of Algernon Charles Swinburne.* London, 1919.

Index

tionships in, 148, 151; mentioned,
4, 18, 78, 79, 82, 115, 158
*Tale of the Emperor Constans and of
Over Sea,* 8
Tennyson, Alfred, Lord: *Idylls of the
King,* 4, 101, 102, 135, 136, 137;
"The Lady of Shallott," 137; mentioned, 4, 5, 16, 81, 159
Thomas of Ercildoune, 81
Tristram of Lyonesse: libertarian values of, 79, 115; and Greek tragedy, 82–83; narrative devices,
89–93, 111; poetic form, 97–114;
epic devices, 98–99, 102–106;
nature in, 103–106, 108, 113, 117,
118–29; philosophy in, 103–106,
108–11, 113–14, 115, 118–32;
characterization in, 104–13; religion of love in, 106, 109, 116, 117,
119–29; pantheistic vision of,
106, 112–13, 118–20, 123–29;
Arthurian matter in, 107–12, 123,
126–27; courtly love elements,
107–14, 118; anti-orthodoxy, 108,
109, 110, 112; role of fate in, 108–
11, 113–14, 116, 126–28; irony

in, 109, 117–18; Merlin's role in,
112–13; "song" in, 119, 127–28;
sensual indulgence, 119–22;
treatment of death, 119–23, 127–
28; battle scenes, 124–25; mentioned, 4, 8, 9, 18, 26, 27, 34, 36,
38–39, 62, 78, 79, 80, 82, 83, 87,
88, 90, 92, 94, 96, 142, 157, 158
Troubadour poetry, 21–36, 37, 38,
45, 61, 69, 157

Vidal, Peire, 29, 33
Villon, François, 7, 10, 12, 14, 15
Virgil, 100
Vogler, Thomas, 99

Wagner, Richard, 81
Warton, Thomas, 141
Watts-Dunton, Theodore, 6, 30,
136
Webster, John, 24
Welby, T. Earle, 134
Whitman, Walt, 2, 33
Wilkie, Brian, 100
William IX, 34
Wordsworth, William, 129, 130, 143